VINTA(
S.D. BURMAN

Anirudha Bhattacharjee, an alumnus of IIT Kharagpur, is a National Award- and MAMI Award-winning author. An amateur musician, he specializes in musical biographies. He lives with his family in Kolkata.

Balaji Vittal grew up in Kolkata and graduated from Jadavpur University. He has worked with Wipro, Standard Chartered Bank and Royal Bank of Scotland, and is an avid follower of Indian cinema. He writes for *Metro Plus*, the Quint and Scroll. Balaji shuttles between Bengaluru, where he now works for Concentrix, and Hyderabad, where his family lives.

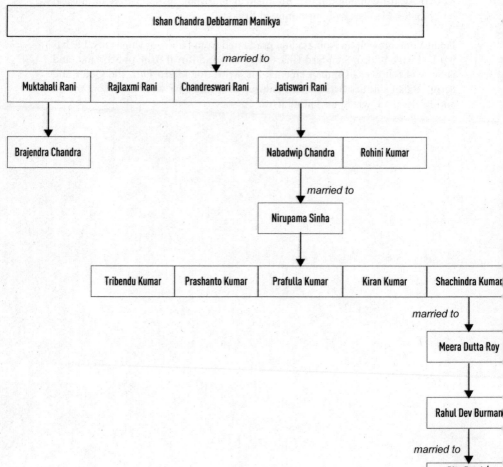

S. D. BURMAN

THE PRINCE-MUSICIAN

ANIRUDHA BHATTACHARJEE & BALAJI VITTAL

FOREWORD BY Pt. HARIPRASAD CHAURASIA

VINTAGE

An imprint of Penguin Random House

VINTAGE

USA | Canada | UK | Ireland | Australia
New Zealand | India | South Africa | China

Vintage is part of the Penguin Random House group of companies
whose addresses can be found at global.penguinrandomhouse.com

Published by Penguin Random House India Pvt. Ltd
4th Floor, Capital Tower 1, MG Road,
Gurugram 122 002, Haryana, India

First published in Tranquebar by Westland Publications Private Limited 2018
Published in Vintage by Penguin Random House India 2022

Copyright © Anirudha Bhattacharjee and Balaji Vittal 2018

ISBN 9780143458531

Typeset by Ram Das Lal, New Delhi, NCR
Printed at Replika Press Pvt. Ltd, India

www.penguin.co.in

In Memory of
the late Samarendra Bhattacharjee
&
the late Sachin Ganguly

Contents

SD

Acknowledgements

This book wouldn't have happened without Sachin Ganguly. We also owe our thanks to Probir Mukherjea, who took special pains to introduce us to the octogenarian.

Anuradha Gupta, Meera Dev Burman's cousin, was all heart when she first spoke to us in June 2014. She wanted to meet us again, and we remember how eager she sounded that day, but unfortunately, she passed away on 4 December 2014, exactly a week after our last meeting. Maybe she had a premonition about her death.... We extend our thanks to her daughter, Sreeparna Sengupta.

Our salutes to the irrepressible Brigadier S.P. Bhattacharjya who also perhaps gave his last interview to us before he bid adieu, rather unexpectedly, on 15 October 2015. Many of his stories were beyond the scope of this book, but we hope someday, they shall form part of a book on Indian history, especially Bengal.

We would like to extend our thanks to the following musicians, film personalities, and their relatives for their invaluable time. We have added their names here, in alphabetic order (as we would continue to do in many instances later, here): Abhijit Dasgupta, Asim Samanta, Basu Chatterji, Bela Sengupta (nee Bose), Prof. Biswajit Bhattacharjee, Chandra Sanyal, Danny Denzongpa, Debabrata Sengupta (aka Debu Sen), Digbijoy Chowdhury, Dinesh Shailendra, Dipankar Chattapadhyay, Prof. Dipankar Dasgupta, Gautam Choudhury, Prof. Goutam Ghosh,

Gulzar, Pandit Hari Prasad Chaurasia, Kalyani Kazi, Kalyani Mitra Pillai, Ketan Anand, Kishwar Jaipuri, Mitali Chowdhury, Pandit Nayan Ghosh, Pintu Guha, Rakesh Anand Bakshi, Ratna Mukherjee, Rinki Roy Bhattacharya, Rupali Guha, Sangeeta Gupta, Subhash Mukerji, and Tulika Ghosh.

We also owe our gratitude to those who layered this book with nuggets of information in their own fabulous ways, and who we interviewed between 1988–2011—Ajoy Chakrabarty, Amrut Rao Katkar, Badal Bhattacharya, Bhanu Gupta, Dr Bhupen Hazarika, Bhupinder Singh, Dev Anand, Homi Mullan, Kersi Lord, Manna Dey, Manohari Singh, Mili Bhattacharya, Sachin Bhowmick, Shammi Kapoor, Simi Grewal, Subir Sen, Sumit Mitra, Tarun Majumdar, and Yogesh. Many of them are no longer with us.

Our trip to Comilla in October 2014, was one of the most important milestones in the writing of this book. The people of Bangladesh, with their intrinsic warmth and affection, are truly unusual and hard to find anywhere else in the world. While the advocate, Golam Faruk invited us for many discussions over hot cups of tea, A.K.M. Moniruzzaman, Head Master, Comilla Yusuf school, and Motaher Hussian Chowdhury, Senior Teacher (Arts), welcomed us as if we were long-lost friends.

Our trip to Comilla Victoria Government College was like reliving history. Even as Prof. Md. Abdur Rashid, the Vice Principal, welcomed us in and treated us to the best samosas in the world, Assistant Professor M. M. Majumdar took us around the college, to help us soak in its past, particularly when Karta was a young college student.

While on Comilla, we must mention our man Fridays, the bikers, Abdul Momen Rohit and Emran Mazumder, who helped us negotiate through the city with great ease—the wonderful autumnal evenings on the banks of the River Gomti, was thanks to these two young men. Any mention about our Bangladesh trip would remain incomplete without mentioning Kamrul Hasan and H.Q. Chowdhury. If Kamrul played our host-cum-chauffer-cum-the 'go-to' man, Chowdhury, the author of *Incomparable S.D. Burman*, apart from sharing little-known facts about the maestro, pressed a thick wad of Bangladeshi taka into our hands, and refused to take it back!

The folk singer, Debasish Roy of AIR, Kolkata, helped us understand Burman's mastery over the genre; we thank him for his time and knowledge. We would also like to extend our thanks to Dilip Kumar Das, a master accordion player, for introducing us to Mr Roy.

In order to understand the impact of Hindustani classical music on Sachin Dev Burman, we sought out Archisman Mozumder, whose enthusiasm and animated descriptions about the evolution of music in Bengal was an unforgettable lesson for us. K.L. Pandey's incomparable knowledge of the influence of ragas on Hindi film songs helped us appreciate the genre better. Our discussions on rhythm were mostly with friends—Indrajit Banerjee, Shivani Zaveri and Subhasish Mukherjee, who would take less than a second to demarcate between a Deepchandi and a Dhamar, and with great aplomb.

Our interactions with legendary footballers, Parimal Dey and Surajit Sengupta, added yet another dimension to the multi-layered personality of S.D. Burman.

Truth be told, we are short of words in expressing our gratitude to Sudarshan Talwar and Kaustubh C. Pingle. As compulsive collectors of memorabilia, they laid bare their treasure-trove of magazine interviews, and rare photographs for this book.

A special vote of thanks is also due to Rajesh Kr. Singh and Srinivasan Channiga for sharing rare films, those which have disappeared from sight, and it is such a pity that they may never be accessible to the general public any longer.

Our gratitude to Anushila Chakrabarti, Uttaran Dasgupta, Devdan Mitra, and especially to Anuradha Warrier for going through the manuscript and suggesting changes, and her husband, Sadanand, whose insights have formed part of this book.

Our several discussions on music and ethnicity wouldn't have been possible without these wonderful people—Amal Banerjee (of SaReGaMa), the Late Biman Mukhopadhyay, Biswanath Chatterjee (of *Hindi Film*

Geet Kosh), Dr Chandrasekhar Rao, Debasish Mukhopadhyay (of *Aajkaal*), Gautam Sarkar, Jayati Gangopadhyay, Mira Hashmi, Pragya Tiwari, and Sanjay Sengupta.

For the innumerable books which helped us navigate through a maze of information better and made this book special, we owe our thanks to writers such as, Akshay Manwani, Anita Padhye, Anuj Kumar, Ganesh Anatharaman, Harish Bhimani, Harmandir Singh 'Hamraaz', Jai Arjun Singh, Dr Mandar Bichu, Nasreen Munni Kabir, Nilu N. Gavankar, Raju Bharatan, and Sidharth Bhatia.

And then, our friends and relatives who helped us during the making of this book—Ali Aftaab Sayeed, Anindya Dasgupta, Anindya Roy Chowdhury, Anita Pai, Anustup Datta, Aritra Bhattacharyya, Arnab Banerjee, Arunabha Roy, Asish Saha, Bhaskar Dutta, Chaitali Sen, Deepa Buty, Gourab Roy Chowdhury, Hemendra Kumar, Indranath Mukherjee, Ishita Bose, Jaideep Mukherjee, Jayanta Ray, Jayita Sen, Joy Bhattacharjya, Joy Christie, Krittibas Dasgupta, Mubasher Bukhari, Dr Nanda Mukherjee, Nilanjan Lahiri, Parthiv Dhar, Pavan Jha, Pratik Dey, Pratik Majumdar, Rajiv Kumar Singh, Raju Bathija, Raman Roy, Ranabir Neogi, Ranjan Biswas, Ritesh Gadhvi, Ritu Chandra, Sabyasachi Biswas, Saurav Chakladar, Sarbasree Bandyopadhyay, Shaunak Bhattacharjee, Dr Srijit Mukherjee, Sudarshan Pandey, Supratik Gangopadhyay, Prof. Surjit Singh, and Yasser Usman.

While it is impossible to mention the entire list of newspapers and magazines that helped us form a perspective on this book, here is an attempt to thank some of them profusely—the *Amrita Bazar Patrika*; *Hindustan Standard*; *The Statesman*; *The Telegraph*; *The Times of India*; the *Imperial Gazetteer of India*; the Journals of Asiatic Society; *Filmindia*; *Mother India*; *Filmfare*; *Star & Style*; *Cine Advance*; *Rasrang* (Marathi); and *Anandalok* (Bengali).

We owe our sincerest gratitude to the following books—*Abarjanar Jhuli*; *Sargamer Nikhad*; the publication by Tripura Government on the centenary celebrations of S. D. Burman, 2006; *Incomparable Sachin Dev Burman*; *Bhati Gang Baiya*; *Bangla Gaaner Sandhane*; *Nawab Faizunnesa*

Chowdhurani; History of Tripura; Sangeet Porichoy; Tomar Geeti Jagalo Smriti; Sangeet Tathva; Bangla Gaaner Bartamaan O Aaro; Ek Hota Goldie; The Desai Trio and *Movie Industry of India; Kothaye Kothaye Raat Hoye Jaye; Bollywood Melodies; Jeeboner Jalsaghare; Guru Dutt: A Life in Cinema; The World of Hrishikesh Mukherjee: The Filmmaker Everyone Loves; Mera Kuch Samaan; Hindi Film Geet Kosh* (Volumes I, II, III, IV and V); *In Search of Lata Mangeshkar;* and *In the Company of a Poet.*

And as we thank our families, we extend the same to Sudha Sadhanand, our editor, who became like family to us.

I, Anirudha Bhattacharjee would specially like to thank my father, the Late Samarendra Bhattacharjee, who introduced me to music, especially to the songs of S.D. Burman.

Authors' Note

It all started in Bhubaneshwar in September 2012. We had gone to interview Pandit Hariprasad Chaurasia at his gurukul. The following morning, we were invited by the well-known artist, Debasis Mahapatra for breakfast, which was preceded by a tour of his personal gallery which had R.D. Burman aka Pancham's portraits.

On the breakfast table, Shravani, Debasis' ever-attentive wife, suddenly said, 'I love S.D. Burman more than RD.'

We found her observation interesting and asked her, 'Ok. So, can you name fifteen S.D. Burman's films apart from the following—*Aradhana, Guide, Jewel Thief, Prem Nagar, Pyaasa, Kaagaz Ke Phool, Sujata, Bandini, Abhimaan,* and *Sharmeelee?*'

Shravani shook her head sideways expressing tacit disapproval, and said, 'That would be difficult!' Shravani's acknowledgement provoked us to think: so, there are facets of this great musician which are unknown even to his hard-core fans. What about his music outside the coveted list of 20–25 films? Are they virtually forgotten, and is that the reason why they seldom form part of even informal discussions on Hindi film music, in general?

A few weeks later, when we shared the idea of writing a book on him with a few close friends, one of them commented, 'S.D. Burman? Isn't he history?'

We decoded that 'history' remark as redundant; outdated;

anachronistic! Strong words, we agree, but even as the fans within us wanted to protest loudly at what our minds conceived as a grave transgression, we felt it was time to tell his story.

Until our publishers contacted us, we knew that there were at least two good books on Sachin Dev Burman, or SD as he came to be known universally, including his short autobiography. And even as we were pondering over the idea, there was one more awaiting release.

Furthermore, we were aware that every little nugget—opinions, views, analyses—had been shared and exhausted about this great composer, and what if we had nothing new to say? As die-hard fans, the last thing we wanted was to sound trite and tired about a man who influenced an entire generation, before and after us, in more ways than one.

However, we took the plunge and thought we would proceed along while recalling his great music; it was almost as if he would guide us to write it the way he would have liked it! And then one day, courtesy our septuagenarian friend, Probir Mukherjea, we fortuitously found Sachin Ganguly, who was SD's secretary in Calcutta! This was almost like divine intervention and there is nothing but gratitude for a man, who gave us hitherto unknown insights into the maestro's life.

We went back to our notes which we'd collected while writing our previous book, *R.D. Burman: The Man, The Music*. We pulled out every shred of paper that we had kept carefully between 2008–2010; old folders on our laptops came alive and out came our days and week-long jottings on discussions with fabulous artists such as, Kersi Lord, Manohari Singh, Sachin Bhowmick, Yogesh, Bhanu Gupta, et al. We realised that we had adequate material that could go into the making of *S.D. Burman: The Prince-Musician*. We wanted to shout out to our friend and many others who had labelled him 'history'—he *made* history and shall always be counted amongst those who gave film music a new grammar.

As is well known, S.D. Burman belonged to a royal family, which like many others in pre-Independent India was ravaged by internecine struggles, palace intrigues, skirmishes and conspiracies. The dog-eared yellowed pages in the archives of Tripura court are evidence of multiple disputes which his family faced for several years, and which one had to rummage through to understand his childhood and youth. What we discovered was that we had to dovetail certain historical facts while describing the various stages of his life—for instance, his childhood which was around the time of the First World War; his debut on radio even before it came to be known as All India Radio or AIR; the city that was once Calcutta (now Kolkata); the Ganges and its impact on his music; Bombay (now Mumbai) which became his beloved after the initial resistance he had towards a city where he arrived with a young wife and a boy in tow; the nation's struggle for Independence and the joy of freedom; the devastating Partition of the subcontinent and with it the loss of his land which was given away to another nation.

Suddenly, the remark that S.D. Burman was 'history' began to make sense. The story couldn't have merely been a chronology of his musical journey; history had to play a significant role in his life's trajectory.

The discovery of a prince, flautist par excellence, singer, sports enthusiast, a devoted family man, etc., took us on exotic journeys to Comilla in Bangladesh, and Agartala in Tripura. From the fossil-covered walls in old crumbling buildings; the rarefied environs of the National Library; a cosy chat by the fireplace with an octogenarian Brigadier of the Indian Army; a sad, albeit fruitful encounter with a woman on her death-bed—this book has been like excavating an ancient site for stories untold.

Unlike several men and women who arrived in Bombay for a career in Hindi films, S.D. Burman was nomadic by temperament. Even within the same city, he shifted around quite a bit. Although he spent most of his working life in Bombay, he never got around to being completely comfortable either with its landscape or its culture. He was Bengali and of a particular type—the financial capital that Bombay was, didn't attract him very much; he spoke Bengali with a Bangal (East Bengal) accent, which anyway made him seem like an outsider even within his own peer group and in a city like Calcutta. The best example of this 'non-acceptance' was his name, which underwent several modifications.

After the initial hiccups, it wasn't as if he achieved instant success. His quality of music in the Forties and Fifties was patchy, but thereafter what he did could very well be a management lesson for young entrepreneurs—despite linguistic and cultural constraints, he hauled himself up and moved with the changing times. It must be mentioned here that apart from extraneous reasons which made him feel like an outsider, it was also his upbringing in a royal household which made it tough for him to run the race along with others. But he did, and with such aplomb that he soon came to be known as a composer who adhered to standards which became unmatchable. Therefore, no book on S.D. Burman would ever be complete without exploring these aspects of his personality.

In the end, whether we make Shravani like him better than before, only time will tell. In so far as we are concerned, we still think that Sachin Dev Burman *has* more than meets the eye, and of course, the ear.

Introduction

The day the great Ustad Bundu Khan forgot about his morning ablutions…

This predates India's pre-Independence days when Ustad Ali Akbar Khan, the court musician of Maharaja Umaid Singh of Jodhpur, had organised a big music festival. Almost all the renowned musicians of the country were in attendance, including Ustad Faiyaz Khan and the great Maihar Baba, Ustad Allauddin Khan. My father, the well-known tabla maestro, Pandit Nikhil Ghosh and my paternal uncle, Pandit Pannalal Ghosh were also invited. My father was extremely close to S.D. Burman (or Burman jethu, as we addressed him) from the time he had started making a mark as a folk and semi-classical singer.

During the music festival, large ornate tents were laid out within the huge quadrangle of Jodhpur palace (later renamed as Umaid Bhawan), for the musicians to stay. Very often, musicians rehearsing in adjacent tents could hear each other and the entire atmosphere would be suffused with several voices and instruments reaching a crescendo.

It was the day of S.D. Burman's performance, and he'd requested my father to come to his tent during rehearsals. Burman jethu was playing the harmonium, while my father accompanied him on the tabla. Many songs were sung that day, and amongst others, *Allah megh de pani de*, a folk song from East Bengal. As the day progressed, this rehearsal session soon turned into a jam session, as my uncle, who could hear the music sitting in his tent, joined them with his flute; Ustad Ahmed Jan Thirakwa, the legendary tabla player, and also my father's guru, began playing the tabla, and soon the room reverberated with music that perhaps should have been recorded for posterity. The mehfil was in full session and the gods were witness to this confluence of great musicians.

It was around midday when Ustad Bundu Khan, acknowledged as one of the greatest sarangi players in the subcontinent, was seen heading for his daily ablutions with a lota in hand. Tents those days did not come with the luxury of an attached toilet, and the bathroom was at the far end of the rows of tents in the quadrangle of the palace grounds.

While the Ustad was briskly walking towards his destination, he suddenly heard S.D. Burman singing in his velvety, high-pitched voice, and was instantly mesmerised. He entered Burman jethu's tent and while expressing great admiration, placed the lota on the ground, forgot all about his visit to the bathroom and went back to his tent to fetch his sarangi! In a moment, S.D. Burman's tent had turned into a veritable stage of India's greatest performers, when suddenly the clock struck four and Burman jethu suddenly realised that he had to perform in the evening.

This fabulous story of how musicians those days forgot everything else due to their devotion to music does not merely end here.

After the musical performances for the evening had come to an end, it was close to midnight and the musicians were being dropped back to their respective tents in a car. Ustad Bundu Khan, my father, and my uncle were the last to leave the auditorium. For some unknown reason, the car was delayed in taking them back to the palace.

Suddenly, Bundu Khan sat down on the footpath in front of the auditorium, and began playing the same song sung by S.D. Burman that afternoon—*Allah megh de pani de...*

There couldn't have been a better testimony than this—a tribute by a great musician to another called, Sachin Dev Burman.

Pandit Nayan Ghosh
March 2018

Foreword

S.D. Burman. The name not only evokes a deep sense of respect, but also a great feeling of love. Not only was he a fantastic musician, he was also a compassionate human being. He was like a child—innocent to the core, with absolutely no malice towards anyone.

Musically, he was the ideal mix of folk and classical. S.D. Burman was amongst the very few composers who had actually learnt and knew Hindustani classical music well enough to know when to use it and when to abstain. This judicious sense of balance, of minimalism, came through strongly in his music. He never overdid things; rather, he kept classical nuances short enough to just garnish the base tune.

He was also someone who understood and composed strictly to a script. It is tough to generalise his music, or restrict it in boxes, as it kept changing with the tenor of a film. From *Taxi Driver* to *Abhimaan*, it's difficult to find a common thread running through his compositions, but even an untrained ear can immediately identify two completely disparate compositions as essentially S.D. Burman's.

I began playing the flute for Dada Burman (as I would address him reverentially) from the early Sixties and *Meri Surat Teri Ankhen* was perhaps the first film when I began working with him. He was also a very good flautist and that became one of the factors which helped us bond even better. Later, when I became part of an independent composer with the film, *27 Down* and collaborated with Pandit Shiv

Kumar Sharma, some of the nuances of composing for films that I had picked up from Dada Burman helped me immensely. My journey with him ended when he left this world, rather suddenly and abruptly, at the zenith of his career.

The authors of this book, Anirudha Bhattacharjee and Balaji Vittal had gifted me their first book, *R.D. Burman: The Man, The Music*, which had won them the National Award in 2011. I wish this book surpasses the earlier one in more ways than one.

Pandit Hari Prasad Chaurasia
Mumbai, March 2018

Prologue

Calcutta: 1943–44 & Shachin Karta

'Of the few hotels near Sealdah, north Calcutta, I remember one called Tower Hotel.[1] Leftover food from the hotel's kitchen thrown into garbage bins near the railway station would trigger an instant scuffle between destitute humans and stray dogs. If there was a disease called hunger, this was it...,' remembered the late Brigadier Shiba Prasad Bhattacharjya, who was then an eighteen-year-old student of Electrical Engineering at the National Council of Education (now Jadavpur University) and lived in a dormitory on 41, Mirzapur Street (now Surya Sen Street) in central Calcutta. It was 1943—the year of the Bengal famine.

Widely acknowledged as a 'Churchill-made' famine, the rumblings in the bellies of the hungry and homeless flooding the streets of Calcutta seemed louder than the bombs. Worse, there was a pervasive threat of communal riots breaking out in and around the city. Further east, Dacca (now Dhaka, the capital of Bangladesh) was hit by a malaria epidemic impacting over 50,000 people.

Newspapers those days would carry a 'daily score' of the dead on its front pages. The 'strictly official' figures were confined to the records of a few registered hospitals, like Campbell Hospital in Sealdah (now N.R.S. Hospital) and the National Medical Institute (now Calcutta

National Medical College and Hospital). Yet another news item which found prominent place was about rescue and relief operations, like South Africa shipping milk products for the hungry.

Shiba Prasad Bhattacharjya,[2] recalled, 'Every morning I would walk from my dormitory to Sealdah station—south, through Circular Road. The destitute and dying would be begging on the streets for a meagre fistful of *phyan* (starch, a by-product of boiled rice) to muffle their hunger. While the living struggled to live, more were born. I even saw women in labour on the roadside.

'In December 1943, the skies lit up. I remember the sound of anti-aircraft guns and rushing up to the roof of 41, Mirzapur Street, and seeing flowery cloud-like things billowing up. Gazing down, I found British soldiers diving for cover behind baffle walls[3] as soon as the air raid sirens went off. Dead bodies, filth, faeces, skeletons—everything was shoved into dustbins and shielded from the living by these baffle walls.

'Shaken by the war arriving at their doorsteps, people began to leave Calcutta. Those of us who stayed back, were encouraged to stay gratis by house owners who wanted to leave the city.'

One of the first fallouts of the war was business and commerce. The bomb scares led to long periods of power outages. Film production, a promising new industry in Bengal, also took a body blow as raw stock was in short supply. The black market flourished, even as regular business was non-existent.

The numbers were sufficient to establish the truth—against twenty Bengali films in 1943, only fourteen released in 1944, and an even lower, eleven in 1945. The egress of film fraternity from Calcutta had begun.

A case in point was New Theatres (NT) in Tollygunge, Calcutta, arguably the best studio in the country at the time, which was struggling to stay afloat. In 1944, it had a solitary Bengali release, *Udayer Pathe*, and that too as late as September. (It was this film which had introduced the renowned director, Bimal Roy to the world.) Its Hindi version,

Hamrahi, was released a year later; *Wapas* (which had received a censor certification in 1943) had a delayed released, in April 1944; and *My Sister*, actor-singer K.L. Saigal's swan song for NT, released in January 1945. Work on *Dui Purush* began in 1944, but it would only see the light of day in August 1945. And *Beduine* (Bengali) went on the floors in 1944, but was axed midway.

This shift from Bengali to Hindi cinema reflected the obvious gloom in Bengal. But, it became an advantage for Hindi films in Bombay (now Mumbai). Films from the region, such as Vijay Bhatt's *Ram Rajya* (1943); Jayant Desai's *Tansen* (1943); Sohrab Modi's *Prithvi Vallab* (1943); and V. Shantaram's *Shakuntala* (1943) had impressive runs of twenty weeks or more in Calcutta. *Kismet,* released in late 1943 at Roxy, ran for three-and-a-half years—a record it would celebrate for thirty-two years!

The migration from Bengal to Bombay began around the mid-1940s and included names such as, K.L. Saigal and K.C. Dey, the blind singer. Nitin Bose, arguably one the best directors then, also packed his bags and left for Bombay. Many others, including the Comilla-born actor-director Sushil Majumdar, followed suit. The port city offered what Bengal was forced to abandon in the face of the horrific famine, strife and war: an opportunity.

However, Sachin Deb Burman, or 'Shachin Karta', as he was reverentially known in Bengal and Tripura, clung on to Calcutta at the proverbial inflection point in his career. He was a singer and composer of *adhunik* or modern Bengali songs, who had jettisoned a life of luxury to pursue a career in music. His faith in Calcutta as the city of his dreams was unwavering. Moreover, he hadn't heard encouraging things about Bombay—his friend, Himanghsu Dutta, whom Salil Chowdhury lauded as 'the father of the modern Bengali song', hadn't had a pleasant experience either in Bombay or Pune. He had shifted in the early 1940s and although his music for *Bhakt Kabir* (1942) and *Bhaichara* (1943) was well received, he'd returned to his native Calcutta. This incident may have had an impact on Burman, and about which he wrote succinctly in his autobiography, *Sargamer Nikhad*:

> In 1942, I refused an invitation from Sardar Chandulal Shah, the owner of Ranjit Studios, to compose music in Bombay as I wanted to compose for Bengali films alone. But opportunities in Calcutta were sparse. Even New Theatres, whose owner B.N. Sircar and other stalwarts Nitin Bose, Debaki Bose, Hem Chandra and Pramatesh Barua with whom I was acquainted with at a personal level, rejected me after their initial assurances. This hurt me and shook my confidence. I can recall scoring music for two films—*Rajgee* and *Rajkumarer Nibashon*.

In all probability, Karta must have forgotten that he had composed for no fewer than sixteen Bengali films during his first phase in Calcutta. The years, 1943–44 were actually busy years for him—*Judge-Saheber Natni* (1943) was a hit, and he was awaiting three releases. Also, 1944 began on a high note for him with *Chhadmabeshi* (not to be confused with the remake which released two-and-a-half decades later). The film was advertised as the, 'Season's merriest film of wild fun, mad frolic, lilting music, and hilarious romance'[4] and, 'If you are afraid of full-throated and bone-cracking laughter, you must not see...'[5] *Chhadmabeshi* was a rip-roaring comedy, which ran successfully for a cumulative thirty-nine weeks at Uttara, Purabi, Purna and Aleya theatres. However, while the comedy worked, the music did not create any ripples. Barring two IPTA-(Indian People's Theatre Association) style tracks, the music of the film was largely forgotten.

His next film called, *Bhed Bhaad* (later renamed as *Pratikaar* and directed by the renowned actor, Chhabi Biswas) premiered at Uttara, but was out of the cinemas in two weeks. The next release at the same theatre was *Matir Ghar*—which fared better than the earlier one, but did not quite shake up the box office. Karta's run as a composer in Calcutta seemed chequered and lacked momentum.

Bombay beckoned him yet again, and he wrote:

Rai Bahadur Chunilal and Sasadhar Mukerji, the proprietors of the Bombay-based film company Filmistan, invited me to compose for a film in 1944. I was in two minds. However, my friend Sushil Majumdar[6], who used to work with Filmistan, advised me not to ignore the Bombay opportunity.

The decision to leave Calcutta for Bombay wasn't driven by professional compulsions alone. His brother, Lt. Colonel Kiran Kumar Debbarman had died prematurely in a gruesome freak accident in Agartala. Also, one of Karta's closest friends—poet, lyricist, filmmaker and teacher, Ajoy Bhattacharya (the director of *Chhadmabeshi*), passed away on Christmas Eve in 1943, a few months before his film's release.

Like they say: time is the best healer; distance is perhaps the second best. In October 1944, a despondent Karta finally moved to Bombay with his family.

Gradually, the bombs quietened down in Calcutta. The unabating fury, hatred and despair gave way to celebrations, albeit partially. Three years later, India gained independence. But she was partitioned too....

Bombay, his *karmabhumi* for the next three decades, would mark the transition of Shachin Karta to Sachin Dev Burman, and finally, to the name by which history would best know him: S.D. Burman and or just, SD.

Karta

Shochin/Shachin Karta, or simply Karta, was the name by which he was known in his native Tripura, and later in Bengal, till he moved to western India.

Historical Musings

The land of Tipperah (today's Tripura) in undivided India consisted of two territories—Hill Tipperah and Plains Tipperah. The region's residents were supposedly identifiable with the Murungs of Arakan in Burma (now Myanmar). Starting late thirteenth or early fourteenth century, Tipperah was administered by the royal 'Manikyas'. In 1760, the capital of Tipperah was shifted to Agartala from Udaipur (not to be confused with Udaipur, in Rajasthan), and the Rajas of Tipperah were honoured with the customary 13-gun salute, important as they were in the pecking order of Indian royalty.

The ruler of Hill Tipperah lorded over large tracts of land in Plains Tipperah, Noakhali and Sylhet which was collectively known as Chakla Roshanabad. In 1761 during the regime of Krishna Manikya, the British, with the help of Nawab Mir Qasim (who went down in history as the quintessential backstabber), won over Chakla Roshanabad. Apart from annexing huge swathes of land, the East India Company showed little or no interest in Hill Tipperah, as the hills added meagre revenue to the British exchequer. Eventually, it was this reason which led to Hill Tipperah's independence. Raja Krishna Manikya was stripped off his authority as plains were no longer under his direct control, but continued to function as the de facto king of Hill Tipperah; he was however treated as a zamindar and not as king in Plains Tipperah.

In 1836, Dampier, the Commissioner of Chittagong division

3

challenged the independent stature of the King of Tipperah. But two years later in 1838, the Deputy-Governor of Bengal agreed that owing to his singular possession from 1793, 'the Raja had obtained a prescriptive right to the territory within the hills,' albeit with less powers. It may be recalled that even coronation ceremonies required ratification from the British Crown.[1]

Ishan Chandra Debbarman Manikya Bahadur, the 180th king of the Manikya dynasty ascended the throne in May 1850, after the death of his father, Krishna Kishore Manikya in April 1849. A mild-mannered and amiable king, Ishan Chandra died young at the age of thirty-four on 1 August 1862, after suffering a paralytic stroke a year earlier.

Ishan Chandra had four wives (Muktabali Rani, Rajlaxmi Rani, Chandreswari Rani and Jatiswari Rani). He had a son from Muktabali Rani called Brajendra; Jatiswari Rani bore him two sons, Nabadwip and Rohini; while the other two queens didn't have any sons.

While ascending the throne, Ishan Chandra had named his younger brother, Upendra as the *Juvaraj* (crown prince), and had anointed his two sons, Brajendra and Nabadwip as *Bodo Thakur* and *Bodo Karta*[*] respectively. Upendra passed away prematurely, and Brajendra died of cholera hours before his father's death. Following the demise of Ishan Chandra, going by the rules of hierarchy and as expressed in his will, Nabadwip was supposed to be king. However, Bir Chandra, Ishan Chandra's younger brother, staked his claim to the throne by presenting a Robkari (Royal Proclamation, deemed as a will) signed by Ishan Chandra

---

[*] The tradition was to name a young prince, Thakur and, not Karta. Nabadwip Chandra was the first in the royal family to be given the sobriquet, Karta. The name held on. As was witnessed in several other cases across India, the British found the pronunciation tough on their tongue, and therefore, the court documents carried 'Kurta' as the spelling for Karta.

a day before his death, on 31 July 1862, which decreed Bir Chandra as the crown prince.

Bir Chandra's claim was challenged in court by his half-brothers, Chakradhwaj and Neelkrishna. Neelkrishna had a stronger argument; after all, he was the eldest of Ishan Chandra's half-brothers. After a lengthy and arduous legal battle, the divisional office at Chittagong accepted Bir Chandra's Robkari and appointed him de facto king until the matter was resolved. (The other theory about the Robkari was that it was created by the Council of Ministers to safeguard the state against British takeover as Ishan Chandra's sons were minors.)

Apparently, a few days before his death, Ishan Chandra had invited his half-brother, Neelkrishna, to Agartala, but since there was a delay in his arrival, the king had drawn up another Robkari that had named Bir Chandra as the Juvaraj. However, Brajendra Chandra's status as the Bodo Thakur and Nabadwip Chandra's as the Bodo Karta remained unchanged.

Meanwhile Neelkrishna and Chakradhwaj appealed to the Dacca High Court, where the judge upheld Bir Chandra's appointment. Next, the brothers moved the Privy Council in England which on 15 March 1869 decreed that the British government had no role to play in land-related issues of Hill Tipperah. A year later, on 9 March 1870, Bir Chandra was finally made the adjure King of Hill Tipperah as well as Chakla Roshanabad by the Commissioner of the Chittagong division, Lord Ulick Brown.

After ascending the throne of Tripura, Bir Chandra promised to nominate Nabadwip Chandra as the Juvaraj but did a volte-face, and on 31 August 1870, appointed his son Radhakishore in place of the teenaged Nabadwip.

Crestfallen, the eighteen-year-old Nabadwip Chandra left Agartala along with his mother, probably also fearing a threat to his life. One story which did the rounds at the time was how the young Nabadwip Chandra had once left home to become a monk, but had returned. This time however, it would be a one-way ferry.[2]

Golam Faruk (a Comilla-based lawyer and historian), spoke about the journey of the disgruntled prince. 'Nabadwip Chandra decided to leave Agartala on boat. He went to the ghat reserved exclusively for royalty, but failed to locate the royal boats. He saw two other boats instead, and requested the boatmen to take them to Comilla. They travelled for ten days on the Gomti, and reached the Khaliajuri area in Comilla. The first person who helped Nabadwip Chandra was Mohammed Gazi Chowdhury, one of the biggest zamindars of Plains Tripura. Chowdhury gave them a place to stay that included a prayer room for Nabadwip's mother Jatiswari Rani.'

After settling down in what was his new home, Nabadwip Chandra filed several cases against Bir Chandra, starting one at the District Court in 1874. But the court ruled that as the adjure king, 'Bir Chandra was within his rights to appoint his son as the *Juvaraj*.' However, he began receiving a monthly dole of five hundred and twenty-five rupees from the State fund, and it was around this time that he decided to get married to the daughters of a Manipuri aristocrat, Hem Chandra (or Hem Barna) Sinha, called Nirupama and Khawmabati.

Kumar Shachindra Chandra Debbarman (later shortened to Sachin Dev Burman) was born, as per his own admission, on 1 October 1906 to Nabadwip Chandra Debbarman and Nirupama Debi, at their Comilla house at Chartha. (It is difficult to ascertain the correct year of his birth. According to his son, the late R.D. Burman, the year of his father's birth was 1901, while some other sources put it down to 1903.) He was the youngest in a family of five male and four female children. While the sons—Tribendu, twins Prashanto and Prafulla, Kiran and Sachin are mentioned in the Tripura genealogy, little is known about the daughters of the family, except for the musically-inclined Tillotama, who finds mention in Karta's autobiography.

Sachin acquired the name Karta as per family tradition and came to be known as *Choto* (younger) *Karta* in Comilla. With time, the prefix Choto was truncated; 'Karta' remained, an identity he would carry all his life....

Comilla Days

Nobody was sure of her real name.

She was addressed as 'Robir ma' (Robi's mother) as she had a son called Robi. She was also Karta's *dai ma* (governess; also, foster mother) who would call him Dalim (pomegranate) Kumar for his pink complexion. As was the convention in a royal household, Robir ma was responsible for Karta's upbringing in the palatial house at Chartha, Comilla. Built on sixty bighas of land (a bigha being 17,452 square feet), the estate of Chartha comprised a tennis court and three tanks, a testimony to Comilla's reputation of being a 'city of banks and tanks'.

One of the first teachers in Karta's life was a family servant, Anwar, who taught the young prince fishing using handmade rods from bamboo shoots. But that wasn't the only lesson which mesmerised Karta. It was Anwar's repertoire of bhatiyali (boatmen songs sung while rowing against the tide; the genre traces its origins to East Bengal) which he sang to the accompaniment of the dotara (a multi-stringed instrument mostly used by folk singers in Bengal) that would leave young Karta awe-struck. Later in life, Karta acknowledged Anwar as his first guide in the world of folk music, a genre which many say has a spiritual connection to the soul. And then there was the elderly Madhav, yet another household hand, whose rendition of the Ramayana every Sunday would transport Karta to another world. Madhav knew neither *taan* nor *khatki* (taan is an intricate phrase of

7

rapidly sung notes without any lyrics, using vowels; khatki is a short and swift inflection). The beauty of his music was in its simplicity.

The Comilla household also served as a stopover for itinerant singers who would sing different forms of folksy music which required no great training to understand—baul, kirtan, bhatiyali, gajan, etc.

In 1909, Nabadwip Chandra, at the invitation of the newly-crowned king, Birendrakishore Manikya, grandson of Bir Chandra, finally joined the offices of the Royal family as President, Council of State, and moved to Agartala, the capital of Tripura (as Tipperah was now called). Thus reinstated, after having been exiled earlier by Bir Chandra, Nabadwip Chandra took young Karta along to Agartala where the youngster's formal education would begin.

In 1901, the literacy rate in Hill Tripura was a mere 2.3 per cent and therefore even after a decade, there weren't many schools in the area. After careful consideration, Kumar Boarding, a school for the children of royal families, was chosen as Karta's first alma mater, and he enrolled in 1911.

Unfortunately, the school turned out to be a big disappointment. The main reason being that the teaching staff, which was clearly in awe of its royal patrons, was hesitant in enforcing discipline on its young students, lest it should displease their masters. Nabadwip Chandra waited for two years and shifted his son to Yusuf School in Comilla where the young boy continued till grade four. Later, Karta was admitted to Comilla Zilla School, the oldest in town (established in 1837), where he completed his matriculation. For his intermediate and graduation, the young man went to Victoria College in Comilla of which Satyendra Nath Basu, a revered educator, was the principal—a position he held for thirty-one years and three months from 24 September 1899 till the day he died, 3 January 1931.

Karta was the first graduate in the Tripura royal family. The year was 1924.

However, along with academics, music was also given equal importance in his home. The reason: Nabadwip Chandra, apart from being an able administrator, was a dhrupad singer and a sculptor. He also played the esraj, and had a flair for writing; Bir Chandra wrote poetry, was an accomplished singer, a photographer, and had a great sense of aesthetics. He encouraged musicians, and had once also invited the giant of a luminary like Jadunath Bhattacharya (known as Jadu Bhatta, one of the pioneers of dhrupad in eastern India, whose students included Rabindranath Tagore) to his court. Bir Chandra also hosted Rababi Qasim Ali Khan of the Senia gharana, who tutored Sadu Khan (father of musicians, Allaudin and Aftabuddin Khan) of Brahmanbaria, a village near Comilla.

What was more, Rabindranath Tagore happened to be a good friend of both Bir Chandra and Nabadwip Chandra, who initially enrolled his twin sons at Shantiniketan, although it is widely believed that Tagore had expressed solidarity with the uncle rather than the nephew when it came to politics.[1]

Shyama Charan Datta was a well-known dhrupad artist in Comilla whose disciples included Himangshu Dutta and Shaila Das, the musician and singer Karta would later work with closely. According to Pankaj Kumar Mullick, Shaila Das may have become the best vocalist of country, had it not been for her sudden death at the age of twenty-six in 1944. Apparently, Datta also wanted to teach Karta, but Nabadwip Chandra had decided to take his son under his own wings. Karta's brother, Kiran Kumar, owner of a deep, resonating voice, also doubled up as his younger sibling's mentor and sounding board.

Under the guidance of his father and brother, Karta started learning dhrupad, and gradually evolved into an artiste of repute. There are stories of how even at that young age Karta's singing left an indelible impact on his listeners, and one which was widely retold was about a station-master's mother who was so impressed with his singing prowess that Karta managed to wriggle out of the warehouse where he and his friends had been locked up for travelling without a train ticket.[2]

Like a wandering minstrel, Karta would also go looking for folk music, meeting many a boatmen and nomadic musicians. Notable among them were Saheb Ali, the Sufi artist, or the noted folk singer, Abbas Uddin Ahmed, who taught Karta the art of 'voice-breaking', considered mandatory to express pain in high-pitched songs.

As per Karta's own admission—on rough and hard pathways, in idyllic neighbourhoods, on rippling waterfronts, everyone, and everything seemed to be infused with music. The chirping of birds hidden in the foliage; the 'everywhere' bauls; the giggles of housewives; the splash of ruddy boatmen; and the humming of respectful babus—music was in the salt, mud and water of Comilla. And Agartala. In fact, the whole of Tripura.

Gradually, Karta began giving public performances. Krishnadas Chakrabarti was his usual tabla 'sangat' in Comilla, while it was Rampada Babu who would play along during the soirees in Agartala.

What may come as a surprise to many, the young musician who was so taken in by the beauty of simple, soulful music was also extremely adventurous by nature and loved going into the forest. Once he and his maternal uncle Madan Sinha—who was more like a friend to him— landed in trouble while on a deer hunting mission, and it was Prafulla Karta who had to intervene and rescued them.

An athletic young man, the six-feet-tall Karta was also a regular at Comilla Young Men's Club, and emerged as one of the best tennis players in the state, travelling for tournaments to different parts in the country. He later enrolled as a member of Tippera Club, which was founded by his father. Amongst several sporting activities, football was one of his favourite games and not only did he play as a forward, he also officiated as a referee in a few Indian Football Association (IFA) matches.

However, higher education beckoned, and Nabadwip Chandra had him enrolled for MA in English literature at Calcutta University. Curious at the prospect of going to a city to study, Karta agreed, considering the options in Tripura were limited. But ultimately, it would be toss-up between either being a prince or a musician.

The strains of Comilla's music faded out as the royal carriage set out on its journey carrying Karta to Dacca railway station to catch the train to Sealdah (Calcutta). But Karta carried all of it in his mind, body, heart and soul. He could never go too far away from it....

Calcutta—1925–1931

S achin Karta's move to Calcutta in mid-1925 was probably auspicious for the East Bengal Club. In what was the first known derby between two football giants, it won the season's league match against Mohun Bagan. Karta, who later became a life member, would remain a fanatical supporter of the club.

Meanwhile it was time for the young man to settle in the new city. The Maharaja of Tripura owned a few houses in Calcutta—one was near the crossing of Park Street and Short Street. Another was called 'Green Park', at Number 59, Ballygunge, the residence of E.T. Sandys, the Manager of Maharaja of Tripura. Nabadwip Chandra, who was the President of the Regency Council in the Ministry of Tripura, settled his son at Number 59, Ballygunge (which was later renamed as Ballygunge Circular road).

In 1925, although Calcutta boasted of both raw and refined intellect in arts and music, there existed an instability factor in its very fabric. Its reputation as the centre of political power had dwindled after Delhi was made the capital in 1911 (the transition began in 1912, and was completed in 1931).

Moreover, Calcutta was at the forefront of the freedom struggle. But the divide and rule policy of the British had shaken the secular foundation of the region to such an extent that it led to the partition of Bengal on religious grounds in 1905.

Although intrigued by the prospects of a life in the new big city, Sachin Karta did not take a fancy to Calcutta. Somehow, the glamour, cold concrete, and bright lights of the city subdued his small-town spirits. He was particularly dumbfounded by the thought that land in the city was a commodity; as he discovered, it was bought and sold, sometimes in pieces!

He would spend most of his days inside the university library, sifting through textbooks and reference material. After the daily grind, the dazzling street lights blinded his view of the virgin skies. Even water bodies, like the one in front of the university buildings, which reminded him of his beloved Comilla, were mere consolations. The river Ganga was probably the only bright spot in an otherwise drab and routine life. The MA degree, which was dangled like a carrot by his father, had failed to whet his appetite.

Nabadwip Chandra sensed his son's disinclination towards academics and thinking that it was perhaps English literature which had made him turn against studies, he had him enrolled at the Law College.

But by this time, Karta had already decided to pursue music. As mentioned in his autobiography, in 1925 he sought to learn Hindustani classical music under Krishna Chandra Dey (Manna Dey's uncle)[1].

'Keshto babu', as Krishna Chandra Dey was popularly known as, took Karta under his care and began training him. However, on the side, the young man continued to pursue tennis at the YMCA and with time, performed so well that the Anglo Indian community, which would refuse to play with 'natives', now waited to play a game with him.

Karta's guru however advised him to give up tennis, as he felt that the constant sweating during the game could prove detrimental for his voice*.

---

* Not medically proven though. In fact, physical exercise helps in clearing mucus, increases fitness levels, which may ultimately lead to a stronger voice. Many classical singers and flautists practised wrestling to increase lung and muscle power. Pandit Hari Prasad Chaurasia acknowledges wrestling as the source of his enduring lung power.

Keshto Babu's style was more light than classical and he had what is known as an 'open-throated' voice, which he used to advantage in his theatrical performances, often singing in D sharp scale. The maestro was also known to hit straight notes, a trait he passed on to his disciple.

Meanwhile, course books continued to terrorise Karta and he gave up Law within a few months. But Nabadwip Chandra was relentless and tried persuading his son to train in General Administration from England, in order to eventually find a high-ranking job in the Ministry of Tripura. Karta was in a conundrum. While he found it difficult to say 'no' to his father each time, his heart was clearly not in academics.

Finally, Nabadwip Chandra respected his son's decision—higher education if any, would only be in the field of music.

Karta's next gurus were Bhismadev Chattopadhyay and Badal Khan. The latter who was a nonagenarian at the time, began taking the young man to musical soirees. Karta also started learning Banarasi thumri from Shamlal Khatri, who exposed the young prince to the classiest of musical gatherings in Calcutta. One of Shamlal's students was Girija Shankar Chakrabarty, the best-known thumri singer in Calcutta, whom Karta had the privilege of hearing on multiple occasions. Among the patrons he met, the brilliant sociologist and musicologist, Dhurjati Prasad (or D.P.) Mukherji was someone who remained a fan of Karta all his life. As did his son, Kumar Prasad Mukherji, arguably the best and last musicologist in twentieth-century Bengal.

Karta's network took roots. The word spread. Radio beckoned.

The Indian Broadcasting Company (IBC) came into being in Bombay in July 1927, and went on air in Calcutta in August. Three years later, the IBC went into liquidation, but was re-launched as Indian State Broadcasting Company on 1 April 1930 (which later became All India Radio [AIR] in 1936). Karta composed and sang two songs for a fifteen-minute slot for the Indian State Broadcasting Company. Although the exact date of the recital is not known, author H.Q. Chowdhury pins down the year as 1928[2], while researcher, Jayati Gangopadhyay suggests it could have been anytime around 1930. Given that in his

14

memoirs, Karta had specially mentioned the Indian State Broadcasting Company and not IBC or AIR, one would tend to agree with Jayati Gangopadhyay.[3] The directors at the radio station included, Rai Chand Boral and Nripen Mozumder, who appreciated Karta's music. It was here that Karta received his first salary, an honorarium of ten rupees!

Calcutta—1932–1944

Renaissance & Basic Songs

The fifteen-minute opportunity on radio was just a beginning. As a singer, Karta's evolution had as much to with his grounding in the basics of folk and Hindustani classical music, as it was to Bengal Renaissance.

Till the late nineteenth century, the audience for Hindustani classical music in Calcutta comprised the affluent—particularly, wealthy zamindars. Although jatra (folk theatre) was open to the masses, the music in such performances was yet to evolve as a separate oeuvre. But it nevertheless came as a respite to the common man, who found the complex patterns of notes and grammar of Hindustani classical difficult to comprehend.

Nineteenth-century Bengal witnessed the birth of four poet-musicians—Rabindranath Tagore; Dwijendralal (D.L.) Ray; Rajanikanta Sen; and Atulprasad Sen.[1] There is no gainsaying the fact that people's acceptance of the poetic quartet's compositions led to the genesis of the modern Bengali song.

With time, the commercial viability of modern Bengali songs increased during the annual festival of Durga Puja, with the release of shellacs coinciding with the four-day festival. This gave birth to the term 'pujor gaan' or the 'puja song'. Muhammad Kasem (who used the pseudonym, K. Mallik), known for his Shyama sangeet (songs dedicated to Goddess Kali), rendered his first puja song for HMV in 1914.[2]

As was the norm, Karta would also begin recording what came to be widely known as basic (non-film) Bengali songs.

However, on 5 September 1931, tragedy struck the Debbarman family when Nabadwip Chandra passed away suddenly at the age of seventy-eight.

Hindusthan

'...*Nasal voice*.... *Faulty pronunciation*.... *Not fit to be recorded*...'

—Verdict by HMV after Karta's audition, 1931

The aforesaid rejection, shocking as it may sound to several, however had precedents. K.L. Saigal was an HMV reject, as was Juthika Roy. However, there were also instances of verdicts being reversed. Amal Banerjee, an HMV (now SaReGaMa) veteran for over three decades, told the authors[1], 'Juthika Roy was rejected when Kazi Nazrul Islam (one of the pioneers of the Bengali song in twentieth century, he is celebrated as the national poet of Bangladesh) was part of the audition committee. She was selected only when Kamal Dasgupta joined HMV.'

Karta's Calcutta chapter may have well ended after the HMV rejection, had it not been for his friend, Naren Dev Burman who recommended Karta to Chandi Charan Saha, the founder of Hindusthan Musical Products. On 5 April 1932, Karta became one of their first recorded artistes. According to Sovon Lal Saha, son of C.C. Saha, who runs his father's company (now renamed Inreco), the serial number of that recording was 19[2].

At this point in his life, Karta was obviously compelled to take the acid test, and gave the recording opportunity all he had. The inimitable stamp of his vocal and composing repertoire—from classical to folk—was engraved in the 78-RPM shellac that was published as record number

18

H11. *Ei pathey aaj esho priya*, written by Sailen Roy, was like a short khayal with intricate taans, in raga Manj Khamaj. On the other side of the shellac was his first recorded song, the bhatiyali-based, *Daakle kokil roj bihane* written by Hemendra Roy. Both the numbers were three minutes and eleven seconds long.[3, 4]

Back home in Tripura, the royal family was not amused at their 'heir's' preoccupation with commercial music. Amongst other things, Karta faced two major objections—one, he had refused to go back to Tripura, and two, he was making music for a living.

What was worse, with his father's untimely demise, he had one supporter less. Legend has it that members of Tripura royalty had stopped sending him money, forcing Karta to shift to a one-room apartment near Bhawanipore in south Calcutta. However according to Sachin Ganguly, who was Karta's fan-cum-secretary in Calcutta in the late 1940s- early-1950s, the royal family did send him money, which Karta refused to accept.[5]

However, Karta's stay at the one-room house was short-lived. According to Goutam Ghosh, head of instrumental music at Rabindra Bharati University, 'That house on Gopal Banerjee Street where Karta lived was part of the houses owned by the Singha family. Chotai Mitra, who used to liaison with New Theatres, had helped Karta get a house there. The house belonged to my *mejo dadu* (mejo meaning the one in the middle in Bengali; dadu, grandfather) Pannalal Singha or Panu babu as he was commonly known, who was in-charge of electrical works at New Theatres studio. Wealthy, pompous and conceited, Panu babu did not accept any rent from his royal guest. While that may have seemed like a respectful gesture, Panu babu, on hearing Karta do his early morning *riyaaz* (practice), asked him to vacate the apartment saying, "If you must continue your music, please leave this place. Your voice is not good. It is high-pitched and sounds like a crow cawing."'[6]

With this began Karta's house-hunting spree—with some difficulty, he found another house which was also a one-room apartment at Bakul Bagan, Bhawanipore, in south-central Calcutta; he next shifted to another apartment on Palit Street, Bhawanipore, as a tenant of artist Rashomoy Bhattacharya who used to address his tenant as 'Raja babu'.

As mentioned earlier, with the ceasing of financial aid from home, Karta found it difficult to sustain in Calcutta. As a result, he began giving music tuitions at home, and also started performing at *jalsas* (musical shows). It was around this time when he seriously tried his hand at music direction in films. Birendra Nath Sircar's studio in New Theatres, which had its humble beginnings as International Film Craft, was the ultimate destination for young aspirants, but in the presence of stalwarts like R.C. Boral and Pankaj Kumar Mullick, there was little room for Karta to find employment as a composer. But there was always an opportunity in the singing department. Even as it seemed that Karta was finally finding his feet, he faced his first roadblock—his Hindi accent was found to be extremely faulty, and he was replaced by Pahari Sanyal (who hailed from Lucknow and therefore spoke Hindi fluently) in *Yahudi ki Ladki* (1933). Karta's friendship with NT's publicist, Sudhirendra Sanyal did not help either. Although he often wrote lyrics for Karta, he couldn't do much for his friend.

By now one would have thought that the man who could have been king, would have packed his bags and bid adieu to music. But Karta, like most successful people, refused to give up. Within a span of a year (June 1932–July 1933), at the recommendation of lyricist Hemendra Roy, Karta composed nine songs for the well-known playwright, Sachindranath Sengupta.

In his memoirs, Hemendra Roy wrote admiringly about Karta's dedication, his voice (particularly, the broken voice which added more charm), and his distinct style of singing. He further added:

> I loved the play of melody in his voice and he loved my words. This created a special bonding and we started visiting each other even without any prior intimation or invitation.... As a composer, he was no less. He has the capacity to enunciate the lyrics through his tunes. I was amazed by the tunes which he

composed for my songs, *Bulbuli ke tariye dili, phool bagan er natun mali* and *Aajke amar ektarate ekti je naam bajiye choli*. His song, *O kalo megh bolte paaro*, not only earned him bouquets from the audience, but also endeared him to music aficionados. He has mastered the art of composing for modern *Kabya geetis* (songs which have both poetry and music).

Roy also took it upon himself to publicise his friend's songs. The celebrated novelist, poet, educator and filmmaker Premendra Mitra, mentioned a particular incident in his Introduction to *Hemendra Kumar Roy Rachnabali*, Volume III, as follows:

> Poet Jatin Bagchi had a house on Hindustan Road. We would assemble there in the evening. On one such evening, around 9 p.m., there was a knock on a window which was at the end of the house. It was Hemendra Kumar Roy, accompanied by a young man.
>
> Hemendra then announced that the young lad would sing a few songs written by him.
>
> We thought it was rather late for such a performance. But the singing mesmerised us. The lyrics, the singing, the voice—all of such high quality. The young lad, then unknown to all of us, was Sachin Dev Burman.

It was obvious that Karta had impressed Premendra Mitra to such an extent that the latter began writing for him. However, soon thereafter both Mitra and Hemendra Roy began to focus on their original literary pursuits and moved away from writing for cinema.

Consequently, Karta called his friend, Ajoy Bhattacharya, the metricist to come from Comilla, as the two had in the past shared a wonderful professional relationship. Bhaskar Bose, a Bangalore-based arts aficionado told the authors a story that was narrated to him by his English teacher, Anjan Bhattacharya, the son of Ajoy Bhattacharya, 'One day Karta told my father, "Ajoy, I have composed a tune. I have been polishing it for some time. Would you like to write the lyrics?" After hearing Karta's rendition, my father cut open a cigarette packet and started scribbling. In no time, it took shape into the famous song, *Tumi je giyecho bokul bichano pothe*.'

It needs to be mentioned here that the ethereal quality in Karta's singing was also because of Ajoy Bhattacharya's simple-sounding, yet reflective poetry. The man was a maverick and understood styles so well that he could almost make his poems sound like the works of Tagore and Nazrul. In the annals of popular Bengali music, he along with Himangshu Dutta and Sachin Dev Burman came to be known as the 'Comilla triumvirate' of melody.

Apart from his forays into light music, there was also the occasional traditional song that brought Karta huge popularity. For instance, *Nishithye jaiyo re phool o bone re bhomora*, which was written by Jasimuddin, based on a Sheikh Bhanu original. (In 1942, Karta recorded a Hindi version of it {*Dheere se jaana bagiyan mein*} and made a grand entry into the Bombay film industry.)

In 1934, Karta was invited to the All India Music conference at Allahabad University. Abhijit Dasgupta, Karta's brother-in-law, narrated to the authors what was hitherto unknown about the musician, 'Ustad Allaudin Khan had gifted Dadababu (as Karta was addressed by his brother-in-law) two tanpuras with huge *toombas* (the base of the instrument). At Allahabad, he was allotted fifteen minutes to sing. Sometime earlier, Karta's guru, Bhismadev Chattopadhyay had advised him—"Don't sing during the first three minutes. Just play the tanpura, irrespective of the public's reaction." The sound of the tanpura created a magical ambience, and the thumri-based composition did the rest.'

After the recital, Sachin Dev Burman was awarded a gold medal from none other than one of the brightest luminaries of Allahabad High Court, Dr Kailash Nath Katju. It was during this trip that Karta also met with Khan Sahib Abdul Karim Khan (doyen of the Kirana gharana). As a musician, although he wasn't a follower of Khan Sahib's style nor had studied under his feet, the meeting was a godsend as the maestro passed away soon thereafter, in 1937.

Subsequent to his performance in 1934, Allahabad University invited him for three successive years. Indrajit Banerji,[7] a Calcutta-based fan of Sachin Dev Burman, whose father was present at the conference, told the authors that during one of those visits, a bare-bodied lungi-clad Karta had kept pacing up and down the terrace the whole night. The reason: he was nervous of missing a front row seat at the Faiyaz Khan (of the Agra gharana) recital, arguably one the greatest vocalists in the sub-continent!

In 1935, in what could be termed as a dream come true, the young musician met Faiyaz Khan at the Calcutta Music Conference and became his *shagird* (pupil). The office of Hindusthan Musical Products at Akrur Dutta Lane in Calcutta became their regular haunt and many an evening would be spent with the Ustad on the ground floor living room, even as the owner, C.C. Saha would arrange for snacks such as, *muri* (puffed rice) and *telebhaja* (deep-fried snacks) with several rounds of tea to keep the duo going.

Meanwhile, back in Calcutta, he recorded his first song in 1935, *Bandhu baanshi* dao mor which went on to become a huge hit amongst the youth. In the same year, Karta also scored the music for two short films, *Sanjher Pidim* and *Sudurer Priya*. Much to his discomfort, he was also made to act in films—for instance, *Sadhana* (1935), in which he played the role of a beggar. As is well known, acting in films wasn't

---

* *Baanshi* (flute in Bengali) is a word which finds repeat mentions in Karta's songs. As a child, he used to play the Tippera flute. It was said that his reputation as a flautist not only preceded, but also exceeded his reputation as a singer in Comilla. Ajoy Bhattacharya once recounted how Tippera flutes were in great demand in Calcutta, and he would get them for budding artistes. Although Karta never played the flute professionally, it became a constant theme in his songs from time to time. Some notable examples being, *Baanshuria re kothaye shikhecho* (1941), *Tui ki shyamer baanshi re* (1945), *Baanshi tomar hathe dilaam* (1949), *Baje na baanshi go* (1949), *Baanshi shune aar kaaj nai* (1960), *Ashamye bajaao baanshi* (1967), etc.

considered respectable those days, and particularly in the case of Karta, it was deemed sacrilegious, and the young man feared being ostracised by his family in case word spread about his foray into acting.

Two years later, Karta felt somewhat more settled in his career. Thanks to Sukumar Dasgupta (who would introduce another legend, Suchitra Sen sixteen years later, in *Saat Number Kayedi*), he signed a feature film called *Rajgee* and had enough work for every subsequent year till 1940 when it increased several folds. In order to help his pupil, Karta's guru, Bhismadev Chattopadhyay would often double up as his associate music director.

Life was good and work was looking better when an unpleasant incident disrupted the teacher-pupil's association which was on its way to becoming a successful collaboration. According to musicologist Suresh Chakrabarti, who had also trained under Bhismadev and belonged to Comilla, Karta had apparently undercut his teacher during an assignment. The incident had impacted Bhimsadev to such an extent that many years later when Karta had travelled a long distance to meet his guru who was living in exile at an ashram in Pondicherry (now Puducherry), he was given a cold shoulder.[8]

While things had started looking up for Karta, his reputation as a film composer was still to be established. In order to better his dwindling finances, he started a music school in his two-room apartment on 1, Raja Basanta Roy Road and called it Sur Mandir. He later moved to yet another two-room apartment at 21 C, Hindustan road, near Dover lane in Calcutta where Paresh Lal Roy, the 'Father of Indian boxing', was his neighbour. Roy's grandson, who spent his childhood in this house, went on to create history in the Indian television industry and the world knows him today as Dr Prannoy Roy of NDTV 24x7.

As a teacher, Karta taught what he imbibed from his gurus. According to Debasish Roy (whose father, a reputed folk singer of the 1960s, the late Suresh Roy who had trained under Karta), 'Sachin Karta was very particular about getting under the skin of a song, and focussed on the correct intonation of words. His lessons were like meditation sessions. Unlike present-day gurus, he would teach only one student at a time. But he was open to suggestions. If someone added value by using a different note or introduced an extra inflection, he would appreciate it. To Karta, orthodoxy did not mean rigidity. And, although my father never told me about the fees etc., I think his guru was happy with a nominal fee,' he said.[9]

During the annual Saraswati Puja celebrations in Sur Mandir, Karta would sometimes join his students with the *dhak* (a large Indian drum played mostly during religious festivals). While he was adept at playing the dhak, there is unfortunately no record of his expertise on the tabla which he played like a professional with accomplished singers during private recitals (known as *ghoroa* sessions). He was left-handed when it came to playing rhythm instruments and angling. To label him a southpaw would be inaccurate, as unlike singer Mukesh or music director Jaikishan, he used his right hand to play the harmonium. His son, Pancham shared his father's ambidextrous trait as well.

The Wedding

In 1937, Amita Sen (the mother of Nobel laureate, Dr Amartya Sen) was teaching Kathak to a young girl called Meera who also was a student of Sur Mandir. The young girl confided in her guru ma that she had fallen desperately in love with her music teacher's voice.

According to Sovon Saha, Karta had first met Meera at a music tuition on the ground floor office of Hindusthan Musical Products, while Meera's aunt, Sukla Dasgupta, mentioned that the two had first met at Karta's guru, Bhismadev's place, as students. Be that as it may, a year later, Meera married Sachin and became Meera Dev Burman.

Anuradha Gupta[1] spoke to the authors about her cousin, Meera and their family background: 'My maternal grandfather was the renowned Dhaka-based lawyer, Justice Kamal Nath Dasgupta. My mother, Mrinal Dasgupta was the seventh in a line of five brothers and five sisters. Indubala was the fifth child, whom I called *ranga mashi*.

'Indubala was a sweet child. As she was from a rich and established family, she was brought up with great care. She studied in English medium, and was one of the first women to graduate from Dacca University. Her marriage was arranged with a barrister from Comilla, Sudhir Dutta Roy, who unfortunately didn't turn out to be a pleasant man. He used to abuse her physically. Finally, pregnant with Meera, Indubala fled her husband's home and never went back. Her husband remarried and sired two sons from his second marriage.'

Dipankar Dasgupta, a retired professor from the Indian Statistical Institute, Calcutta, and nephew of Indubala Devi, also recounted the torture his aunt had borne.[2] 'It was inhuman—from kicking her in the stomach during pregnancy, to drenching her in sugar syrup and tying her to a pole in the courtyard during a scorching summer afternoon! Her father-in-law who was a kind soul, dropped Indubala back to her father's house (my grandfather's house) in Dhaka. While in her natal home, my aunt spent most of her time with her brothers, and later moved into the house built by her son-in-law. In all probability, Meera never saw her father.'

Meanwhile, as was expected, several members of Tripura royalty strongly disapproved of the alliance—firstly, Meera was a commoner and second, she was almost half her husband's age. Moreover, an amorous relationship between a teacher and student was considered morally inappropriate. But Karta had made up his mind and married Meera on 10 February 1938.

After a grand wedding, the newly-married couple went on their honeymoon and spent time at the Louis Jubilee Sanatorium in Darjeeling. Some twenty-seven years later, their son would also find his first love in Darjeeling.[3]

Despite the opposition to his marriage by family members, Karta proceeded to Agartala with his bride. In what mustn't have come as a surprise but predictably hurt him for several years, the women of the royal household cold-shouldered the young Meera and that left Karta terribly upset.

A year later, on 27 June 1939, Meera gave birth to a baby boy who was named Rahul. The child was the apple of his parents' eyes and went by several nicknames—Tublu, Tulamu, and the name by which he would be known and admired by music lovers across the world—Pancham.

Anuradha Gupta spoke about her nephew who was only a few years younger than her.[4] 'I was very close to him, more a friend than an aunt. Pancham was very mischievous. I remember the day my mashi (Indubala) had returned from Dhananjay Das babaji's *diksha* (initiation) ceremony and had her head covered with her sari *pallu*. Pancham pulled the pallu off her head and ran out, exposing his grandma's clean-shaven head. (She had shaved her head as part of the dikhsha ceremony).

'Pancham was emotional, shy and used to be ridiculed by elders in the family, especially his mashis (maternal aunts). The consensus was that he would be a failure in life, as he hardly had any inclination towards academics.

'I remember as a child, he was extremely fair, and would turn red while blushing. Also, he was good at forging signatures. One of the best that I remember was the round face of character actor, Om Prakash, with his signature inside. Of the lot, the boy was very fond of my maternal uncle, his *mani dadu* (Nirmal Dasgupta), and looked up to him for inspiration.'

With a wife and child to care for, Karta was now looking for a steady source of income, which happened a year after his son's birth. Even Rai Chand Boral used him in one song, *Ke jeno kandiche* for the film *Nari* (1941). By the early 1940s, Karta's twin facets as an artist—folk singer and composer—were distinctly manifest in the Bengali *adhunik gaan* (modern songs) genre. He was equally comfortable with semi-classical, which lent him an edge over his peers who chose to limit themselves to either folk or the semi-classical variety of music. Karta and Tarapodo Chakraborty were the first to master the *raagpradhan gaan* (classical-based light music), a term coined by Suresh Chakrabarti.

Incidentally, most of Karta's hits happened to be composed by his friends, Himangshu Dutta or Nazrul Islam. The former understood his friend's voice rather well, as he made him perform intricate inflections in the most uncomplicated way. The most significant aspect of this kind of style was that a listener could instantly identify with it and found the tunes easy to repeat. Some of Dutta's compositions like, *Jodi dokhino pobon, Alo chhaya dola, Premer samadhi teere* or *Natun phagune jabe* rank among the best songs of Karta then, as they are even today. The last song has a *nat* phrase that must have undoubtedly inspired Karta, as he used it in several subsequent compositions, an early example being, *Ki maya laaglo* from the film *Pratishodh* (1941).

The four Nazrul geetis (songs that were written and composed by Nazrul Islam) sung by Karta—*Padmar dheu re; Chokh gelo pakhi; Kuhu kuhu bole koyeliya;* and *Meghla nishi bhore* impressed the urban gentry as much as they touched the hearts of the rural folk. To add to this repertoire were melodies that he learnt during his childhood from Abbas Uddin and the itinerant fakir, Saheb Ali.

By the early 1940s, Karta's voice underwent change—from forceful, it became sweeter with softer and sharper inflections. This 'new voice' was what was popularly termed as a *wailing timbre*. While his reputation as an accomplished vocalist was abundantly manifest, little or unconfirmed accounts abound regarding his evolution as the front-ranking composer of modern Bengali songs. There is evidence to show that during the decade spanning 1932–1942, Karta leaned more towards semi-classical music. For e.g., *Tumi je chile mor* and *Jago mama saheli go* were both composed and sung around 1938. But in Karta's folk vs. semi-classical battle, the former clearly won in a knockout.

Gradually, even as folk and Sachin Dev became synonymous, in retrospect, there has always been a raging debate about the type and style of folk he sang. According to the musicologist, Rajeshwar Mitra, Karta's repertoire had its origins in the interiors of Mymensingh, Brahmanbaria and Comilla (now in Bangladesh), and thus cannot be confined to the similar-sounding, bhatiyali. However, there was no doubt that as a musical genre, bhatiyali was indeed intrinsic to his nature. Moreover, as was evident, his exposure to various forms of music helped him break out from the existing trends and helped him later in life.

'Bengali folk tunes are primarily pentatonic. Bhatiyali is an exception as it places no restrictions on the use of notes. The only constraint is on the use of tabla as it is expected that the sound of lapping of oars on still waters be duplicated. Given the all-encompassing nature of bhatiyali, it can easily be called the king of Bengali folk music,' said Debashis Roy.[5]

Further research threw up an interesting connect between bhatiyali and Hindustani classical music. Several well-known bhatiyali tunes follow the seven basic notes with a 'ni' (komal ni), mirroring the Khamaj thaat in classical music. Curiously, Karta's very first composition, *Daakle kokil roj bihane*, was indeed bhatiyali, as was his debut film song, *Ore sujan naiya* from *Sanjher Pradip*.

Varman—Bombay, 1944–1949

Though there were many deviations to the name Shachin and Deb, Bombay rechristened Barman as 'Varman'. This continued till the beginning of the 1950s.

Filmistan

Circa 1943. While Bengal wilted under an engineered famine, the Bombay film industry was witnessing the birth of one of its most famous start-ups, albeit under unpleasant circumstances.

For the iconic Bombay Talkies, it had been a fabulous run from the time of *Jawani ki Hawa* (1935), till *Kangan* (1939). But with the outbreak of the Second World War in September 1939, everything changed. The German technicians working under Himanshu Rai, the genius of an owner of Bombay Talkies, were forced to return home. Within a year, Rai who was not only under tremendous stress owing to the abrupt changes, but also overworked, died during the making of two films—*Bandhan* (1940) and *Jhoola* (1941).

It was during this chaotic phase of Bombay Talkies' history when Himanshu Rai's deputy, Sasadhar Mukerji and Devika Rani (Rai's widow and later the de facto owner of Bombay Talkies) began having differences over several issues. Resorting to the time-tested divide-and-rule policy of the British, Devika Rani brought in Amiya Chakraborty as a co-writer and assistant, and later promoted him to producer-director, on the rolls of Bombay Talkies. This upset S. Mukerji, who was not only the producer, but often the ghost director for most of Bombay Talkies' films. After a series of meetings with Devika Rani, a compromise was worked out—henceforth, S. Mukerji and Amiya Chakraborty would produce and direct alternate films for Bombay Talkies.[1]

33

However, even this failed and things reached a flashpoint in mid-1943, when *Kismet* was in post-production. S. Mukerji issued an ultimatum to Devika Rani: 'Either Chakraborty or me.' She stuck to her guns. Mukerji walked out and so did some of the other major stakeholders of the studio such as, Rai Bahadur Chunilal, Gyan Mukherjee, and Ashok Kumar.[2]

The mass exodus resulted in the birth of a new studio and Shaheed Latif, who was married to the famous writer, Ismat Chugtai, christened it, Filmistan. The rebel group lost no time and announced its first production titled, *Chal Chal Re Naujawan* (1944).

Shachin Deb Barman came on board as part of the recruitment drive. Probir Mukherjea, a Calcutta-based musician and lawyer who was acquainted with both the Deb Barmans and Mukerjis said, 'S. Mukerji was very fond of the Nazrul song, *Chokh gelo pakhi*, which was sung by Karta. Mukerji wanted the song for his new film.'[3]

Kalyani Kazi, the daughter-in-law of poet Kazi Nazrul Islam, told the authors that Nazrul, much to his consternation, had had a tough time getting Barman's diction right for '*chokh*'. Barman would pronounce it as 'chalk' (English) as he had a strong East Bengal accent.[4]

One fine morning in October 1944, the well-known novelist Saradindu Bandyopadhayay, who was then working for Filmistan, received Shachin Karta, Meera, Pancham, Nirmal Kumar Dasgupta and his wife, Sukla, at the Victoria Terminus. They were first put up in a shanty in Borivili and later relocated to a small flat owned by a Gujarati couple.

As was and still is a common pre-condition for tenancy in some parts of India amongst certain communities, there was a complete embargo on the consumption of non-vegetarian food in the house. The Barmans, who were strictly non-vegetarians, paid little heed to the sine qua non. Fish was a staple diet for the family, and the Barmans devised an ingenious method to clear the fish bones by collecting them in a packet to be thrown away elsewhere. One fine morning, when the landlady invited herself to their house, fish was being cooked in the kitchen. The Barman couple, assisted by their cook Suryamani, frantically arranged for incense sticks to suppress the strong odour of fish![5]

So far as his surname was concerned, it is quite likely that Barman was unheard of in the Bombay film industry, which incidentally had the similar-sounding 'Varman' in large numbers. It was perhaps because of this reason why Barman was erroneously referred to as Varman. Sometime later, Barman had a letter pad printed where his name was spelt as S.D. Varman, and he also began using it as his signature. However, there were also instances where he would spell his surname as 'Deva Varma'.

After settling down in Bombay—which included getting familiar with musicians at Bombay Talkies—Varman had to wait for over a year for his first release. The film was called, *Shikari*.

It all began as a salvage operation. Filmistan's first production, *Chal Chal Re Naujawan* was a commercial failure and the studio had run into heavy debts. S. Mukerji was known to place a huge premium on public opinion and wanted to be doubly sure that his team gets it right the second time. Saadat Hasan Manto (one of twentieth century's greatest writers, who migrated to Pakistan after Partition) was commissioned to write a story to appease the British government. Varman was roped in to compose music for *Shikari*, while Savak Vacha was to be its director.

However, *Shikari* went through a series of delays. Nalini Jaywant, who was signed up as the film's leading lady, opted out because of a contractual fall-out with her then husband, Virendra Desai and studio honcho, Rai Bahadur Chunilal. She was replaced by Mumtaz Shanti, who was unfortunately found to be unsuitable for the role. Finally, two new actresses, Veera and Paro, were cast opposite Ashok Kumar. Wartime rules mandated that scripts be cleared by the Censor Board in Delhi, and Gyan Mukherjee was forced to spend a considerable amount of time lobbying in the capital. Eventually, all these factors had a domino effect on other Filmistan productions like *Safar* and *Lokmanya Tilak*.

The publicity material for films like *Shikari*, *Safar* or *Lokmanya Tilak* did not carry the names of music directors. As part of their overall strategy, Filmistan was probably selective while publishing the names of music directors on such material.

After the initial hiccups, *Shikari* was ready for release and the promotions began with some interesting catch-phrases—'The arrows rushed to their strings, when they challenged his right to live his own life,' and, 'See the tug of war between these two damsels to capture their prince charming', and so on. Finally, on 5 January 1946, *Shikari* saw the light of day and had a decent run at Roxy Cinema, Bombay.

Varman's first composition in Bombay was sung by none other than Ashok Kumar. Interestingly, it was a bhatiyali song, *Dol rahi hai naiyya*, and was based on Nazrul's, *Chokh gelo pakhi*. The song was used strategically in the narrative, almost like a war cry by the chieftain (played by Ashok Kumar) while attacking the Japanese in Burma. It was probably also the only memorable song in the film.

In his autobiography, Varman wrote about how the music of *Shikari*[6] had not only earned him praise from the cast and crew, but also the press. However, in the February 1946 issue of *Filmindia*, Baburao Patel, who was known for his acerbic reviews, wrote:

The lyrics of Gopalsing Nepali are quite good and written in a very simple language with words which help musical phonetics. The musical tunes, however, must be considered as very poor (sic).

Nevertheless, the film had several firsts to its credit—for instance, in the song, *Chupo o marne se darne walon*, the phrase, '*Ding lala oyi lala*,' was later used to great comic effect in *Paanch rupaiya barah anna* from *Chalti Ka Naam Gaadi* (1958); *Rangila re, rangila re* was Kishore Kumar's first recorded song as an adult in a Hindi film, although he was not officially credited for it; this song also has the distinction of being the first Hindi version of Burman's Bengali song—*Rongila rongila* which he composed and sang in 1945.

Additionally, *Shikari* in all probability may well have been the first Hindi film in which the lyrics were written to tunes. Varman knew precious little Hindi, and even lesser Urdu, and thus inadvertently, pioneered the concept of writing to tunes. According to the renowned journalist, Raju Bharatan, there were also disagreements during the recording of *Shikari's* songs as Varman had difficulties in the arrangement[7]. Finally, C. Ramchandra, the composer-singer, who was working on Filmistan's *Safar*, was summoned to sort things out. The reason: orchestration was not Varman's strength, and in Bombay, it was extremely important, than it was in Calcutta. One must also mention here that even in this department, about which he was still learning, Burman relied heavily on the guidance of his guru, Bhismadev Chattopadhyay.

While the Bombay run of *Shikari* would subsequently find mention in the autobiographies of both Ashok Kumar and Varman, the Calcutta run, which was scheduled for a single-hall release at Paradise on 23 August[8] was marred by an extremely horrific incident in the history of pre-Independent India.

On 16 August 1946, Calcutta woke up to one of its worst nightmares as the city was brutally assaulted by unprecedented communal violence owing to Direct Action Day which drove a deep schism in an otherwise peaceful city.

Not only did Bengal face severe shortages of food and other amenities, Calcuta seemed to be in the grip of a terrible fear. In cinema halls, night shows were suspended indefinitely,[9] and there were advertisements in newspapers announcing—'Please note the change in timings.' Not only was the production and distribution of Bengali films stalled, not a single Hindi film was released during the period, forcing theatre owners to screen films that were lying with local distributors. Thus, quite a few of Varman's films came back in circulation including, *Chhadmabeshi* and *Rajkumarer Nirbashon*. *Matri Hara*, the last film Varman worked on before leaving for Bombay was released in December 1944, and which had generated little interest at the time of its release, surprisingly had a decent re-run at Rupbani theatre.[10]

Unfortunately, communal riots had also spread to Bombay and partly due to which, despite concluding the film on time, Filmistan's production number five, *Eight Days* (or *Aath Din*), was put on hold. Varman was also working on Mohan Sinha's period drama, *Chittor Vijay*, but even that had to be postponed for some time. Much like Calcutta, starting September 1946, night shows were suspended in Bombay as well[11].

A month later, the situation improved and augured well for the film industry. *Eight Days*, a story which had its genesis in a conversation over brandy between Saadat Hasan Manto and Savak Vacha, was released shortly thereafter. It is a well known fact but merits mention here that the film which later went on to become a huge hit was ghost-directed by Ashok Kumar, although it was officially credited to its editor, Dattaram Pai.

This was also Varman's first Hindi film in Calcutta for an audience which had waited endlessly for *Shikari** and was pining for some entertainment in their otherwise tumultuous lives. On 9 May 1947, *Eight Days* was released simultaneously in Paradise, Bina, and Park Show House, but the demand

---

* Eventually, *Shikari* never made it to Calcutta. In April 1947, there were ads in the papers about the film's release at Roxy. For reasons unknown, the reels of the film didn't arrive. Instead, *Basant* (1942), a five-year-old Bombay Talkies' production was rushed in as a replacement, which ended the grand run of *Kismet*.

for the film was such that its distributor, Kapurchand Ltd., had to order two extra prints which were later screened at Chitralekha and Aleya. On week four, the print was sent from Bina to Bhabani theatre and post week six, the film was finally withdrawn after having run simultaneously at four different halls. In effect, it completed a cumulative run of close to twenty-five weeks, which was a feat in itself.[12]

It is often said that the best person to sing a composition is none other than its creator, as was proven in the case of *Eight Days*. *Umeed bhara panchi*, the Varman solo continues to be popular even today. The film also included his first ever duet with a male singer, S.L. Puri—*Babu babu re dil ko bachana*.

After all the adulation, it is intriguing why Varman sang his next Hindi film song thirteen years later.

Despite the early success with Filmistan, Varman found the city of Bombay a bit too regimental for his liking. As mentioned earlier, not only did he miss the magic of Ganga, he found the rationing of water strange, considering he had always been blessed with abundance since childhood. But gradually, Bombay endeared itself to the musician. While his basic Bengali songs with lyricist Mohini Chowdhury[13] were applauded in Bengal, Varman would never return to Calcutta permanently. The city's tumultuous political situation and dwindling commerce deterred him.

However, he did take a while to make up his mind, because during one of his subsequent trips to Calcutta, he left his family with his mother-in-law, Indubala.

On 18 March 1955, *Filmfare* published an article by Sachin Dev Varman

in which he explained the mechanics of Hindi film music:

> I had just joined Filmistan and at an informal gathering at Malad, I was giving a recital of my songs before S. Mukerji, the Filmistan chief, Ashok Kumar (Dadamoni to all of us), Pradeep, the lyric poet, and others. In the midst of it I heard a jarring sound which was supposed to be a message of appreciation from an admiring listener. Who could it be? I looked in the direction of the sound and turned pale. The culprit was none other than my boss, Mr. Mukerji, whom I knew to be a true lover of music and whose style of singing was like my own. How could I satisfy his ear?
>
> As days went by, I made further discoveries regarding his sense of rhythm and harmony. Every day after lunch I had to carry my harmonium to his room. Lying comfortably on a sofa, he listened to my compositions, then closed his eyes, and presently snored! The snore was a signal that my composition was disapproved.
>
> This ordeal continued for nearly two months and I came to the end of my patience. I also came to the conclusion that if I could not please my boss, there was no point in my staying on at Filmistan, just to sing lullabies to him. The next day I went prepared for a showdown.
>
> As usual I started playing the harmonium and went on humming my new tune till my boss's eyes closed. There was nothing more to do. I had only to wait for the inevitable snore. But suddenly the boss woke up and said, "Mr Burman, why don't you get it recorded?"
>
> "Record what?" I asked.
>
> "I mean this tune. You may call the musicians and start rehearsing right now," he said.
>
> I was puzzled and wondered why of all the tunes I composed for him all this time he liked this one. I found out the same evening.

As I was coming out of the rehearsal room the 'room-boy' (door-keeper) was humming the tune and quite correctly too! This gave me an idea. From that day I made it a point to get my tunes 'approved' by the 'room-boy'. It worked. In almost all cases the room-boy's approval carried.

The secret of Mr Mukerji's judgement was, as he told me one day, the formula of universal appeal. He said, "You see, Mr Burman, you have your own style of music, which I like. By all means keep it up but present it in such a way that film lovers may like it and feel at home with it—not only in Bombay or Bengal but all over the country."

With this and many other pieces of sound advice the man who had apparently no rhythm or harmony guided me over the difficult road to success for which I shall always remain grateful to him.

Back then, music directors enjoyed the luxury of music rooms inside a studio. Varman too had one in Filmistan, which he shared with Khemchand Prakash, who was on contract with the studio for a film called *Sindoor* (1947). As was the norm, a room-boy would run errands like serving tea and food to musicians. It was during this phase when Varman once mentioned how the room-boy, who would be listening to his compositions for most part of the day, would instead sing Naushad Ali's songs from *Rattan*!

The room-boy's preference for *Rattan* had more than one reason. This modern-day Laila-Majnu story was the biggest hit during the mid-1940s. Released a week after *Shikari* at the Imperial in Bombay, it celebrated a 100-week run at metros, including at Paramount in Calcutta. A special colour version was also readied and exhibited in other theatres around the country.

Naushad Ali's picture would adorn the ads of his forthcoming films, a rare achievement for a composer those days.

While the music of *Eight Days* worked, Varman who had his roots in classical music, discovered that composing a catchy tune wasn't easy. Filmistan had given him the liberty to freelance and as mentioned earlier, he had already begun composing for Mohan Sinha, but unfortunately his work in such films was somehow eclipsed. *Chittor Vijay* (1947) which was delayed inordinately was one, while *Dil ki Rani* (1947) was another.

Historically however, *Chittor Vijay* was significant as Geeta (nee Roy) Dutt sang her first song for Varman in this Raj Kapoor–Madhubala starrer. Alas, the songs aren't available today and are perhaps tucked away in someone's private collection.

Dil ki Rani also had Raj and Madhubala as the lead pair, and this was the film in which Varman was credited as Kumar Sachindra Deo Varman. He used Raj Kapoor to sing his own songs in the film (the star was indeed a good singer, and had previously sung in *Jail Yatra* under the baton of Ninu Mazumder), and *O duniya ke rehene walo bolo kahan gaya chitchor*, ran like a motif all through the film. It was also Varman's first tandem composition in the history of Hindi cinema, as a multi-singer version of the same number was used in the film.

What was most surprising was although the press went hammer and tongs after *Chittor Vijay* and *Dil ki Rani*, Varman was spared the ignominy. Although it is difficult to guess if Varman was even aware of it, considering he somehow always managed to have the press on his side. It was as if the critics had reposed great faith in this promising composer whose next big hit was waiting to happen.

The next big release from S. Mukerji's stable was *Do Bhai* which was screened in Bombay on 2 April 1948[14] at Novelty, a cinema hall that along with Roxy, was host to most of Filmistan's releases. The publicity vehicle had been jolly wagging along well ahead of the release and in a happy departure from the norm, the film turned out to be a musical success. Even Baburao Patel, who had previously rubbished Varman in *Shikari*, had kind words to say:

The picture has a few songs nicely worded and well-set to music and that is the only relieving feature of an otherwise silly, boring and meaningless picture.

Do Bhai had a lengthy playlist of nine songs and heralded the debut of Mohammad Rafi and G.M. Durrani for Varman. While Rafi would go on to become one of Varman's favourite playback singers, Durrani, the star singer of the 1940s, faded out, ending up as a junior artiste in films.

There is interesting trivia about Rafi's song in the film—*Duniya mein meri aaj andhera hee andhera*. In his autobiography, Manna Dey spoke about his days of internship under Varman, which included teaching singers, and mentions how Rafi was also tutored by him. Given that this was the only song Rafi sang for Varman in the 1940s (see, *Hindi Film Geet Kosh*, Volume II), this could have been the only song that Manna Dey ever taught Rafi while working for Burman!

The number that earned Varman accolades was also Geeta Roy's first hit in Hindi cinema. Featured on Kamini Kaushal who was swathed in a beautiful sari and wore exquisite jewellery, it was Varman's first experimentation with Rabindra Sangeet in a Hindi film. In his autobiography, Varman mentioned how the 'all-important' room-boy had also given his approval for *Mera sundar sapna beet gaya*!

As a medium of musical expression in cinema, Rabindra Sangeet had found a place from the early 1930s. In his autobiography, singer-composer Pankaj Mullick wrote how he along with Rai Chand Boral had used Tagore's tunes as the background score for the first talkie by New Theatres called, *Dena Paona* (1931). Rajib Gupta, Pankaj Mullick's grandson told the authors, 'During my grandfather's childhood, *Rabi Babur gaan* (Rabindranath Tagore's songs) were almost mandatory amongst the adherents of Brahmo Samaj. There were instances where one or two words would be changed as per convenience. The 78 RPM of *Mukti*, which had alterations to the original words and musical notations had been sent to Tagore by New Theatres for approval. Tagore, after hearing the songs, signed the record with the words, "APPROVED".'

Rabindranath Tagore was generally known to be inflexible about any modifications made to his compositions. In 1925–26, he had apparently got into a lengthy debate with musician and aesthete Dilip Kumar Roy, son of D.L. Roy, and it was probably this conversation which had ultimately convinced Tagore to soften his stand. Unfortunately, Viswa-Bharati University, the vanguards of Rabindra Sangeet, were less generous than the poet Nobel Laureate himself! However, there was no adverse reaction by the university on the use of *Rodon bhora e bosonto* as *Mera sundar sapna*, a song Tagore wrote and set to tune for the dance drama, *Chitrangada* in 1892. Perhaps the cordial relationship between the Varmans and Tagores had something to do with the university's generosity!*

The song was a fabulous hit and Varman made most of it by proactively publicising his role as its composer. The beauty of it was in the way he had rephrased the second antara or paragraph. *Mera sundar sapna* was basically a sad song, which was rendered in a slightly dragging fashion by Geeta Roy, and although emoting beyond a point does sound unnatural and over-the-top at times, Geeta's measured singing made it sound utterly contemporary. Her voice carried weight and bass and for a girl her age (she was just sixteen), her understanding of the emotional quotient was impeccable.

The dusky doe-eyed girl with a Mona Lisa smile and a voice that could fluctuate between joie de vivre and the calmness of an ocean, went on to become one of the most sought after female singers in the next decade. A student of Pandit Hanuman Prasad, Geeta Roy had a unique style which was particularly suitable to cinema, which involved

---

* Tagore's compositions were influenced by various genres of music. Folk, baul, Western, Carnatic, *tappa*, *thumri*, etc. But the obvious inspiration was dhrupad and its phrases (*asthayi*, *antara*, *sanchari*, *abhog*), of which Tagore used the first three in most cases. Use of the sanchari is predominantly a Bengali feature in Indian light music. It may be noted that Karta, despite drawing inspiration from Tagore from time to time, hardly used the sanchari in his compositions. It was more pronounced in the songs of New Theatres (composed by Pankaj Mullick, R.C. Boral), and later, O.P. Nayyar, who inspired by these masters, did use it on more than one occasion.

showcasing a gamut of emotions in a span of three to four minutes. Geeta's other solo, *Yaad karoge yaad karoge ek din humko yaad karoge* has tremendous recall value even today, nearly seventy years after the release of the film.

Do Bhai was Varman's penultimate film for Filmistan in the 1940s. The film's success and the money earned from several other assignments helped him shift to a large apartment called, R.V. Sanatorium on a small hillock in Sion, and soon his family joined him from Calcutta. It was during this phase that he began travelling in local trains to film studios.[14]

The Partition

While Varman's career in Bombay was still to take off, the ground beneath the subcontinent was witnessing a tectonic shift as India and Pakistan were being formed over a mammoth tragedy called the Partition, in 1947.

A year earlier, on 7 March 1946, Varman accompanied by Meera and Pancham, travelled to Agartala to condole the death of his brother, Prafulla Kumar. After the shraddha ceremony, marking the last rites for the departed, he sold off whatever little he had in Agartala and never looked back. It is not known what had triggered a dispute of this proportion, but it was said that neither was Varman willing to forgive nor forget. He had never bothered about his royal status and had avowed to give up his association with the family altogether. Although there are no written accounts to substantiate such claims, it was widely speculated that Varman had been deeply impacted by his father's financial status and the indifference shown towards his wife, by his family. Even today, there is an unwritten code of silence amongst members of the erstwhile Tripura royalty as they deign to discuss the topic.

But truth be told, his heart still craved for his place of birth. During the Partition, Varman had tried staking claim to his Chartha house in Comilla. He had even written a letter to his cousin, Kamini Kumar Singha, who was a retired minister of Tripura state, which was published in 2006 by Suresh Kumar Singha, a relative from Varman's maternal side.

46

Even seventy years later, the Partition of the subcontinent is recalled as a mindless and cruel reality. The Boundary Commission of Bengal headed by Cyril Radcliffe ensured that Tripura virtually ended up in no man's land. On 15 October 1949, Hill Tripura joined India, while most of 'Plain territory Tripura' became part of East Pakistan. Comilla ceased to be part of India; Varman had become an outsider; he would never go back to his birthplace.

The Would-be Stars

The octogenarian Sachin Ganguly went back in time and recalled a particularly interesting incident to the authors. 'A few decades ago, I had seen a documentary on S.D. Burman. If I remember right, it was perhaps shown at St. Xavier's College, Calcutta. The film had multiple shots of Sachinda dressed in a white dhoti and panjabi (kurta) walking past studios. His face was not shown, only a pair of legs walking endlessly. This conveyed a basic fact. Sachinda was struggling. No one outside the fraternity knew him. He was not getting work.

'I was with him for a few days during his initial days of struggle. He once told me, "Look, Bobby (the name by which Burman addressed Sachin Ganguly), I have been offered another film by Filmistan, starring Dilip Kumar and Kamini Kaushal. They are offering me twenty-two to twenty-four thousand rupees for it. Shall I take it or go back to Calcutta?"

'I suggested that he accepts the offer.'

Varman's predicament was the result of a lesson learnt from an earlier film titled *Vidya* (1948), which revolved around the theme of untouchability. *Vidya* had indifferent music, for Varman had recycled some of his Bengali songs—for instance, *Prem jamunaye hoyto keu* became *Pyaar banake mujhpe koi chaa gaya*, which was sung by Lalita Dewoolkar (who later married composer Sudhir Phadke and was known as Lalita Phadke). The Suraiya–Mukesh duet, *Layi khushi ki duniya* was the Hindi version of the Varman–Meera duet, *Ke dilo ghum bhangaye*. Both songs sounded contrived, devoid of any surprise elements which was expected of a film starring Dev Anand and Suraiya, as it was speculated that the two were romantically involved. Moreover, Mukesh as Dev's playback wasn't a great choice either.

The director of *Vidya*, Girish Trivedi belonged to the Mohan Sinha school of filmmaking. His amateurish efforts had almost succeeded in jeopardising the career of a young actor called Dev Anand and if it hadn't been for *Ziddi* (1948), the industry might have had one megastar less.

It was reported that the then Prime Minister of Bombay, B.G. Kher who had come to the premiere of the film with his wife in January 1949, had excused himself politely during the interval, so tedious was the pace of the film.[1]

The failure of *Vidya* had left Varman disappointed. He sent Meera and Pancham back to Calcutta and gave up two rooms in his four-room apartment in Sion. Varman now decided to punt on his next film titled, *Shabnam*. This 1949 film was loosely adapted from Arthur Crabtree's *Caravan* (1946) and was a potpourri of genres—social drama, fantasy, and a highway robbery involving migrants from Rangoon. The success of Kishore Sahu's *Sindoor*, which was partially a road movie, had probably encouraged S. Mukerji and Chunni Lal to repeat the formula. The film had absurd elements like the heroine (Kamini Kaushal) disguised as a boy, till she is discovered during a bathing sequence and the hero, Dilip Kumar playing a gypsy for most part of the film. Be that as it may, it was perhaps the chemistry between the leading stars which gave a great pre-release fillip to *Shabnam*.

Filmistan's publicity material for the film wasn't particularly innovative either, but it was certainly upfront: 'Entertainment Full to the brim'; 'Universal Applause—a grand musical extravaganza with 11 outstanding songs and 6 magnificent dance numbers.'[2]

Following in the footsteps of two stalwart music directors, Anil Biswas and Naushad, Varman also used Mukesh as Dilip Kumar's playback.

The actor was rather happy with the choice of Mukesh and said it in no uncertain terms in his biography penned by Urmila Lanba titled, *Life and Films of Dilip Kumar*.

Despite the stupendous success of *Mera sundar sapna beet gaya*, Varman chose Shamshad Begum over Geeta Roy as the main female voice for *Shabnam*. Even though the film's music can't be defined as unforgettable, *Shabnam* did make a mark.

Varman recounted the popularity of *Shabnam's* music as follows:

Once I was waiting at Bandra station to catch a train for Malad. Suddenly, I discovered that the train had come, halted and left, but I didn't realize. What was I doing? Well, I was mesmerised by a group of labourers singing a song from *Shabnam* to the rhythm of the movements made by their hammers and shovels.

An interesting point in the film was that in a sequence, the heroine is heard humming a number from *Saajan* (1947) which was composed by C. Ramchandra and not Burman!

Sachin Ganguly recollected another incident about a song from the film, as follows, 'Karta had composed a multi-lingual song—*Ye duniya roop ki chor*—for the film. We were coming out of the premiere show in Bombay and Karta was almost assaulted by a group of people who he thought were reaching out for his autograph. The group came up to us and asked him, "Are you the composer of *Shabnam?*" Karta was literally pulling out the pen from his button-hole when he realised that they were Tamils and were incensed by the fact that he had derided their community by composing the parody song.'

While Varman was not to be blamed—he hadn't written the song—he decided to apply caution when it came to respecting the sentiments of all communities in the country.

The success of *Shabnam* gave Dilip Kumar his first car. Varman continued travelling in local trains, but on a first-class ticket.

HMV, Bombay & Bengali Songs

In the late 1940s, Varman recorded a large number of songs. For instance, in 1948, he recorded two with his wife, Meera, who later earned the rare distinction of being the only person to have recorded basic Bengali and Hindi songs under her husband's baton.

Varman's sudden leaning towards Calcutta, which he had left for opportunities in Bombay, was because he needed more work and had begun recording for HMV.

It is important to mention here that Varman's loyalty towards Hindusthan Musical Products was questioned in 1946 when he had sung for *Eight Days*, the audio rights of which were controlled by HMV. It was rumoured that the owner of Hindusthan, Chandi Charan Saha, and his family harboured a grouse against Varman who had shifted loyalties, as against K.L. Saigal who had signed fifty blank contracts as a mark of respect to Saha before leaving Calcutta for Bombay and had kept his promise by never recording for HMV.

But then, Prince Varman was a struggler whose negotiating power in Bombay was limited, unlike Saigal, who went to Bombay as King and remained one till his death, in 1947.

In 1949, when Varman arrived, accompanied by Sachin Ganguly, composer N. Dutta (originally known as Dutta Naik), and sitar player Suhrid Kar at the HMV studio in Bombay for recording, there was no welcome party to receive them. After wandering around aimlessly for a while, the quartet sought help from a member of the HMV studio staff who checked the register and confirmed that there was a recording slot booked by a certain Sachin Dev Varman. He asked the team to proceed to room numer 11 in which the four men found the classical musician, Gangubai Hangal rehearsing. This went on for quite some time after which Varman lost his temper. Sachin Ganguly stepped in to pacify him and led the rest into a vacant room and the recording proceeded without any major disruption.[1] Lo and behold, Varman's career as a singer of Bengali basic songs in Bombay had commenced without the customary fanfare due to an artiste of his calibre. He recorded two songs that day—*Baaje na baanshi go* and *Ami potho cheye robo*, written by Gauri Prasanna Mazumder.

In the meantime, *Kamal* (1949), advertised as the 'Year's best in entertainment'[2], proved to be enervating. The only interesting point was the Hindi version of Varman's Bengali hit, *Haye ki je kori e mono niya* (which was later redone by Pancham as, *Toone o rangeele kaisa jadu kiya* in *Kudrat* in 1981).

The trend of the Bengali version scoring more brownie points than its Hindi counterpart continued even when the Hindi version and not the Bengali was the original. In 1948, for a change, Varman recorded the Bengali version of *Pehle na samjha pyaar ka* (*Eight Days*) as *Ei chaiti sandhya jaye britha*, and it went on to become one of his most popular songs. The intonation, style, and especially the pathos was particularly heart-rending.

The other song that Varman recorded in 1948 was *Bodhu go ei madhumaas*. He later used the first line of the sanchari multiple times; for example, this became the first line of the refrain of *Chup hai dharti chup hain chand sitare* (*House Number 44*, 1955).

One of the reasons *Kamal* didn't soar was probably because of Varman's distance from the lyricist, Prem Dhawan. The man who is credited with one of the most iconic songs in the history of Hindi film music, *Ai mere pyare watan* (*Kabuliwala*, 1962), was somehow unable to convert his talent into success.

Varman was a worried man. The gains of *Shabnam* were unfortunately negated by the rejection of *Kamal* at the box office. As a result, he had to give up his two-room apartment and move to Evergreen Hotel in Khar. By now, Pancham was studying at Ballygunge Government School in Calcutta. Later, Meera would leave him with his grandmother, who also taught him English, and return to be with her husband in Bombay. It was during this period that Mrigendranath Lahiri, a friend of the family, became Pancham's local guardian and continued his association with him until his death in January 1994.[3]

In so far as Varman's career was concerned, there was a storm brewing over using Kishore Kumar as the voice of Raj Kapoor in *Pyar*, which was ready in 1950, but had a delayed release in May 1951. Despite the fabulous chemistry between Raj and Nargis, the film flopped. Baburao Patel's review of *Pyar* had gems like, 'Another Dave-Vyas trash (M.G. Dave and V.M. Vyas respectively); Stupid old tale fails miserably,'; and 'Vyas's direction is stupid in the extreme and the only one thing that beats it in stupidity is Dave's story.'[4]

Curiously, not much has ever been discussed about the music of the film. *Ek hum aur doosre tum*, a duet between Kishore and Geeta was Varman's first attempt at using the refrain from a Hollywood background theme, *Algiers* (1938), as the prelude to a song. There wasn't anything particularly remarkable about the experiment, except that the last line had Geeta singing the harmony, while Kishore sang the melody. However, the Kishore solo in the film, *Jalti hai duniya, tera mera pyaar hai* became more popular in the Bengali version, *Shei je dinguli* in 1951. This was one, while the other being, *Jhilmil jhilmil joler dhare*, after which Varman gave up professional singing for five years till the Durga Puja in 1956. This indicated good tidings for him between 1951 and 1956, in Bombay.

It is interesting to note that even after he'd decided to pursue a career in Bombay, and had virtually bid goodbye to Calcutta, he still had a desire to retire in the city and bought four kathas of land (1 katha being 720 square feet) near Dhakuria lake. Abhijit Dasgupta said[5], 'A certain gentleman owned four plots around west Dhakuria. Three friends, Keshto kaku, Dadababu, and my father purchased them. Keshto kaku, who had bought two plots of land sold one off to Justice Mitra. This was in 1945–46. The construction of the house began in 1947. It was a two-storied building and each floor had three bedrooms. Dadababu's house and ours were mirror images of each other. I remember that even the *grihapravesh* (house warming ceremony) happened on the same day.'

Varman's house was completed around 1949 and was registered in Meera's name. Soon, Varman's mother-in-law, Indubala and Pancham moved into the new house. On his subsequent trips to Calcutta, Varman would hold musical sessions on the ground floor drawing room of the house until he was forced to shift to the first floor (where he used to play Patience when not practising music), unable to deal with curious onlookers who would peep into his room.[6]

Subsequently, he kept the first floor to himself, and offered the ground floor to prospective tenants. Soon thereafter, he signed a lease agreement with Metal Box and Company (now defunct), and took in the company's General Manager, a Tamilian[7] as his first tenant. While the extra income helped Varman financially, it also assured the maintenance of the building. Abhijit Dasgupta[8] however failed to recall any tenant, but remembered that Varman would take in paying guests, who were well looked after by Pitambar, his full-time retainer who had a long innings at 36/1 South End Park. Interestingly, this house happened to be the only property which bore his name prominently—'Shachin Dev Barman'.

Sachin Dev Burman

From 1950, courtesy Bombay Talkies and Navketan, Shachin Deb Varman was rechristened as Sachin Dev Burman.

Romancing Bombay Talkies

Nydia, the blind flower girl in *The Last Days of Pompeii* written by Edward Bulwer-Lytton had inspired the eponymous sculpture by the great American artist, Randolph Rogers. Further extrapolation suggested that the novel might have even inspired Sir Charles Chaplin in *City Lights* (1931). Be that as it may, the renowned novelist Bankim Chandra Chatterjee accredited Nydia for his story, *Rajani*, a blind girl who sold flowers in late nineteenth century Bengal.

Following a short stint at Filmistan, Ashok Kumar and Savak Vacha returned to Bombay Talkies after Devika Rani married the celebrated Russian painter, Svetoslav Roerich and bid adieu to the studio. In his autobiography called *Jeewan Naiyya*, Ashok Kumar mentions how Bombay Talkies was not only reeling under the burden of a huge debt amounting to 2.8 million rupees (or twenty-eight lacs), but what was even worse was that in September 1948 the studio was ravaged by a fire and a part of it had to be rebuilt. During his second stint at Bombay Talkies, Ashok Kumar commissioned *Majboor* (1948) and *Ziddi* (1948), and their respective successes pulled the studio out of a grave financial crisis. But all wasn't over yet as Bombay Talkies still remained under a huge debt of three hundred thousand rupees.

Mashal, which was based on Bankim Chandra Chatterjee's *Rajani* was launched by Ashok Kumar almost in tandem with *Mahal*, India's first ghost movie directed by Kamal Amrohi—released on 29 December

1950, at Roxy, Bombay, replacing *Mahal*, which, after its release coinciding with Ashok Kumar's birthday (13 October) in 1950, was moved to another theatre.

The making of *Mashal* was a stop-start ride. Originally, Sunanda Banerjee was contracted to play the female lead, but the choice had created such a controversy amongst some stakeholders that she was replaced by Sumitra Devi. During the making of the film, Bijoya Das, who was playing a supporting role, married her cousin Satyajit Ray, who was then a graphic designer! Ruma Ghosh, who was playing the role of the blind girl in love with Kanu Roy (not to be confused with the music director of the same name), fell in love with Kishore Kumar, and this became a subject of concern for Ashok Kumar as love marriages were taboo back then. On top of it all was the challenge of shooting the film simultaneously in Hindi and Bengali (*Samar*), and it therefore took two long years to complete.

Directed by Nitin Bose, *Mashal* was a success and its music somewhat steadied S.D. Burman's career. According to Ashok Kumar, as quoted in his autobiography:

> I was instrumental in getting Sachin Karta from Calcutta to write the music for *Shikari* and *Eight Days*. Unfortunately, he was not getting a strong grip in Bombay. After trying for around 3-4 years, he decided to go back to Calcutta. The work for *Mashal* was in the initial stages at that time. I told him to do the music for the film. He was noncommittal, and expressed the desire to return to Calcutta. I inveigled him and gave him the option to go back to Calcutta after completing the work for *Mashal*.

> The songs of *Mashal* became immensely popular and he abandoned the idea of leaving Bombay altogether.

Mashal also put the spotlight on Burman's assistant, Manna Dey, who apart from completing the work on the background score, had his first hit song.

In the early 1940s, Probodh Chandra Dey aka Mana (he became

Manna after his nickname was mispronounced and misspelt in Bombay) arrived in Bombay to assist Krishna Chandra Dey and began his career with a song in a 1942 film called *Tamanna*. In the year of India's Independence, Manna Dey decided to leave Bombay for Calcutta along with his ailing uncle, but fate had something else in store for him. The well-known director, Phani Majumdar required an assistant for composer Hariprasanna Das and called Manna back to Bombay, where the singer began his second stint.

Initially however, Bombay wasn't kind to the young and supremely talented singer. His ideas evinced cynicism from composers, and his playback attempts were openly scoffed at. Even as mediocre singers found regular work and prospered, Manna struggled each day, till *Mashal* happened to him.

In his autobiography, he made a reference to the film and particularly to the song[1], as follows:

> My search for work would take me from one studio to the other, mostly without result. There would be times when I feared that fate had nothing much in store for me, except for music direction in inconsequential films, or singing songs featured on Balmiki or on Hanuman wagging his tail.

> Rafi, Mukesh, Talat Mahmood, all of them had music directors who were dedicated to them. I did not. Also, Sachinda who in spite of knowing me from the time he was my uncle's student, had never composed a song for me, despite my having assisted him and trained his singers. Ultimately, my wish came true. Sachinda gave me *Upar gagan vishal*, the song which helped me prove my musical credentials to the whole country.

However, in an interview with the writer, Ganesh Anantharaman,[2] Manna Dey contradicted himself partially, stating that the melody for *Upar gagan vishal* was originally composed by Kavi Pradeep. The reason could have been because lyricists of yore would often sing their words set to a base metre, and certain music directors were known to take that as the final tune for a song. There is also a possibility that Burman may have developed the original tune suggested by Pradeep. Be that as it may, *Upar gagan vishal* became Manna Dey's first hit in Hindi films.

The background score of the film made waves and the man behind it was someone who assisted Burman for several years thereafter—N. Dutta, who wasn't credited in the film, but did a stellar job. In 1960, when Dutta scored the music for *Jaalsaaz,* he reset and recast the title score of *Mashal* in the song, *Mere dil, meri jaan.*

Mashal had another milestone—one of historical significance to music lovers—this was the film in which Lata Mangeshkar sang for S.D. Burman for the first time. Sachin Ganguly shared an interesting anecdote about this incomparable coming together of two legends, 'Those days studios were not sound proof and recordings would often take place post 8 p.m., once the city had gone to sleep. It was well past midnight during a *Mashal* recording. Sachinda didn't have a car. Lata was already a star and one of the youngest singers to own one. She offered to take us home. Manna and Sachinda insisted on being dropped off near a bridge from where they planned to take a public conveyance despite Lata's insistence. Sachinda considered taking a favour against his principles. He also told me categorically to not let Meera *boudi* (sister-in-law in Bengali) know about this incident.'

In the Bengali version of the same film titled, *Samar,* Kishore Kumar sang his first ever Bengali song. Sachin Ganguly regaled us with yet another nugget in the context[3], 'During the recording of *Sundari lo Sundari*, Kishore entered Bombay Talkies wearing a cream-coloured silk kurta, a white pyjama, and a black-and-white polka-dotted muffler. While teaching him the song, Karta started singing the portion meant for Kishore, while Kishore was asked to do the female part of the song, as Geeta Dutt was not present just then. So the whole song was rehearsed with Karta doing the male portions and Kishore singing in a woman's voice!'

Mashal was probably the first film which had his name as composer: 'Kumar Sachin Dev Burman', a name by which, sans the 'Kumar', he would be known in years to come. The change of spelling on the letter pad, however, came much later.

In February 1951, *The Motion Picture Magazine* carried a glorious review of the film. About the music, the magazine reported:

> Music by S.D. Burman and Munna Dey (*that is how his name was spelt in the title card;* italics ours) was distinctly different from the type of music which is in vogue these days with the music directors and because of this, more than its real merit, it succeeds in appealing to the listeners. Its great asset was its soft and pleasant orchestral compositions. Lyrics by the onetime top notcher Pradeep were so simply worded that they clicked with everyone because of the philosophy they seemed to preach.

If *Shabnam* helped S.D. Burman connect with the masses, *Mashal* brought him acceptance from the elite. Most importantly, it cemented his long association with future legends such as, Lata, Manna and Kishore.

Finally, or so it seemed for the time being, Burman was well settled in his musical career and began pursuing his childhood hobbies of fishing and football. He was known to have never ever missed any game at the Cooperage stadium, especially if East Bengal was playing. One can imagine that their 3–0 win over Eastern Rail (then East India Railway) in the finals of the Rovers Cup in 1949 must have made him ecstatic. On days when East Bengal was either not playing or had crashed out of the tournament, Burman would support other Calcutta teams like, Mohun Bagan or Mohammedan Sporting. He would also arrange football matches for his team of musicians and needless to say, play the referee.

It was around this time when Ashok Kumar's protégé, Dev Anand, was firming up plans for his future projects and S.D. Burman would begin his decades-long association with him.

41, Pali Hill: The Anands

In the mid-1940s, 41, Pali Hill was a sprawling bungalow in what was then the outskirts of Bombay. The monthly rent for the house was a meagre fifty rupees, which was paid by its young resident called Chetan Anand. After a short stint as a teacher at the famous Doon School, Chetan entered showbiz. But even before he began making films, he along with some of his friends wanted to start a theatre group and soon, 41, Pali Hill began to be frequented by writers, directors, poets, technicians and musicians—Guru Dutt, Mohan Segal, Raj Khosla, Balraj Sahni and his wife, Damayanti (who passed away tragically in 1947), Pandit Ravi Shankar and Ustad Ali Akbar Khan. These luminaries were also part of the IPTA's theatre group which was run by K.A. Abbas and was affiliated to Leftist ideology.

In one of his interviews with the authors, Chetan Anand's son, Ketan Anand recalled those halcyon days and said, 'They all argued and played chess throughout the day and rehearsed at night and performed whenever they could, at various venues like Azad Maidan, Jai Hind College auditorium or Sundar Bai Hall....' The bunch would then travel in the late night local train which would be full of milkmen and fisherwomen on their way to sell their wares.

After his stint with theatre, acting and writing, Chetan Anand made his critically acclaimed (but a failure at the box office) *Neecha Nagar* in 1946. Three years later, he floated a film company and called it Navketan—named after his son Ketan who was born on 19 July 1947 in undivided India. The first film under Navketan's banner was *Afsar* (1950), which was based on Nikolai Gogol's *Inspector General*, the film version of which had Danny Kaye in the title role. S.D. Burman, who was also a member of the 41, Pali Hill group, was signed on as its music director.[1]

However, *Afsar* starring Dev Anand in the title role, flopped, and Burman's music, which was a mix of multiple genres, received a modest response. One wonders if his overzealousness had tired him out, but it did seem like he had tried too hard and ended up creating a confusing potpourri! For instance, the mukhda of *Nain deewani* featured on and sung by Suraiya, was a note-by-note copy of Tagore's extremely popular song, *Shey din dujone*. Contrary to normal practice, even the antara had snatches of the original tune. Another Suraiya solo, *Gun gun gun gun* was a cleverly crafted Hindi version of the well-known Bengali kirtan, *Bhojo gourango*. However, *Man mora hua matwala* was a song which registered with listeners and had a wonderful sitar obligato by Suhrid Kar, who was assiting Burman in the film.

In the overall scheme of things, *Afsar's* music didn't have a prodigious recall value, which included two parodies sung by character actor, Manmohan Krishna, who was also an active member of the 41, Pali Hill group.

❧

Cometh 1950, and the Bombay music scenario underwent an overhaul.

Khemchand Prakash passed away suddenly, bereft of the accolades that he received, albeit posthumously for his brilliant score in *Mahal* (1949); Anil Biswas was also losing his hold in the film industry; only C. Ramchandra and Naushad Ali were living up to their reputation. As the decade of Fifties progressed, Lady Luck blessed the young duo of

65

Shankar–Jaikishan with several successes, followed closely by a certain O.P. Nayyar.

In 1950, Burman had some catching up to do. He knew the intricacies of his oeuvre, but commerce was still Latin and Greek to him. But given his control over melody and his innate sense of humour, he was not only supported by his team members, but also revered by singers and composers alike. Once during the recording of *Nain diwani*, Suraiya made an error, and Burman jokingly waved his silver-topped walking-stick in the air and pretended to hit her on the head. Suraiya giggled in embarrassment, but immediately rectified the mistake.

If seen through the prism of an important contemporary marketing principle, what was missing in S.D. Burman's music was a distinctive style to make him stand apart from the rest in a crowd. Additionally, he also needed a big hit and even as he must have wondered about the way forward, a young man called Sahir Ludhianvi happened to him. And a film called *Baazi*.

The Gamble

As Lord Meghnad Desai mentioned in *Nehru's Hero Dilip Kumar*, 'Dev Anand was the young urbane man straddling the boundary between the police and the criminal.' The grey elements in the characters that he played with such great aplomb was inspired by the Forties' genre of noir prevalent in Hollywood. But then, it was Ashok Kumar—whom Dev Anand considered his guru—who was the first to portray such a character in Gyan Mukherjee's *Kismet* (1943). In the fitness of things, a certain Guru Dutt, who was Gyan Mukherjee's assistant, would go on to define Dev Anand's screen persona, which completely mesmerised an entire generation in a film called *Baazi*, which was released on 15 June 1951 at Swastick Cinema, Bombay.

In an interview to the *Open* magazine in 2007, Dev Anand had mentioned that *Baazi* was inspired from *Gilda* (1946), which he had either seen in Bombay or Pune, when he was employed with Prabhat Studios.

It was at the hostel in Prabhat where he first met Guru Dutt, owing to a gaffe made by a washerman who had given Dev's shirt to Guru and vice-versa. The hostelmates' friendship grew and often, Dev and Guru, now also accompanied by Rehman (who was a lead actor then) would be seen riding bicycles in and around Prabhat Studios—where the FTII stands today.

In 1946, Guru Dutt and Dev Anand's first film titled, *Hum Ek Hain*, directed by Pyare Lal Santoshi (father of Raj Kumar Santoshi) was released. Dev's next film was out a year later in 1947 called *Mohan*, which was directed by Anadi Nath Banerjee, a member of Uday Shankar's academy in Almora of which Guru Dutt was a member in the early 1940s. As is common amongst young friends, as strugglers in the film industry, Guru and Dev had made a commitment to each other. If Dev were to ever produce a film, Guru would direct it; and if Guru directed a film ever, Dev would play the lead.

Having spent his childhood in Calcutta, Guru Dutt was drawn to Bengali literature and the cinema of Pramathesh Chandra Barua and New Theatres. He was also very fond of Bengali music, particularly that of Sachin Dev Burman. Abhijit Dasgupta narrated a wonderful incident about the two men. It was when Guru Dutt was staying at Burman's house in Calcutta. 'One day I was summoned by Dadababu to his house for something that he said was important. On entering the ground floor drawing room of his house, I saw that Guru Dutt, Tulamu (R.D.Burman) and he were standing in three out of the four corners in the room. I was told to occupy the fourth. There were some toy buses and all four of us were to play a game called "Accident", whereby buses would bump into each other. Such was the youthfulness of the man (Burman), and the same spirit seeped into his music.'

It can be safely assumed that the on-boarding of Sachin Dev Burman for *Baazi* must have been a unanimous decision on the part of Guru Dutt and Dev Anand[1]. Sahir, of course was the fourth ace in the pack.

Sahir Ludhianvi (born Abdul Hayee) had a tumultuous childhood and as a result of which, he grew up to be a loner. His poetry brilliantly captured the angst of the underdog and those who lived dangerously on the periphery of society.

Although personally, Sahir never recounted how and when he met Sachin Dev Burman, Akshay Manwani in his book, *Sahir Ludhianvi, The People's Poet, says:*

Having spent a year in Bombay, following a protracted period of struggle, Sahir finally got the break that he had long waited for. Mohan Segal, a friend of Sahir's, told him that S.D. Burman, the music director, was on the lookout for a lyricist and that Burman appreciated new talents.

Acting on Segal's tip, Sahir went to meet Burman at the Green Hotel in Khar. As the story goes, there was a 'Please do not disturb' sign outside Burman's room, but Sahir took this to be of no more significance than the 'Please don't make noise' sign in a coffee house. He walked straight into Burman's room, introduced himself, and gave his reasons for being there. Because Burman was a Bengali, and essentially a composer, he was unaware of Sahir's stature in the world of Urdu literature. Yet he greeted Sahir and gave him the film's tune and situation and asked Sahir to write the lyrics corresponding to the tune.

As the notes wafted out of Burman's harmonium, an inspired Sahir wrote *Thandi hawaein, lehra ke aayein...*

This melody, which was used in Kardar productions' *Naujawan* (1951), directed by Mohan Segal, became Sahir's first song for S.D. Burman.

However, contrary to popular belief, Sahir and Burman were supposed to work together even before this iconic song happened to them. Sahir had met the Anands and consequently Burman, as he was part of the group (including, Pandit Narendra Sharma and Vishwamitra Adil), which was selected to write the lyrics for *Afsar*. The publicity posters of the film even had his name[2], but somehow, the partnership had failed to take off for reasons unknown.

It was because of Guru Dutt's undying passion for music that *Baazi* was embellished with eight songs. And in true Bombay tradition, even the muhurat shot was a song sequence, a ballad that became stuff that legends are made of. The story goes that Sahir wrote *Tadbeer se bigdi hui taqdeer bana de* as a ghazal without the customary *takhallus* (nom de plume). But Burman effortlessly turned it into a zany club song.

For someone whose knowledge of Hindustani classical music was never in doubt, but who wanted nothing to do with Western music, the song was a fabulous surprise. Sadanand Warrier, an NRI musician told the authors, 'There are points in the interlude where you find the use of chromatic notes both in the ascent and descent. Even the "hey hey hey hey" is essentially a chromatic movement. Chromatic notes are seldom used in ragas.'[3]

One could actually extrapolate the chromatic notes in the interlude of the James Bond theme of the Sixties, but may we quickly add that this must have been a mere co-incidence?

In 1963, while writing for *Film Sangeet*, Burman had said, 'I deliberately used the phrase, *hey hey hey hey, hey hey*—to capture the feeling of being truly liberated as portrayed by the young woman.'

There were stories about cinegoers entering the hall just in time to view *Tadbeer se bigdi hui* and leaving just when the sequence ended. If Sahir was appreciated for his pizazz, Burman had emerged in a new avatar with this song—there were no traces of any 'Bengaliness' in the melody; the antara with dholak beats sounded more Punjabi than anything else.

In March 1955, Burman wrote in *Filmfare* magazine:

Fishing is one of my hobbies. Once, I was fishing at a village about twenty miles from Calcutta. It was an unlucky pond, and at the end of a fruitless day I had only my patience to flatter. Thoroughly disappointed, I was about to call it a day, when a boy of about ten jumped into the pond and started singing my *Baazi* song (*Tadbeer sey bigrhee hui taqdeer banaley;* sic) not knowing that the man who composed its music was on the opposite bank with his fishing rod. It was the biggest catch of my life.

Later in life, Burman would pass on the mantra to his son: make music for the common man; it is he who matters the most.

S.D. Burman was an active angler and often frequented the Powai Lake, and even had a boat reserved in his name. Many from the film fraternity were also fellow anglers, like Naushad and Shammi Kapoor, who once claimed to have caught a bhetki (barramundi) weighing twenty-eight-and-a-half pounds in September 1960, and set a record which was unbroken for a decade. In Bengal, farmhouse owners considered it a privilege to invite Burman for fishing. He would often visit places like Howrah, Amtala, and even Purulia.

Baazi was a riot of regional flavours—a combination of Punjabi, Gujarati, Bengali and Western. Except for what he had imbibed over the years, Burman was virtually alien to all other forms and had so far worked within a strict framework. Most importantly, the story of *Baazi* didn't lend itself to the traditional, salt-of-the-earth kind of score. But Burman managed rather well—from *Dekh akeli mohe barkha sataye re* (which was based on a garba song sung by Geeta Roy in the 1949 film, *Mangal Fera*), to *Aaj ki raat piya*, which somehow evoked the opening line of Nazrul Islam's *Padmar dheu re*—it was a sound that was hitherto unexplored.

Kishore's first solo for the Burman—Dev Anand combine—*Tere teeron mein chupe pyaar ke khazane hain*—was featured on a character who is jay-walking and singing to complete strangers. The scats, *danda ra danda ra*, breaking into the next octave at the fag end of the number, were a novelty in Hindi cinema.

A distinctive feature for a film of that era were the club songs—*Sharmaye kahe* and *Suno gajar kya gaye*, the latter structured around the theme of Arabian Nights, replete with castanets.

As a singer, Geeta Roy shone like a beacon in *Baazi* and displaced Shamshad Begum who had always been Burman's first choice till the late 1940s. It was also during the recording of *Tadbeer* that Guru Dutt fell in love with Geeta Roy and subsequently married her.

Baazi's songs kept the cash registers ringing for a very long time and helped Burman make up his mind—Bombay it was.

Sabbatical, Insignificance & More...

A jit Chatterjee was a well known character actor and mimic artist in Bengali cinema. In 1951, he cut an album which included a parody titled, '*Padabi Badal*' about two misprints in the pamphlet of a music conference leading to a terrible confusion. The names on the brochure were, *Sachin Kumar Mullick* and *Pankaj Dev Burman*. As a result, the songs get interchanged and while Burman is assigned to render a Rabindra Sangeet, *Daakbona aar daakbona*, which was actually made famous by the other artist, Mullick is asked to sing *Nishithye jaiyo re phool o bone re bhomora*! The hilarious act concluded with the singers training each other in their respective genres.

Humour apart, the act highlighted a significant point—Burman and Mullick were more than just household names in Bengal. Hence it was surprising when Sachin Dev decided to take a sabbatical that year and completely dissociated himself from Bengali music after Durga Puja. He was perhaps overworked in Bombay or maybe, the size of his Bengali audience had diminished. It was however a fact that a huge chunk of his admirers were now in East Bengal, an independent administrative unit under Pakistan, where the use of Bengali language was prohibited. On 24 March 1948 at Dacca University, Mohammad Ali Jinnah, while showing utter disregard for 54.6 per cent of people in Pakistan who

73

spoke Bengali, declared Urdu and English as the official languages of the country. This was reiterated in January 1952 by the then prime minister of Pakistan, Khawaja Nazimuddin, which had led to a bloodbath in Dhaka on 21 February.

Although people on the other side were restricted due to a draconian regulation, the airwaves connected them to their favourite composer and his lilting melodies. In a conversation with the authors during the writing of this book, H.Q. Chowdhury said, 'In the early 1950s and later, fans in Dhaka and East Pakistan were hooked on to AIR, Calcutta. A programme called, *Anurodher Aashor* was in huge demand. Listeners would patiently wait till the last song of the show was played out. When S.D. Burman sang, there would be pin drop silence.'

His temporary absence from Bengali music was perhaps a well-thought out decision. As mentioned earlier, he had multiple assignments in Bombay, while back home in Calcutta, several new singers were beginning to make a mark.

The last two songs that Burman recorded for the 1951 Durga Puja were, *Jhil mil jhil mil* and *Shei je dinguli*, and curiously, both revolved around recalling one's past, the halcyon days, as it were. The songs somehow pointed towards a 'planned sabbatical', if not a farewell.

Mitali Sen and Digbijoy Chowdhury (the daughter and son of Mohini Chowdhury, who wrote the lyrics for both songs), said, 'Our father was sad when S.D. Burman cut himself off totally from the Calcutta music circle. He was eager to write for Burman, and was also asked by him to visit Bombay. Our father was introverted and wasn't sure if he could adjust there. Consequently, these two songs became his last for Mr. Burman. Our father and Mr. Burman remained good friends though, and Pancham was very fond of his "Kaku". Mr. Burman looked rather serious most times, and it was difficult to gauge what he was thinking. But Pancham was gregarious and spoke from the heart.'

Digbijoy Chowdhury continued, 'But alas, time creates distance. Our father lost contact with Mr. Burman later in life. In 1990–91, I was assisting Anjan Chowdhury (the well-known Bengali film director) and went to meet Pancham in Bombay for some work. During the return trip, our flight got delayed and we decided to go to Pancham's house which was nearby. It was evening time and Pancham was entertaining guests at his home in Santacruz. He offered drinks to the crew that included Anjan and Haranath Chakrabarty. Both being teetotallers, declined politely. So did I as I didn't drink as well. Someone from the team then told Pancham that I was Mohini Chowdhury's son. Pancham immediately came to me and said, "What? You are Mohini Kaku's son? He was my father's friend. This makes us friends too. How can you refuse the drink?"'

Now that Sachin Dev Burman had finally decided to live in Bombay, he deftly adapted himself to the ways of the industry, or so he thought. He signed many films during this period and the most publicised amongst them was *Saz*, the muhurat for which was held in Bombay Talkies on 21 January 1951.[1] The cast boasted of Nigar Sultana, Nasir Khan, Yakub, and two new finds, Arti Kamat and Kamal, who was Madhubala's sister. However, the project was shelved eight months later and Burman's songs languished in the cans, including one by Lata Mangeshkar and a duet by Kishore Kumar and Geeta Dutt.

Baba was yet another film which remained incomplete.[2] Finally, *Ek Nazar* (January 1951), which was a love triangle starring Rehman, Nalini Jaywant and Karan Dewan, became Burman's first release that year. Alas, it tanked at the box office and in any case, Burman's music in the film sounded jaded, almost as if he was forced to compose the so-called ornate pieces. With the possible exception of *Ja dekh liya tera pyaar o sajan bedardi* by Lata Mangeshkar and a Kishore Kumar song featured on comedian Gope, *Naye zamane ki mohobaat nirali*, there was little to take away from the album.

However, in a few days, 1951 started looking better. It all began around September 1950 when Abdul Rashid Kardar, the maker of box office hits like *Dard* (1947) and *Dulari* (1949), agreed to finance a project by Mahesh Kaul called, *Naujawan*. The film took time to be made, but was well received when it released in mid-1951. The rustic image of Premnath, post Raj Kapoor's *Barsaat* (1949), helped steer *Naujawan* as he looked convincing playing a motor mechanic in the film. But Kishore Kumar as the voice of Premnath in the song, *Kahan le jaiyo Ram*, wasn't convincing. For those interested in film trivia, Kishore Kumar probably yodelled for the first time under S.D. Burman's direction in this film, lip-synched by choreographer Krishan Kumar in the song, *O pi pi piya*. Burman used Rafi and Geeta for two sequential duets in the film. One was, *Panghat pe dekho*, cast in a kirtan-folk mix, the first line of which was later moulded to, *Gazab chamkayi bindiya tori aadhi raat* in *Sagina* (1974).

Lata Mangeshkar sang exclusively for the heroine of the film, Nalini Jaywant. While *Dil ka dard na janey duniya* was moderately popular, *Thandi hawayein* came like a gale and blew everything away. Nalini Jaywant's graph which had dipped post *Ek Nazar*, climbed back on with this song.

The song became one of Lata Mangeshkar's three significant hits for Burman in 1951. The other being *Tum na janey kis jahan mein kho gaye* from *Sazaa* (1951). It had a lovely slide guitar obligato by Van Shipley and was composed in Rabindra Sangeet style, starting on low notes and rising to a crescendo in the antara. (One may notice a similarity with the first line of Tagore's *Mone ki dwidha rekhe gele chole*.) The waning notes in the antara—'*Tum kahan*', was a throw back to '*Tumi kothaye*', from Himangshu Dutta's composition, *Rater o moyur choralo je*. Years later in 1974, Lata Mangeshkar would sing both *Thandi hawayein* and *Tum na janey* during her first concert at the Royal Albert Hall, in London.

While reminiscing about S.D. Burman, Lata once narrated how he would coach her and sing in his typical folksy style with the customary voice-breaks and reiterate the parts that she felt uncomfortable rendering. At times, he would pat her back affectionately and when satisfied with her performance, offer her a paan in appreciation.

Gopaldas Parmanand Sipahimalani (popularly known as G.P. Sippy), who began his career as a dealer in carpets and real estate was the producer of *Sazaa*. While the film was still under production, he announced two more films with Burman, both to be directed by Fali Mistry, including *Sazaa*. One was an untitled costume drama starring Madhubala and Nimmi, based on a Hasrat Lucknavi story. The second was a social drama, tentatively titled *Dao*, starring Dev Anand and Shyama.

Going by the immense popularity of *Tum na janey kis jahan mein kho gaye*, one would imagine that *Sazaa* must have been a successful album. On the contrary, as was the trend in the industry, Burman had to force-fit songs and frankly, many sounded like intrusions in the narrative. But even this had a silver lining, because Burman used some of the snippets for popular melodies later. For instance, the prelude of *O roop nagar ke saudagar* sung by Lata, became the refrain for *Jahan bhi gaye hum* (*Naughty Boy*, 1962); an interlude in *Yeh baat koi samjhaye re* sung by Sandhya Mukherjee may have been an inspiration for the antara of *Oonche sur mein gaye ja* (*House Number 44*, 1955) and subsequently, even *Babu samjho ishare* (*Chalti Ka Naam Gaadi*, 1959). Well, almost.

Sandhya Mukherjee was an upcoming singer from Calcutta who got to sing two numbers for Sachin Dev Burman, thanks to Sachin Ganguly's recommendation.[3] In a deviation from her original style, which was instantly identifiable by the vibrato, she began imitating Geeta Dutt, thereby offering nothing new to Hindi film music. Her career in Bombay did not progress beyond a few songs; however, she became the top singer in Bengal and remained so for over two decades.

Meanwhile, Burman was thoroughly enjoying himself while composing. Sample this—the dummy, nonsensical lyrics which he inserted, *Tangoli o tangoli, nake mukhe chunkali* as the prelude to the romantic duet, *Aao gup chup gup chup pyaar karen*. This song happened to be Hemanta Mukherjee's first Hindi song for Burman and actor Dev Anand, as it was for Sandhya. The other voice that Burman used for Dev was that of Talat Mahmood. Although both Hemanta and Talat were accomplished singers in their own right, it was as if Burman was still searching for the right voice to do justice to Dev Anand's on-screen persona.

Meanwhile, even as it was evident that the composer of *Sazaa* had interjected a romantic ballad with crazy-sounding words, there was a great deal of ambiguity about the intense lines in another—*Maut bhi aati nahin, aas bhi jati nahin.... Tum na janey kis jahan mein kho gaye....* Although it was Sahir, somehow his name got omitted in the end credits, while it mentioned Rajendra Krishan, who had written all the other songs in the film.

But if there was one thing about which there was no debate and an overall admiration bordering on reverence, then it was about Burman's decision to use Lata Mangeshkar's voice for the leading lady of the film, as also for other films before *Sazaa*, particularly when the tune demanded vocal calisthenics. As in the classical dance-based number featuring Cuckoo in Shaheed Latif's acclaimed *Buzdil* (1951), *Jhan jhan jhan payal baaje*, which was a revised version of Burman's own, *Jhan jhan monjir baaje*. This film with Kishore Sahu in the title role received a raving review even from someone as fastidious as Baburao Patel, and performed fairly well at the box office.

That done, Burman would now move down South before scaling several other heights in what had now become his beloved city—Bombay.

The AVM studios in Madras reached out to S.D. Burman for a film they strongly believed was '100% entertainment'—*Bahar*. The contract was signed around late 1950; his name was still spelt incorrectly, and perhaps owing to regional differences, as Verman instead of Burman.

The renowned author-lyricist and Burman's old associate, Hemendra Roy was against him going to South India looking for work. But at that stage of his life, although the purity of an art form that he had adopted as a profession did matter to Burman, it was survival which required immediate attention.

His sojourn to the south of the Vindhyas proved fruitful as evidenced by *Bahar's* music. In what can only be speculation, Burman seemed to have deliberately reverted to his comfort zone and used folk, albeit sparingly, in the first line of the antara in *Duniya ka maza le lo*. (The phrase was later used by music directors Kalyanji–Anandji, also as the first line of the antara in *Saat saheliyan khadi khadi*, *Vidhata*, 1982.) The film introduced the beautiful Vyjanthimala to Hindi cinema and as she was an adept Bharatanatyam dancer, a couple of light dance numbers were mandated, including, *O pardesia pyaar ki bahar hai* and *Saiyaan dil mein aana re*, sung by Shamshad Begum.

After the grand success of *Mera sundar sapna beet gaya*, Geeta Dutt had become typecast and was somehow thought to be most suitable for melancholic numbers. In *Bahar*, she continued in the same vein and sang for Padmini (an actress who debuted in the film; not to be confused with 'the' Padmini of 'Travancore sisters fame'), which was sluggish and immensely forgettable.

Curiously, till the 1950s, S.D. Burman tended to use more female singers than male and *Bahar* was no exception. Kishore Kumar for instance, sang his solitary song in the film, *Qusoor aap ka*, which was featured on Karan Dewan and was revived in the mid-1980s after HMV re-released it in a double cassette compilation of the singer's songs. The phrase, *'Left Right Left Right'*, obviously borrowed from a military march or drill, had become so popular that several additions or slight variations have been in use ever since, mostly in the form of parodies. This was Burman's second tandem song in Hindi; Shamshad sang the version featured on Vyjanthimala. Interestingly, although *Ai zindagi ke rahi*, the only background song in the film was featured on a female character played by Padmini, it was sung by a male, Talat Mahmood.

Some of the songs in *Bahar* were conducted by the then trusted lieutenant of Burman, N. Dutta along with AVM's in-house music director, R. Sudarsanam. One such was, *Qusoor aap ka* and it is possible that the metre of this song may have inspired the Bengali music director, Sudhin Dasgupta to compose, *Ki namey deke bolbo tomake*, which was sung by Shyamal Mitra. Years later, Pancham used it in the antara of *Kaun mil gaya* (*Azaad*, 1978). Interestingly, all three phrases were actually pacier versions of the refrain heard in Israel's national anthem, *Hatikvah*.

An interesting episode which was unfolding during the recording of *Bahar*'s songs was Kishore Kumar's impending wedding. After the recording in Madras, Kishore Kumar flew to Bombay for his marriage registration and went directly to Evergreen Hotel to request Burman to be one of the witnesses at the event. According to Sachin Ganguly, Burman was playing badminton on the lawn adjacent to the hotel and after hearing Kishore out, excused himself from the singer's personal affairs. In all likelihood, he was showing caution and didn't want to strain his relationship with Ashok Kumar, who was against the alliance between his brother and Ruma Ghosh.

On 26 October 1951, *Bahar* released all over India and brought good cheer for AVM. But Burman had other pressing matters to attend to. Like his truant son!

∝✕∾

Priya Cinema on 95, Rashbehari Avenue is a well-known landmark in today's Kolkata. However, in 1951, the open space adjacent to Deshpriya Park used to be a desolate expanse and served as a haunt for a few layabouts and mischievous schoolkids. Rahul Dev Burman or Pancham would be often seen idling in the park with friends—smoking a cigarette, when he was not cycling or playing the harmonica. As was well known, Sachin Dev doted on his only child and indulged him to such an extent that he bought a bicycle and badminton racquet as gifts for the boy after he failed in class at Ballygunge Government High School!

However, with Pancham's dismal performance in school, Burman was forced to think of other options and he thought of Tirthapati institution on Rashbehari Avenue, which wasn't very far from his house. Burman sent word to Jiten Banerjee, the school principal, requesting admission for his son. The principal was quick in his response and put forward a condition for granting Pancham admission—if Sachin Dev Burman would give him the honour by singing at his residence.

Burman obliged. Sachin Ganguly took Pancham to his new school and completed all the formalities.

Soon thereafter, Burman returned to Bombay and started work on Fatehchand's *Jaal* which was inspired by Di Santis' 1949 film, *Bitter Rice (Riso Amaro)*. Guru Dutt was roped in to direct his second film and he shifted the original backdrop of rice plantations in *Bitter Rice* to a fishing village in Goa, although the actual shooting of the film took place in Ratnagiri, Maharashtra.

As the story was set in a Goan village, Burman blended the region's fabulous folk forms with some from his native Bengal, a genre he was most comfortable using. His assistant, N. Dutta, proved to be an asset for he knew the nuances of his state's music. As a result, the combination created magic. For instance, in the carnival song's mukhda, *Chori chori meri gali* by Lata Mangeshkar, one finds the interjection of a local Goan folk tune, *Chio chio chi*. Much like *Baazi*, majority of songs in the film were featured on the film's heroine, Geeta Bali, while Dev Anand was left with less.

The group dance during the climax of the film, *Kaise ye jaagi agan* by Lata and chorus stood out, for it evoked classical music especially the interludes, but overall worked wonders against the backdrop. Lata's *Pighla hai sona* was probably inspired by Tagore's *Neel dwigontey*, more in poetic imagery if not the tune. In the duet, *De bhi chuke hum dil nazrana dil ka*, Kishore marked his presence in the usual frivolous manner. Burman hadn't yet bought into Khemchand Prakash's view that Kishore could also sing serious songs. Perhaps this was the reason why the piece de resistance of *Jaal*—*Yeh raat yeh chandni* went to Hemanta and became synonymous with the film. It also resurrected several careers and this requires a minor digression.

In 1951, when S.D. Burman ceased to be a salaried employee of Filmistan, S. Mukerji was looking for a composer with sound Bengali credentials for his ambitious project, *Anand Math* which was based on the eponymous novel by Bankim Chandra Chatterjee. In 1945, the reputed Bengali director Hemen Gupta had made a film on the Bengal famine and S. Mukerji had invited him and his young associate called Hemanta Mukherjee, a budding Rabindra Sangeet exponent, to Bombay. Some of the songs he sang for Salil Chowdhury during 1949–50 played a great role in reviving modern Bengali music and has been acknowledged as such.

Although Hemanta came with a good reputation, also having sung with the Calcutta chapter of IPTA, he had to fight for a place while recording *Yeh raat yeh chandni*. The reason being that Guru Dutt's assistant, Raj Khosla wanted to sing it; on the other hand, Sahir was keen on either Rafi or Talat singing it. But Burman stood his ground and went for a stark newcomer who had come to Bombay to become a composer on the payroll of the Mukerjis.

While Burman had to work on Hemanta and rid him of his earlier influences, which included Rabindra Sangeet, what went in the singer's favour was the high pitch and long note structure of the song.

In the duet version with Lata, Hemanta was given a solitary line, almost in muted pitch, which acted like a counter melody to the catch-phrase, *Chandni raaten pyaar ki baaten*. This was classic Burman, a composer who could embellish the same song with such precious nuggets that it almost seemed like a different song.

Yeh raat yeh chandni gave Hemanta a firm foothold in Bombay, and he soon became one of the most sought after voices—Shankar–Jaikishan roped him in immediately as the voice of Dev for the epochal duet with Lata, *Yaad kiya dil ne kahan ho tum* in *Patita* (1953). As did C. Ramchandra for Pradeep Kumar in *Anarkali* (1953), a film in which Hemanta also wielded his baton as a composer for a solitary song (unacknowledged).

With *Yeh raat yeh chandni*, even Dev Anand finally established himself as the quintessential romantic hero in the industry. Although he would never let go of his devil-may-care attitude and essay roles which had certain negative shades, he essentially came to be synonymous with an amiable hero who found himself hemmed-in due to extraneous reasons.

As a throwback to *Baazi*, *Jaal* had one club song—*Soch samajh kar dil ko lagana* sung by Geeta Dutt, featured on a junior artist called Kammo. Much like *Baazi*, Guru Dutt made a cameo appearance in his second film as a fisherman in the song—*Zor laga ke*, as did his assistant, Raj Khosla, in *Chori chori meri gali ana hai bura*, as a trumpeter.

Jaal became the high point of S.D. Burman's career. The films that followed in the next one year were somewhat of a drab.

❧

The debacle started with *Lal Kunwar* (1952). While Suraiya, the heroine-cum-lead singer would recover with *Mirza Ghalib* (1954) and *Waris* (1954), *Lal Kunwar* was almost like a blot on her career.

Even *Shahenshah*, which was produced by G.P. Sippy, failed to register at the box office despite the fact that it was India's first Gevacolor film with lavishly shot dance sequences. The film was obviously a high budget venture and in order to tide over the financial debacle, Sippy had collaborated with a fellow builder called R.H. Hiranandani. He also roped in Amiya Chakraborty who was an established director and had had previous successes with *Daag* (cleared in 1952; released in 1953).

Unfortunately, Amiya Chakraborty was going through a difficult marriage at the time and wasn't at his creative best. As a result, *Shahenshah* could not live up to its so-called grandiose. Burman's music was languid—perhaps because the songs required a lot of instrumentation which he hadn't yet mastered—barring a few which he composed on high notes and with an 'Arabic' feel like, *Koi raag chedhe* (sung by Asha Bhosle); the Lata songs, *Khaakh hua dil jalte jalte* and *Gham kyon ho*; or Shamshad's *Jaam tham le*, which was the only hit in an otherwise indifferent album.

As it transpired, G.P. Sippy had had a fallout with R.H. Hiranandani, which is why *Shahenshah* was released under the banner of G.P. Productions (and not 'G.R.'). But Sippy, the quintessential Sindhi businessman refused to throw up the sponge and immediately announced his next Gevacolor film titled, *Radha Krishna* in 1954. Kamini Kaushal, who played a princess in *Shahenshah*, was signed up to play Krishna's consort, Radha in the film, while Master Rattan Kumar, who was in demand after Raj Kapoor's *Boot Polish* (1953), was to play Lord Krishna.

Raja Nene, the director of *Radha Krishna*, did no better than Amiya Chakraborty. The part-fantasy part-mythology movie was a huge disappointment, as was its music. Although it may be unfair to dismiss the songs altogether, the fact is that not a single one has any recall value today. Given the genre, the expectations from Burman, whose Bengali repertoire included a plethora of bhajans and kirtans, was rather high, but yielded no results.

Raja Nene then directed yet another film that year, the title song of which would be played on the first of every month on Radio Ceylon for the next thirty odd years. *Din hai suhana aaj pehli tarikh hai* sung by Kishore Kumar and composed by Sudhir Phadke in *Pehli Tarikh* (1954).

In 1953, *Dao* now rechristened as *Armaan*, finally saw the light of day. The Dev Anand starrer, directed by Fali Mistry certainly had a better score in terms of variety, fitment and orchestration. Sachin Dev Burman shifted to Talat Mahmood from Hemanta Mukherjee for Dev Anand, and it was not without reason. In contrast to the full-throated singing which was mandatory for a song like *Yeh raat yeh chaandi*, Burman used the more dulcet and 'unassuming' voice of Talat to suit the grain of the film. Also, the composer was in an innovative mood—in *Bharam teri wafaon ka*, a soliloquy where the guitar plays in arpeggio style almost doubling for the rhythm, was virgin territory for him. Asha saunters in, almost like Geeta Dutt in *Baazi*, scatting with *Jab duniya badli hai phir kyon na badle hum*, which had the piano interspersed with melody throughout. One is tempted to assume that the song may have inspired Kishore Kumar to compose *Matwale hum matwale tum* (*Jhumroo*) eight years later.

Meanwhile, in between all the experimentation, Burman went back to the traditional Bengali kirtan, *Bhojo Gourango* for *Krodh kapat ke andhiyare mein*. In several interviews, Manna Dey would rue over the fact of having to sing 'unromantic' songs and this particular one would have surely made him cringe. What was most intriguing was although Burman had a long and close association with Manna, he was somehow reluctant to try him out as the lead voice for a romantic hero.

Close on the heels of *Armaan*, the Hindi version of Agradut's (Bibhuti Laha) bilingual *Babla* (1951/53) was released. While the Bengali version was a success, the Hindi remake was panned mercilessly by critics for the melodrama. Burman, who was the composer for the Hindi version, as opposed to Robin Chatterjee for the original, used a young Hridayanath Mangeshkar as the voice of Babla, and his song, *Leheron ke rele sang naiya mori khele*, which had fleeting similarities to Tagore's *Jagorone jai bibhabori* and *Tora je ja bolish bhai*, was one of the bright spots in an otherwise drab score.

Meanwhile the Burman–Sahir partnership continued unabated, the outcome of their films notwithstanding. The year 1953 also marked the debut of two young actors, one of whom, the late Shammi Kapoor, spoke to the authors in 2009 about his first film. 'S.D. Burman was the music director of my first film, *Jeevan Jyoti*. Sahir Ludhianvi wrote the songs. The heroine was also a debutant, Chand Usmani. The film was not a big success, but had some nice songs of which I recall a folk-based number, *Chayi kaari badariya* sung by Lata Mangeshkar. There is an interesting story behind one of the songs, *Tasveeren banti hai*. The male singer who was supposed to sing the part at the end of the song didn't arrive on time, and Mr. Burman convinced me to sing. That was the only song I ever sang for films.'

In *Jeevan Jyoti*, while Sahir wrote the maximum number of songs, Pandit Narendra Sharma, yet another doyen of a poet-lyricist, also played a cameo as a song writer—for *Nazar lag jayena*. An interesting fact about this wedding song was that it had a longish coda which used the tune of *Aaj ki raat piya* from *Baazi*. One wonders if Burman kept recycling some of his tunes to ensure that the original would find a new lease of life and perhaps impel the listener to revisit the songs; a perfect example of yet another marketing principle of Top of the Mind Recall or TOM!

A peculiar trait in Burman, as was evident with *Jeevan Jyoti*, was that no singer was ever sure if he or she would finally end up recording a song for him! Hemanta Kumar once said rather sardonically, 'I'm on my way to Sachinda's place to rehearse a song, but do not know who would record it finally.' In *Jeevan Jyoti*, two solos—*Chayi kaari badariya* and *So ja re so ja* were sung by the Mangeshkar sisters, Asha and Lata. While the Lata version made it to the film, Asha's renditions were later released as version songs (alternative version, or cover version of a popular film song).

Jeevan Jyoti was doomed from the word go and it was undoubtedly because of Mahesh Kaul and his melodramatic treatment of the subject. What may come as a surprise to many of his fans, Shammi Kapoor had failed to impress in the film, while Chand Usmani, the other debutant, held out a promise which unfortunately remained unfulfilled.

In a way, the failure of these films was countered by the moderate success of *Angaray* (1954). With a multiple location shooting schedule in Darjeeling, considering it also had Nargis as the main lead, the film took over three years to complete. In order to make up for the delay, various marketing gimmicks were adopted to keep the film alive in public memory, including certain provocative pictures of Nargis which had nothing to do with the film.

But alas, *Angaray* failed to make its mark at the box office. A formula-driven lost-and-found story, its amateurish production values, made worse by over the top acting by its lead stars, proved a death knell for the film. But the good news was its music, which lingered on, especially the climax song, *Tumhe kho kar* (sung by Lata), and the romantic duet, *Mitwa mitwa* (sung by Lata and Talat). And truth be told, the songs certainly deserved a better film.

However, the same couldn't be said of Burman's songs in the Kamini Kaushal production, *Chalis Baba Ek Chor*, although *O piya pyaare* and *Teriya teriya* were indeed catchy. However, what was also interesting was the song, *Kismet ne baag lagaya hai* which sounds extremely similar to the first line of the antara in *Jeevan ke safar mein rahi* (*Munimji*, 1955). Despite a surfeit of twelve songs in the film, *Chalis Baba Ek Chor* was yet another addition to the long list of Burman's failures, notwithstanding a disclaimer by the producer that the songs were serene, almost as a counterpoint to the frenetic pace of the script involving children.

Although by now Sachin Dev had become part of the great Bombay film bazaar, he was noticeably self-effacing. Unlike his peers, he hardly ever socialised, wasn't surrounded by the ubiquitous acolytes or hangers-on and followed a lifestyle that was pedantic by any standards. So far as taking vacations was concerned, it was mostly limited to his annual trip to Calcutta during winters, while his son would visit Bombay during summer vacations.

The only perceptible change in Burman's life post the success of *Baazi* was when he moved into Sea Green Hotel on Marine drive. But even that was forced due to practical reasons—the man neither had a home in the city, nor a car, which was now mandatory for him to further his career. He was content either taking the local train to work or travelled by taxi. There was one cab which later became the subject of a film.

The Noir Turnstile—One

Taxi Driver

Guru Dutt's first throw of dice in his directorial career, *Baazi*, gave him a '6-up'. Even as many were envious of the young man's success, Guru Dutt's stint with Navketan was coming to an end. It was said that there came a time when Guru Dutt felt so deeply alienated from the Pali Hill group and particularly, from both Balraj Sahni and Chetan Anand, that he'd vowed never to work with them again.

In any case, the Pali Hill gang was also fast disintegrating. One of the reasons being a disastrous performance at Azad Maidan where the IPTA was scheduled to stage a play at the invitation of the Mazdoor Sabha. Not only had the IPTA failed to check the stage, lights and sound arrangements, there were long-winded speeches by union leaders, followed by a collection box which was circulated amongst the audience for funds.

This proved to be the last straw for Chetan Anand and he decided to confront the IPTA. What had been simmering for a long time came to the forefront—for Chetan and Uma, theatre was an art form, while most members of the IPTA saw it as a vehicle to propagate their political ideology. Chetan Anand decided to quit the group without any further delay and formed his own outfit called the Hind Manch.

According to the artist, Shiv Shankar Bhattacharya[1] (whose father, Satya Jeeban Bhattacharya was a member of the IPTA), S.D. Burman who was a member from 1943–44, also discontinued as he was uncomfortable with its political beliefs. He later became a member of IPTA's Bombay chapter in mid- to late-1940s.

In his book, *Cinema Modern: The Navketan Story*, veteran journalist Sidharth Bhatia elaborates on the failure of Chetan Anand's second film called *Aandhiyan* (1952). While speaking to the authors during the writing of this book, Ketan Anand put it satirically, 'The theme of *Aandhiyaan* could not sustain the cumulative effect of the tragedy! Even the music, which was undoubtedly the coming together of India's musical geniuses—Ali Akbar Khan, Ravi Shankar and Pannalal Ghosh—unfortunately failed to make a mark.'[2] However, amongst the group of musicians was a young man called Jaidev Verma who also doubled up as the assistant music director of the film. He was a student of Ali Akbar Khan and would later assist S.D. Burman in *Taxi Driver* in 1954. An extremely talented and a fine music director, Jaidev never made it to the big league and remains somewhat unknown and less celebrated.

However, despite the failure, *Aandhiyan* made a lasting contribution to Navketan by giving the studio its title music—a twenty-two-second-long recital by the three maestros of Hindustani classical music. This signature tune would herald every Navketan film for the next eleven years until *Tere Ghar Ke Saamne* (1963).

Navketan's next film, *Humsafar* (1953) which was directed by Anadi Nath Banerjee resulted in pushing the studio to near bankruptcy. Following a severe financial crunch, the Anand brothers found it increasingly difficult to collaborate any further. While Chetan was fixated on idealism, Dev wanted his image to resonate with the audience.

In an interview with Sidharth Bhatia, Dev Anand recalled those days and said:

> We had a friend who used to come to the office and ask for money. It had become a standing joke among us. One day he came and suggested that after the success of *Baazi*, the next character I play should be that of a taxi driver. I put the idea forward to Chetan bhai who nodded, non-committal, as if thinking about it, though I could make out he had liked it.[2]

It is then that Chetan's wife, Uma, and his youngest brother, Vijay aka Goldie, wrote a script around a taxi driver and Navketan was given a second lease of life.

Such was the enthusiasm for the film that the Éclair camera which Dev had bought from France was mounted on his Hillman Max, and Chetan would be off shooting the streets of Bombay at dawn. The maximum city's overcrowded streets and unending chaos became part of the film, lending it a look which was so far unheard of in the industry.

If *Baazi* was the beginning, *Taxi Driver* was the priming of S.D. Burman who was now acknowledged as a specialist in club songs. There was also an uncanny similarity in both films—*Baazi* had eight songs; *Taxi Driver* had seven, with one song each which had two versions.

Embedded deep within the story of *Taxi Driver* was a real romance brewing between the lead actors of the film. On 3 January 1954, Dev Anand and Kalpana Kartik shifted to an adjacent room at Modern studios during a recess and got married. Mona Singha, a Punjabi-Bengali-Christian girl from Simla (now Shimla) was related to Uma Anand and had made her debut in *Baazi*. Ketan Anand recalled his lovely aunt and said, 'My father was fond of the letter K. He had christened Mona Singha as Kalpana Kartik, just like he had christened Uma Sood (nee Kashyap) as Kamini Kaushal during her debut in *Neecha Nagar*.'[3]

Yet another milestone in the making of *Taxi Driver* was the fabulous entry of Asha Bhosle with *Jeene do aur jiyo*, hailed as her first cabaret number in Hindi cinema. In what can only be termed as boisterous,

Burman merged the mukhda and antara in the song so seamlessly that it produced a lilt which was pitch-perfect for the ambience of a club. The track was featured on a debutant from Simla, the beautiful Sheila Ramani. Interestingly, the film had two leading ladies who were both winners of beauty contests in Simla.[4]

It is noteworthy that Sachin Dev Burman, who had a fondness for everything Indian, including films revolving around local themes, not only adapted to unusual scripts, foremost of which was noir, but succeeded in creating electrifying tracks to suit their modernity. The songs of *Taxi Driver* were arguably among his best—*Dilse milake dil* was just as lovely as a romantic song and became a benchmark of how a club dance number could actually sound pristine; *Dil jale toh jale* had Burman using the Blues, perhaps a first in Hindi cinema.

However it wasn't as if everything was perfect with the score. For example, *Ai meri zindagi aaj raat jhoom le*, the climax song which was used in the same fashion as *Suno gajar kya gaye* in *Baazi*, had limited impact when compared to its predecessor. For all its brilliance and pathbreaking work, the Navketan banner was known to be lethargic on the editing table—the climax of many of its films would stretch with long shots lingering on the subjects of songs, making the audiences restive. No wonder then that today after six decades, *Ai meri zindagi* is all but forgotten.

As was expected, Lata outnumbered Asha and this despite the fact that the film required a modern and hip female voice. But then this was 1953 and Asha was to yet become the voice of 'modern, Western-based' numbers. Lata was as always dazzling and even sang short phrases of taans within songs, thereby elevating them to a different level.

Asha's duet with Jagmohan Baxi, *Dekho mane nahin*, had an interesting nugget and that being its antara which was based on a folk tune native to undivided Bengal (including Bihar). Unfortunately, Jagmohan's career as a singer did not progress beyond a few songs, but he later partnered with Sapan Sengupta and the duo known as

Sapan-Jagmohan, composed some interesting songs in the late 1960s and Seventies.

However, if there is one song which sparkles like a bright jewel in the crown of *Taxi Driver*, it is the dulcet, *Jayen toh jayen kahan*. The song was based on Tagore's *Hey khoniker athithi* and is a shining example of how enmeshing genres can create unparalleled magic. Although on closer inspection the two songs sound different—Tagore's tune was firmer and had a masculine quality, while Burman's version was melancholic, he stretched the lines, made them sound lighter, and had the right singer in Talat Mahmood who sounded as if he was singing from the depths of his soul. His intonation, his sighs at the *swaranths* (the end-points of phrases where the singer is often at risk of going out of breath/ lowering of flux) reflected the protagonist's state of mind so aptly that even Lata Mangeshkar in the tandem version, sounded plain and a tad screechy in comparison.

Jayen toh jayen kahan brought Sachin Dev Burman unprecedented fame. Not only was it a regular number one in the iconic Binaca Geet Mala show, it won Burman the best song Clares award (rechristened later as, Filmfare Awards), which was into its second year. According to Raju Bharatan in *Filmfare* (dated 1–15 November), the votes in favour of *Jayen toh jayen kahan* outnumbered the cumulative votes garnered by songs placed in second and third positions.

That year Naushad Ali lost the award to S.D. Burman's *Taxi Driver* by 4,767 votes. His fabulous Lata–Hemant lullaby from *Shabab*, *O Chandan ka palna* was left behind with a mere 2,361 votes. His disappointment (like C. Ramchandra's the previous year) was all the more greater because his Lata solo from *Shabab*—*Jogan ban jaongi* finished third with 1,896 votes.

The award notwithstanding, Burman was still on the lookout for the voice which could do justice to Dev Anand's stature as a star. He had used Kishore Kumar in *Chahe koi khush ho chahe gaaliyan hazaar de.* While the exuberant nature of the song (based on the well-known melody, *Tarantula*) was apt for Kishore, it underlined a basic loophole in the method of designing a song sequence in Hindi cinema, which was that the suitability of a playback singer for an actor often took a backseat in preference to the voice's fitment for a given situation. Rarely did Burman ever circumvent this rule, and in *Taxi Driver* he had used three different voices for Dev. This unreal aspect of a Hindi film song was often ridiculed by many, including a luminary no less that Satyajit Ray. But let it also be known that the listeners and audiences of those times were far more benign and forgiving than they are today.

At this point in the book, a slight digression may help evaluate the trajectory of S.D. Burman better. Even as early as the 1940s, Indian film composers were advised to see American and British films and obviously to use certain aspects as part of their creations later. Burman was no exception to the rule and had little qualms about borrowing tunes from the West. And *Chahe koi khush ho* was not the first time either. Back home in Bengal, there were murmurs about Burman resorting to plagiarism.

Although there is no doubt, and as mentioned earlier, that Burman had a proclivity towards sounds and genres that were Indian or rather subcontinental, he was not the 'Indian fakir' as was publicised in certain sections of the media, or a composer who had a strong aversion for the West. As was evidenced in *Baazi* and *Taxi Driver*, he never shied away from accepting the Western sound as a preferred alternative. Hence, if Burman was labelled a plagiarist, it wasn't due to the Tagore-inspired *Jayen toh jayen kahan* or *Mera sundar sapna*, but for the Western influences in *Baazi* and *Taxi Driver*.

But since his childhood, Burman who had been inspired by wandering minstrels and ustads alike, the motivation to embrace all kinds of sound perhaps came from his guru, Bhismadev Chattopadhyay.

In an interview to the magazine, *Ganer Kagoj* in 1976, he said:

> A few people in Calcutta complained to me that Burman was bastardizing Indian music by composing cheap songs. I told them that I was happy that this experimentation was finally successful, and went on to explain that film music mandated adhering to sequences on the screen. How ridiculous would it sound if he used the sarod or raga Jaijawanti during a cabaret sequence? Would the viewer be in a position to tolerate the stupidity?

And soon thereafter, S.D. Burman would redeem his 'Indian fakir' tag yet again.

Devdas

Talsonapur, a fictitious place in undivided Bengal was the birthplace of the best known lover in Indian cinema, Devdas Mukherjee. Written by Sarat Chandra Chatterjee at the young age of twenty-five, and published in 1917, *Devdas* remains the best example of a failed, drunk, albeit quintessential, 'man in love' in the annals of Indian cinema.

The first known cinematic adaptation of *Devdas* was a silent version, directed by Naresh Chandra Mitra in 1928. Seven years later came the Bengali–Hindi bilingual from New Theatres, directed by Pramathesh Chandra Barua, which managed to create such an impact, that the film was remade into various languages from time to time, the most recent of which was Anurag Kashap's *Dev D* (2009). However, of all its versions, if one were to cherry-pick the best for its simple storytelling, visual glory and musical excellence, then it would have to be Bimal Roy's in 1955.

Interestingly, the film was a stop-gap arrangement, almost like a palliative to help Bimal Roy Productions tide over a severe financial crisis. The reason: *Do Bigha Zamin* despite its cinematic brilliance had failed to make money because of the financier 'who had eaten off the funds.' A year later in 1954, Bimal Roy made *Naukri* which wasn't a commercial success either. By now, Bimal Roy was a worried man for he desperately needed money to not only support his art, but scores of others who depended on him for survival.

Roy had shot P.C. Barua's *Devdas* for New Theatres and had been witness to the unprecedented frenzy that the film had generated. *Devdas* was not merely a piece of popular literature or a well-made film, it had actually become a word to describe a tragic male lover. Despite the film's maudlin theme, audiences would see it repeatedly and revel in what they believed was the ultimate representation of a romantic tragedy.

The Hindi version of *Devdas* brought Bimal Roy and S.D. Burman together for the first time. Frenetic arrangements began to firm up the cast—Dilip Kumar as Devdas, Motilal as Chunilal, Meena Kumari as Parvati or Paro, and Nargis as Chandramukhi, who declined the offer, for she wanted to play Meena Kumari's role. Bina Rai was approached next and she too declined, her reason being the same as Nargis'. Next to refuse the role was Suraiya.

While several actresses kept refusing the role of Chandramukhi, the production house decided to finalise Meena Kumari to play Parvati. However, Kamal Amrohi, the poet-turned-director-turned-producer and Meena Kumari's husband, laid down certain ground rules for his wife—no outdoor shooting schedule with the hero of the film, Dilip Kumar, nor any intimate scenes.

Bimal Roy refused to be cowed down and immediately got in touch with Bengali cinema's upcoming actress, Suchitra Sen, who accepted the offer. Moreover, Sen and Roy had family connections, and perhaps that also helped seal the agreement between the two. (Roshanara, Bimal Roy's eldest sister was the first wife of Adinath Sen, Suchitra Sen's father-in-law. Roshanara had died young, and Adinath Sen had remarried, but the ties between the Sens and Roys remained intact.[1])

Meanwhile, Meena Kumari, despite her husband's diktat was extremely eager to play Parvati's role, but as her marriage was just two years old, she abided by him and finally, let go. A few days later, Vyjayanthimala came to meet Bimal Roy and offered to play the role of Chandramukhi. Considering he had been disappointed twice in a row, Roy was now banking on saleable names to ensure the success of

Devdas. Although Vyjayanthimala was relatively new (*Nagin* {1954} was yet to happen), but her dancing skills were the talk of the town, and she was on board.

It is difficult to fathom why Bimal Roy moved away from Salil Chowdhury for *Devdas* as he had not only composed for *Do Bigha Zamin* and *Naukri,* but was a full-time employee of Bimal Roy Productions at a salary of 500 rupees a month.[2] What seems plausible is perhaps the distributors wanted a more saleable name and by that time, S.D. Burman was much sought after. His *Taxi Driver* was a commercial success, and he had also bagged the coveted Clares award for the best song.

In order to seal the contract with Burman, Bimal Roy took his screenplay writer, Nabendu Ghosh who described the meeting succinctly in his autobiography, *Ek noukor jatri:*

> We went to Sachin Dev Burman's house at Bandra. It was a two-storied house. The staircase connected to the veranda on the first floor which had four ornate chairs, a table and a teapoy. Sachinda welcomed us with a smiling face. He was a tall and lean man, not more than fifty, dressed in a spotless white *dhuti-panjabi.*

> Bimalda reciprocated the greeting. I kind of bowed and greeted him with a namaskar.

> Sachin Dev Burman said—Namaskar, and hesitantly enquired about me.

> Bimal Roy gave a brief introduction, presenting me as one of the promising writers in Bengali literature. This failed to elicit any response from Sachin Karta, so Bimalda went on—He has written the screenplay of my films—Ma (1952), Parineeta (1953), Biraj Bahu (1954), Naukri (1954) and Yahudi. (*Nabendu Ghosh's memory played spoiltsport here, as Yahudi was made much later in 1958 and the script was certainly written after Devdas was released.*)

> Sachin Dev Burman said: "Oh, I know about these great films and I will remember his name. However, I have not read any of

his literary works." By this time, I noticed that he was speaking in an East Bengal dialect. He let his wife know of Bimal Roy's visit and asked us about our intent.

Bimal Roy said, "Please do not disappoint me. I am re-filming *Devdas*. I want you to do the music."

"Sarat Chandra!"—exclaimed Sachin babu with hands folded as if in prayer and turned towards Bimal Roy, "Sarat Chandra with Bimal Roy—I consider myself doubly lucky. Thank you; I accept this offer with extreme pleasure."

His eyes and face lit up like a child's.

Bimalda paid him an advance and said, "Nabendu babu will let you know the details of the song situations and shall also discuss the meaning of the songs. We shall then get down to sittings."

"Fair enough," nodded Burman.

Nabendu Ghosh met S.D. Burman after a few days to explain the song situations, and gradually became a regular visitor at his home.

Nabendu Ghosh had to make several visits to S.D. Burman's house for the story sessions, and said that if there was one thing he missed, it was tea! While this was put down to Burman's parsimonious nature, the tea at the Burman household was something to look forward to. Good quality Darjeeling tea made with concentrated milk and sugar would be served in large cups made of the finest porcelain. The cups were gifted to Burman by the Tripura royal family.

Devdas was released in 1956. Advertised as 'A new and authentic transcription of Sarat Chandra's immortal classic, *Devdas*,'[3] it was a wonderful amalgamation of literature and cinema, while keeping the lyrical and historical context of the original novel intact.

Burman's music for the film could be best classified as diegetic. It was perhaps the result of working with Bimal Roy which gave him the freedom to break away from the tried and tested methods, which had willy-nilly become his trademark. He took six months to work on the film and in the end, delivered an album which narrated the film through a sound track. What made *Devdas* so superior was its sheer variety—situational songs, folk songs, songs with minimal instruments, songs without any particular rhythm, use of raga-based *gats* (a term used in Hindustani music denoting phrases) for transitions, etc. Every musical motif was rolled out with utmost care.

For instance, the title score was enough to reveal what was to play out on screen in the next two hours and forty minutes—a sense of cinematic deja vu, as it were. One also notices the fabulous interjection of a thumri based on raga Gara—*Mohe panghat pe nandalal* (by Bindadeen Maharaj of Wajid Ali Shah's court) hinting at the nautch girls of Calcutta, which was an integral part of the story.

In his previous film with Dilip Kumar (*Shabnam*), Burman had used Mukesh as his playback voice. In *Devdas*, he went with Talat Mahmood who had earned him his Clares award. The solos, *Mitwa laagi re* and *Kis ko khabar thi* are by far the most recalled poignant moments in the history of Hindi cinema. Talat's voice also had an uncanny similarity to Dilip's and his natural vibrato added an extra dimension to the 'tragic' element of the male protagonist. If in the classic template of method acting, Dilip Kumar succeeded in transforming into Devdas and vice-versa, then through his musical prowess, Talat also sounded like Devdas.

The first and the better-known song, *Mitwa*, exploded the myth of a light song falling into the traditional mukhda-antara pattern. It had two sets of couplets, but was constructed on the metre of a blank verse and was an interplay of melody and visuals that gave the audience an insight into the psyche of a jilted lover.

Incidentally, Sahir's use of blank verse in the second Talat solo, *Kis ko khabar thi*, a soliloquy based on raag Malgunji is one of best examples of situational music in Hindi cinema. One also wonders if Laxmikant–Pyarelal were inspired by it for *Gore gore chand ke mukh pe* in *Anita*, 1967.

As a courtesan, Chandramukhi obviously had the maximum number of songs in the film. Devdas' visit to her dwelling on the eve of his lover Paro's wedding has the lissom nautch girl explode on screen with *Ab aage teri marzi*, dancing to the steps of Hiralal, the choreographer. The first four words of the song—*Dildaar ke kadmon mein*—were probably referenced by Kalyanji–Anandji as *Ishk walon se na poocho* in a similar situation in Prakash Mehra's version of *Devdas*, *Muqaddar Ka Sikandar* (1978).

The most popular song featured on Chandramukhi was, *Jisse tu qubool karle*. According to K.L. Pandey[4] (an expert on the influence of Hindustani classical ragas on Hindi cinema), this song is a combination of four ragas, Bhairavi, Charukeshi, Nat Bhairavi and Jaunpuri. If viewed from the prism of musical purity and grammar, one isn't sure if the mix was well thought out because Burman, as per his own admission, composed spontaneously and not with any specific ragas in mind.

An unpublished Lata Mangeshkar song in the film, *Dhan-dhan bhagye, jaage mori* was only used briefly, signifying Chandramukhi's contentment after Devdas takes refuge in her house. A brilliant 'song-let' (given the short length) in raga Ahir Bhairav, it was pruned to cut short Chandramukhi's happiness, as Devdas experiences his first bout of pain triggered by the cirrhosis of liver.

Devdas' journey to Paro's marital home—unfulfilled as it remained—finds Burman using *Woh na aayenge palatkar* in the background. Based on Khamaj, it is a typical 'nautch girl song' and the voice of Mubarak Begum adds just the right quantum of character to it.

The use of light ragas in the background help in alchemising the love between Devdas and Paro. These include a longish sitar piece in raga Basant Bahar, a significant element in the film's score, highlighting Paro's femininity; the traditional kirtan piece, used later by Burman in *Pyaasa* in the song, *Aaj sajan mohe ang laga lo*, is used in the background when Parvati is seen dressing in front of the mirror. Bahar is also played to celebrate Devdas' arrival in Paro's home, almost ushering in the season of spring, as is the tune of Tagore's *Aaji dokhin duar khola, esho hey, amar basanta esho* (The southern doors are open, come o beloved spring, come right in).

The Bahar spirit continues unabated. When the zamindar of Hatipota, Bhuban Mohan Chowdhury (played by Moni Chatterjee) arrives at Talsonapur to marry Parvati, a phrase on the shehnai similar to Tagore's *Aaji basanta jagrta dwar e* (Spring has come to my door) is used in the background.

As mentioned earlier, the music sufficed in telling the story of the film. Even small slivers of the background score deftly indicate the kernel of the central theme. The scene when Devdas discovers that Chandramukhi has taken to ascetism, one notices Burman fleetingly using the tune of the second line of his own song (composed by Subal Das Gupta), *Katha kao dao saara*. The score reaches a crescendo at the end of the dialogue between the two characters on a high *sa*, signifying a closure between the tragic lover and the courtesan.

In a pivotal scene in the film, when fruits rain on the asbestos shed at Paro's residence, Burman uses a sitar-sarod jugalbandi (duet) with brisk and taut notes, reminiscent of morning ragas. The piece repeats when Devdas, now all grown up, lets Paro know of his arrival by throwing a pebble on the same asbestos roof.

Although there is no recorded evidence, it may be safely assumed that Ali Akbar Khan, who had shifted base from Calcutta to Bombay and would often visit recording studios (and was incidentally close to both S.D. Burman and his assistant, Jaidev) played the sarod pieces in the film. Suhrid Kar, Burman's assistant, was a regular on the sitar; as was Jairam Acharya on the sitar from the late 1950s.

One instrument which he used in abundance was the flute, almost as if it was mandatory for the score, as was alcohol to Devdas' persona. In the early 1950s, Sachin Dev Burman wrote to Sachin Ganguly, asking him to find a good flautist in Calcutta. 'Sachinda asked me because he couldn't find one in Bombay. I went to HMV studios and met songwriter Pabitra Mitra who was employed there and asked him about a good flautist in HMV. Pabitra recommended Kamal Mitra. I asked for his address, but reiterated to Pabitra that Karta wanted a good flute player in Bombay. As it turned out, Kamal Mitra was game,' said Sachin Ganguly.[5]

Kamal Mitra claim to fame were the flute pieces in Salil Chowdhury's composition, *Kono ek ganyer bodhu*[6.] Gradually he became a Burman regular, before Sumant Raj took over. Among the many flute pieces in *Devdas*, one of the most heart-rending interjections was when an enraged Devdas leaves for Calcutta after his father threatens to disown him in the event of his marriage to Paro.

The climax of *Devdas* merits special mention, not only for its robust and cathartic end to an eternal love story, but also for its background score which elevates the scene by several notches. In what may come as a surprise and also serve as an example of camaraderie amongst fellow-musicians, that particular piece was done by Salil Chowdhury as Bimal Roy was not satisfied with the original score. Late one night, Burman accompanied by Bimal Roy went to meet Salil Chowdhury and the composer concluded the climactic piece in a matter of a few hours.

However, the music of *Devdas* also had its weak moments. For instance, *O albele panchi*, *Aan milo aan milo* and *Saajan ki ho gayi mein* added little value to the script. The most celebrated of the lot is undoubtedly *Aan milo* which was the Hindi version of Burman's own, *Rongila rongila rongila re*. Although both Manna Dey and Geeta Dutt were gifted singers, they somehow failed to replicate the pain of the Bengali original. Ironically, *Aan milo* is acknowledged as the biggest hit by audiences and is sung even today by aspiring singers at several reality shows.

The Noir Turnstile—Two

House Number 44

After Taxi Driver, Navketan's next production was also a dark crime fiction, based on one of John Ford's lesser-known films, *The Informer* (1935). *House Number 44* (1955) would have also remained a lesser-known film, had it not been for three songs....

It was Dev Anand and Kalpana Kartik's first film after their marriage. Meanwhile, S.D. Burman was still on the lookout for that elusive 'voice of Dev'. Despite the monumental success of *Taxi Driver* which was mainly due to Talat Mahmood, Hemanta Mukherjee was back in the reckoning for *House Number 44*. Strangely thereafter, Talat never sang for Dev Anand under Burman's baton and no one knows why.

As in *Jaal*, in which Hemanta established himself with the rage of a song, *Yeh raat yeh chandni*, his *Teri duniya mein jeene sey* in *House Number 44*, came to symbolise the underbelly of Bombay city during the early 1950s. Set to Sahir's fabulous poetry, Hemanta's sonorous flight proved that he was a singer who had ripened beyond compare.

The song had a fleeting resemblance to Tagore's *E pothey ami giyechi baar baar*, and a harmonica piece in the interlude, which many said was played by none other than Pancham.

There was this other uncomplicated melody, *Chup hai dharti chup hai chand sitare* which quietly tiptoes to envelop a night in Bombay city. It was definitely more rhythmic compared to *Teri duniya mein jeene* se, as it used shorter notes and as per the norm, its antara was constructed on higher notes than the mukhda. That it was actually an imposition on a rather lucid screenplay did the song no harm. The late musicologist, Biman Mukhopadhyay, in a telephonic interview with the authors spoke about the jalsas which used to be held in and around Calcutta, especially during the Durga Puja season and how Hemanta had become a rage during such events[1]. 'Even before he became a household name, Hemanta was the most imitated singer in the mid-1950s in Calcutta. Most of the amateur singers would make it a point to sing songs from *Jaal, House Number 44, Anarkali* (1953, composed by C. Ramchandra) and *Patita* (1953; Shankar–Jaikishan). While his Bengali songs for Uttam Kumar were gaining popularity, his songs for Dev Anand established him and probably made him acceptable to urban audiences.'

Here was a singer who got to sing for the lead actor of the film, but one wonders why he was allowed to merely hum in the refrain notes of the duet, *Peeche peeche aakar*, with Lata! It was perhaps because of *Phaili hui hai sapno ki baahein*, a reinforcement of the power that Lata Mangeshkar had come to wield, as a singer. A dream sequence in which the leading lady is seen dancing in a meadow in Panchgani, surrounded by silver oak trees, it has a haunting, almost celestial effect, held taut by waltz. In this song, Burman employs a simple but piquant melody where the mukhda does not have the fourth note, *ma*, while the antara has both *shuddha* and *teevra ma*, creating the twin feelings of euphoria and intoxication at the same time. Burman also employed two short phrases in the manner of an alaap, beginning unconventionally with *teevra ma* but easing on to *shuddha* notes. Apart from each element which went in making the song perfect, the arrangement was particularly tantalising. As mentioned earlier, Jaidev who was Burman's assistant, had a working knowledge of string instruments—mainly the sarod and guitar—having learnt the basics under the tutelage of Ali Akbar Khan. Nevertheless, the choice of obligatos (counterpoints), fillers and harmonies aren't associated with a Burman or Jaidev song. The backup to the melody uses multiple instruments, and the manner in which the sitar, flute, the piccolo and percussions are used, it reminds one of Salil Chowdhury's orchestration. Of significant interest are the counterpoints in the antara, which sound like whistling winds, and evoke the feeling of breeze caressing the leaves of trees.

Unfortunately, the song had almost faded into oblivion until HMV resurrected it in two compilations in 1985—the first was a twelve-song album called *35 youthful years—Dev Anand, Navketan,* and the other one a collection of S.D. Burman's songs.

The other four numbers in the film were somehow always in the periphery, amongst which was Asha Bhosle's *Dum hai baqi toh gham nahi,* a club song picturised on Sheila Vaz. Although the song was similar to *Tadbeer se bigdi hui* from *Baazi,* one wonders why Burman left out Geeta Dutt, except that he was perhaps trying out various other options as back-ups. Or who knows, Guru Dutt was perhaps the missing brick in *House Number 44.*

While the background score of the film wasn't exceptional, one particular scene needs special mention, especially in the way it treats the music thematically. The hero of the film, Ashok (Dev Anand) is seen running for his dear life while being pursued by the villain's (played by K.N. Singh) henchmen. Ashok is anyway distressed—poor, hungry, homeless and a jilted lover—and in the next scene is seen staggering out of a bar. The incoherent blabber of men in the modest watering hole gives way to the line: *Tere wade ka kya aitbaar, sitamgar...*which is part of the famous Mirza Ghalib ghazal, *Yeh na thee hamari qismat,* wafting out from somewhere in the neighbourhood. As Ashok totters out into a dingy street looking for the source of the melody, the shadow of a nautch girl dances on the wall, a throwback to Hollywood noir cinema. Simultaneously, another tune merges into the night, *Kaisi bansiya bajayi shyama* (uncredited). Here is where Kishore Kumar saunters in with his cavalier hiccupping, yodelling, scatting and segues into *Oonche sur mein gaye jaa,* his solo in the film.

Like in *Jaal* and *Taxi Driver,* Burman used Kishore for the lighter side of Dev Anand's character in *House Number 44*, while retaining Hemanta for the brooding young hero.

Despite a near-cult status, Dev Anand was still to find his 'voice'. Amongst the 'holy trinity' of Hindi cinema, Raj Kapoor had already sealed a lifetime pact with Mukesh, while Dilip Kumar, for all his love for Mukesh and Talat, accepted Rafi as his voice, recommended highly by none other than Naushad Ali.

Meanwhile, two films for which Sachin Dev Burman composed the music—Shahid Lateef's *Society* and Hemchunder's *Madh Bhare Nain*, were cleared in 1955. The latter had some fascinating compositions, amongst which, *Aa palkon mein aa* could easily be counted amongst one of Lata's best for Burman. As would *Meri umar se lambi ho gayi bairan raat judaai ki* from *Society*. However, Kishore Kumar, the hero of *Madh Bhare Nain*, could have got a better deal as a singer in the film. But then, it was only a matter of time and it would happen in the form of Chetan Anand's swan song for Navketan.

Funtoosh

While *Taxi Driver* (1954) revived Navketan's fortunes, *House Number 44* had a decent run. Navketan announced their next film, *Funtoosh*, which was a term of endearment between Dev Anand and Kalpana Kartik in *Taxi Driver*. Although as a word, it meant nothing, according to the late Uma Anand[1], 'The word Funtoosh emphasises what you're trying to say.' Despite labelled as gibberish, curiously the word found its way into Bengali and is used for a man who lives beyond his means.

The moderately enjoyable film with a 'name which had no meaning' was important for S.D. Burman, and for a very specific reason. It ended his search for Dev Anand's 'voice'—it was out there for everyone to see in the credit titles of the film, 'Songs of Funtoosh rendered by Kishore Kumar'.

One can almost visualise Burman telling Kishore to, 'Just go out there and enjoy yourself!' It was clear that both the director and composer of the film were punting on Kishore, despite the main protagonist of the film being a brooding character. Now conventionally, one would imagine a 'serious' male singer to be the hero's voice, but the choice of Kishore Kumar worked brilliantly as he lent Dev a tragic-comic dimension which was hitherto unknown.

However, it was also a time when flamboyance or comedy in music was equated with superficiality; the audience was reluctant to accept anything which fell outside a set pattern. As a result, not only did the brooding musical soliloquy, *Dukhi mann mere* become the most celebrated song in the film, it also formalised the Burman–Kishore association and remained a personal favourite of Kishore Kumar, as told to veteran journalist Pritish Nandy in a 1985 interview.

Funtoosh also had a few other landmarks. For instance, it was an out and out Asha Bhosle album and gave her the opportunity to display her repertoire, be it *Phool gendwa na maro* or *Johnny, jeene me kya hai*. Additionally, Pancham also made a few significant contributions to the film's music. For instance, *St James Infirmary Blues* from his personal collection helped his father fashion the third antara of *Dene wala jab bhi deta*. Most importantly, *Aye meri topi palat ke aa* was his composition which found its way into the film.

While *Funtoosh* was like a bond of trust in the making between father and son, it was a wrap for Chetan Anand, who bid adieu to Navketan to form his own film company called, Mahashakti Films. 'They decided to part ways in an amicable manner. Chetan did not take anything from Navketan,' said Uma Anand.[2]

There's no doubt that the Pali Hill association played a significant role in S.D. Burman's life. It shaped his career, helped him connect with the industry, and most importantly, added the much-needed glamour quotient to his life as a film musician. While Chetan Anand leaving Navketan was akin to cutting the proverbial umbilical cord, Burman had firmly cemented his relationship with the other Anands—Dev and Vijay and regardless of who the director was, he was considered, 'Navketan's family composer.'

Alas, Chetan and Burman never worked together again. Not even when Chetan Anand returned to Navketan during its silver jubilee celebrations to direct *Jaan-e-man* (1976) and *Saheb Bahadur* (1977), remakes of *Taxi Driver* and *Afsar* respectively.

It was twenty-five years later during the making of *Kudrat* (1981), when Chetan Anand was taken by the film's music director, Pancham to meet his mother, Meera Dev Burman. They wanted to seek her permission to use her husband's *Haye ki je kori ami mono niya*, which was turned into the memorable, *Tune o rangile kaisa jadoo kiya*.[3]

Pyaasa—The Haves & Have-nots

'Paintings sell for millions. Poetry does not.'

Pyaasa was based on a story called *Kashmakash* (1947–48), in which the protagonist is a painter. In the film, Guru Dutt turned him into a poet. It is a well known fact that poetry is rarely if ever a favourite genre with the common man. In *Pyaasa*, Guru Dutt makes ordinary working people like nurses, even prostitutes, recite poetry. Had poetry been a favourite with the masses, then would poets like *Pyaasa's* Vijay languish in penury? What was also strange and least expected of Guru Dutt was the anomaly while writing the character of Vijay—he is shown to be a Brahmin, in all probability a Bengali from Calcutta, who not only speaks chaste Hindi, but is also lauded as a brilliant Urdu poet. A nigh impossibility in the 1950s.

After dabbling in noir and comedies, one wonders what propelled Guru Dutt to make *Pyaasa*. In the absence of any other argument, one would have to go by what is best known and that being his method of dealing with catharsis.

In an interview to Henri Micciollo, a French critic who had viewed Guru Dutt's *Pyaasa*, Satyajit Ray had praised the director's 'remarkable

111

sense of rhythm and fluidity of camera,' which he attributed to his years spent with Uday Shankar. He also described Guru Dutt's approach to cinema as 'musical'. In the history of world cinema, particularly among French viewers, *Pyaasa* is acknowledged as a classic film even today.

Musically speaking, the film was a combination of two albums—one comprising songs, and the other shayari or poetry, as it had five blank verses which weren't written to tunes. The film opens with the most striking one, *Ye hanste hue phool* rendered by Rafi in the traditional 'nazm' style, showing Vijay stretched out on his back in a sunlit park, enjoying the sight of a bee sucking nectar from a flower. Next, the audiences see a foot encased in a shoe crushing the insect[1]. The two scenes pretty much establish the film—an idealistic poet who was fast trundling towards the abyss of a real world.

The other stunning verse, *Tang aa chuke hain kashmakash-e-zindagi se hum* was sung in a metre which was traditionally used during mushairas and was heard earlier in other films as well. However, for the other major scenes in the film involving poetry, Burman had no role to play. All the actors, including those playing well-known poets like Majaaz Lucknawi and Jigar Moradabadi, recited blank verses. The party sequence which unfolds at the residence of a leading publisher, Mr. Ghosh (played by Rehman) is a scathing commentary on the commodification of artists over centuries by rich patrons. The forced laughter of guests, the over-the-top appreciative noises from people who are in attendance because it is a rich man's house, stands out in stark contrast to a poet who realises the futility of it all, but stays on for he has no other option. When Hemanta's sonorous voice wafts in, scything through the chaos and disorder, it almost feels like rain on parched earth.

Jaane woh kaise, composed in raga Bilawal is an epic of a tragic song, without being a regular tear-jerker. Its seminal status in the firmament of Hindi film music is not only because of its depth and poignancy, but also for its hummability. Burman arranged the song with delicate piano notes and what later became synonymous with Guru Dutt's films, there was no prelude.

In a conversation with lyricist Pulak Bandyopadhyay[2], Sachin Dev Burman had mentioned that the second line of the national anthem—*Punjab Sindh(u) Gujarat Maratha Dravid Utkal Banga*—had inspired the line, *Humne toh jab*. The reference to the national anthem is so subtle that unless someone points it out, it is next to impossible to spot a similarity.

The other two solos featured on Guru Dutt and sung by Mohammed Rafi show Burman in a completely different avatar. The first of the two to burst forth on the screen was, *Jinhe naaz hai Hind par woh kahan hain*, which was a watered down version of Sahir's poem *Chakley*. The simple Piloo-based melody, interspersed with sporadic twists starts with humming and follows through with a few eerie-sounding notes on the organ almost like a choir. Interestingly, *Jinhe naaz* is not a nazm, because, it returns to the refrain. It isn't a ghazal either, but sounds like one. The metre of the song is set in dadra (a rhythm cycle in Hindustani classical music invoving six beats which are split into two divisions of three each), but the song is without any strong percussion support.

Amongst other things, this song over several decades is considered as a severe indictment on a nation which reveres women by elevating them as goddesses, but does little else in the way of empowering their bodies and souls. The poet minces no words and openly rejects an inept country which is guilty of reneging on its duty of protecting its women; one could even extrapolate that Meena who rejects Vijay and marries the rich publisher, also succumbs due to economic compulsions. Burman had also recorded a shorter version of the song by Manna Dey, which was later left out of the film. The Rafi version was therefore padded up by adding additional lines to the original lyrics.

It was a well acknowledged fact that Guru Dutt was a master of song picturisation. *Yeh mehlon, yeh takhton, yeh tajon ki duniya* is remembered as much for its very simple melody and firebrand poetry, as it is for the spectacular backlighting. As Vijay stands silhouetted Jesus-like (post Resurrection) in the doorway, Rafi's first few words are barely audible. The phoenix gradually rises, so does Rafi's voice. Until the end of the first mukhda, one hardly hears any background music. Then Burman thrusts a cascade of angry violins to the increasing discomfort of the audience who have come to mourn Vijay's 'death'. Sahir's verses fall like hard slaps on the faces of those who make it their mission to control the destinies of others.

On the day Vijay arrives at a function which is held to felicitate him posthumously, he is relaxed as he is purportedly assumed dead. Rafi's nuanced rendition manifests this freedom of the 'dead' poet. Burman's orchestral pitch ascends, as Sahir continues to proclaim his judgement. Gulabo, the fallen woman, played by Waheeda Rehman, looks ecstatic for the poet is alive; several others on stage are bewildered and they mutter, huddle, and exchange furtive glances. Finally, the publisher makes it clear that Vijay has to be thrown out of the auditorium—he is more of a liability being alive. Meanwhile, the bust of the 'unsung poet' remains covered.

'Jala do, isse phoonk dalo yeh duniya...' In this line, Burman blends in high-pitched notes to signify the 'Last Post', the end, the denouncement. Rafi displays raw passion by scaling stratospheric levels in 'Tumhari hai tum hee sambhalo ye duniya...' It is almost as if Vijay unhooks himself from this wretched world and walks out with Gulabo who never belonged to it in the first place.

It has been argued ad nauseam in several forums how it was Sahir's poetry and the director's eye which elevated the scene, and not S.D. Burman, to make it look spectacular. However it was indeed the music which sounded overwhelmingly divine because of its sheer simplicity. Burman moves from note to note, from *sa* to *re* to *ga* etc., and in the process touches all the normal notes of the scale, except the seventh (*ni*) which is flat. The Khamaj thaat which endeared itself to Burman all his life, manifested itself yet again.

It is believed by a section of people in Pakistan that Sahir took the first few lines from Majeed Amjad's poetry and informed him later. Majeed was generous; he never claimed the lines to be his. This was Sahir's *tazmeen* to Majeed....[3]

Pyaasa was also one of the highest points of Geeta Dutt's singing career. From the romantic, *Hum aapki aankhon mein* to *Jaane kya tuney kahi* (the Hindi version of the Bangla, *Mono dilo na bodhu* sung by Burman in 1956); the picnic song, *Ho laakh musibat raste mein*; the kirtan, *Aaj sajan mohe ang laga lo*, and the unreleased, *Rut phire par din hamare*, her voice had élan which one acquires with experience in the real world.

The kirtan in *Pyaasa* has often been the subject of research for students of cinema. The build-up to the love angle with multi-dimensional shots and the lyrical content is not just interesting, but is also expansive—many find similarities with the Radha-Krishna story; some highlight the conflict between physical proximity and mental distance between lovers; while others contrast the hero's cynicism with the heroine's acceptance of love.

As a song, never before was the kirtan of Bengal better represented in Hindi cinema. The use of multiple khols in unison—led by Sudarshan Adhikari, a percussionist from Midnapore district in West Bengal whom Burman had groomed in the traditional *bostom* (itinerant kirtan singers in Bengal) style was unparalleled.

However, when evaluated for its sheer melodic quality, *Jaane kya tuney kahi* sounds supreme. Burman strides over the notes by creating an eminently hummable melody, which in reality isn't as simple as it sounds. As a singer, Geeta meanders through the notes buoyantly, something she strictly reserved for her husband's films. The music arrangement comprising three principal instruments—the Chinese blocks played by Kersi Lord, the sitar by Jairam Acharya, and the flute by Sumant Raj effectively anchors the song. Mukul Bose who was Burman's recordist, placed the mikes strategically to maximise the rhythm set by the Chinese blocks.[4]

Mono dilo na bodhu marked S.D. Burman's return to Bengali music after five years. He'd teamed up with Rabi Guha Majumdar for his 1956 Durga Puja album for HMV. The huge popularity of the song led to Burman being invited to Calcutta for a solo recital, although he would frequent the city for shows held at Ranji Stadium (Eden Gardens). The other Bengali singer to participate in the event was Hemanta Mukherjee.

A few lines about the lesser heard, *Rut phire par din hamare* from *Pyaasa*. It was picturised on Waheeda who was shown rowing a boat in a lake. The initial response to the song was lukewarm; people walked out of the hall for a cup of tea or to take a quick smoke. As a result, Guru Dutt decided to withdraw the song from the film, which in hindsight wasn't perhaps a wise thing to do. The reason being that the song, which in more ways than one sounds like a lament from deep within a woman's soul, is still popular amongst music lovers. One notices how its antara sounds like *Chand phir nikla* from *Paying Guest*, a film Burman was doing simultaneously with *Pyaasa*. Most importantly, *Rut phire par din hamare* was one of the very few songs where Burman used a sanchari, as in the lines:

Pahunchi na apni naiyya aaj tak kisi kinare
Koi naheen jo humko apni taraf pukaare

It is now common knowledge that the Geeta Dutt–Mohammed Rafi duet, *Hum aapki aankhon mein* was added later at the behest of distributors who felt that the intense story needed a break for audiences to breathe easy! The song, shot like a typical dream sequence in flashback, had all the elements of a ballroom dance, but Burman decided to not use the waltz. Instead, he went for an off-beat 2/4 rhythm which came as a pleasant surprise for the audiences who awaited the waltz to play out in a scene such as this! In contrast to his other songs, Sahir's lyrics sounded more in the Majrooh Sultanpuri or Hasrat Jaipuri mould, with lovers challenging each other by throwing romantic questions.

By and large, although *Pyaasa* was perceived as a serious and 'literary' album, it did have its quota of peppy songs. *Ho laakh musibat raste mein*, the Geeta–Rafi duet is one, and so is the brilliant Rafi solo, *Sar jo tera chakraye*, which became the most popular song of its time. Along with this, the other song composed by O.P. Nayyar, *Ae dil hai mushkil* (*C.I.D.*, 1956) made Johnny Walker the most sought-after comedian in the industry.

However, even as *Pyaasa* was on its way to becoming a benchmark in the annals of Indian film history, a controversy was brewing between two talented members of Guru Dutt's team.

Sahir, who was known to be brusque, once commented how his lyrics made the songs of *Pyaasa* unforgettable and also a commercial success. In a way, it was true because his straight-from-the-heart lyrics had created a paradigm shift in the way songwriters visualised tragedy in Hindi cinema. But S.D. Burman, who had encouraged the young lyricist from Ludhiana and given him the decisive break in *Baazi* was pained by his high-handedness and refused to work with Sahir ever again. Thus ended one of the finest collaborations in Hindi film music which extended to 134 songs spanning eighteen films.[5]

For *Pyaasa*, S.D. Burman had teamed up with Guru Dutt after a gap of almost five years. Following the success of *Baazi* and *Jaal*, Guru Dutt had offered him *Baaz* (1953)[6] which Burman had turned down, and thus paved the way for O.P. Nayyar to become part of films like *Aar paar* (1954), *Mr. and Mrs. 55* (1955) and *C.I.D.* (1956).

Although *Pyaasa* was mainly shot at Kardar studios, the outdoor was on location in Calcutta, and Guru Dutt arrived in Burman's favourite city for an extended period. Sachin Dev had redone his Calcutta house and had moved to the first floor. Guru, who normally stayed at the Grand Hotel, occupied the ground floor at Burman's South End Park residence. And thus *Pyaasa* became a perfect reason for Dutt Productions' cast and crew to mix business with pleasure. Burman would go on fishing expeditions in Amtala and Howrah, often accompanied by Guru Dutt, Geeta Dutt, Pancham, and Sushil Chakrabarty (of Melody, the music shop on Rashbehari Avenue). Even the shooting schedules were more like picnics, and the director who was fond of his drink would often carry a bottle to the sets. Sachin Dev would abstain, for he would be accompanied by his teenaged son, but would indulge in 'mishti paan' (sweet paan) from Chedilal's shop off Rashbehari Avenue. The Bengal variety of the betel leaf was a rarity in western India, but Karta had discovered a shop in Bombay's Chowpatty area and would buy his daily stock without fail.

Meanwhile, Pancham had appeared for his Senior Cambridge examination in 1955 and had arrived in Bombay from Calcutta. In an article titled, "My God, That's My Tune" published in *Filmfare* dated June 16–30 1984, Pancham said:

> I was very bad in studies, and my grandmother used to complain constantly. My father was in Calcutta one day when he made the decision to take me to Bombay. My grandmother objected, saying the industry would be a bad influence on me. Father, however, was adamant. He said: 'My son is not a good student. I am getting old; I must take him to Bombay and groom him. In ten years, I may be able to make something of him.' A quarrel ensued and father left Calcutta. Before leaving, he asked me if I'd composed anything. I played the 15 tunes I had ready.

> In December 1955, Guru Dutt came to Calcutta for the shooting of *Pyaasa*. He was close to my father, and I asked him to use his influence to get me to Bombay. It worked. *Pyaasa* was the first film

I helped my father with. I not only composed one of the songs, but also played the mouth organ and some other instruments at the recording. Seeing me work like this my mother's fears were laid to rest and she was convinced I was in the right line.

However, contrary to what Pancham had said to the magazine, according to music composer Dipankar Chattopadhyay[7], who was also Pancham's friend during his student days, he was reluctant to join his father in Bombay. The reason: the young lad was more than happy in Calcutta, smoking and flirting with other substances which kept him occupied. Sachin Ganguly added that Indubala was very fond of her grandson, and unlike her daughter Meera, gave him a lot of leeway which Pancham misused.[8] Burman sensed that it needed more tact than pep talk to bring his son back on track. Although Meera was dead against Pancham coming to Bombay, Burman reasoned with her that their son's present guru, Ali Akbar Khan was doing more work in Bombay than in Calcutta, and it would be wiser to move Pancham for his musical training.

Pyaasa was Pancham's first film as an assistant, albeit uncredited. Apart from composing *Sar jo tera chakraye*, he also played the raga Shivaranjini-sounding 'Meena's theme' on the harmonica which was used during the opening titles and in the background whenever Mala Sinha appeared on screen.

Dev & Filmistan

In the mid-1950s, Sachin Dev Burman signed two films for Filmistan. The last time he had worked with the Mukerjis was during *Shabnam* (1949). This time, he teamed up with the younger brother of Sasadhar Mukerji, Sobodh. In an exclusive interview with the authors, his son, Subhash discussed his father's relationship with S.D. Burman.[1] 'My father and Mr. Burman were friends from the 1940s. Apart from films which united them, it was also the language, and most importantly, football. My father was a Mohun Bagan supporter while Mr. Burman was the quintessential East Bengal fanatic.

'They had their football fights, almost like children, and mostly it was a case of agreeing to disagree. But it was all in good humour, and the two were temperamentally suited to each other. So when my father decided to make films, it was difficult to think beyond Burman. He was the choice for both *Munimji* (1955) and *Paying Guest* (1957) by default.'

The Kishore–Lata tandem, *Jeevan ke safar mein rahi* from *Munimji*—a film in which two of Hindi cinema's greatest poets, Sahir and Shailendra, wrote lyrics—achieved a near cult status.

A particular recording session during the making of the film was testimony to Burman's bizarre sense of humour, or rather his strange way of appreciating good work! After the final rehearsal of a song with Kishore Kumar, Burman suddenly jumped towards him and is said to have shouted, 'Stop the rehearsal!' There was complete silence all around as Burman approached Kishore menacingly and said, 'Kishore, if you sing like this, the film is a sure shot hit. Wonderful!'

Unfortunately, apart from the Kishore version of the song, most of the other songs (sung by Lata Mangeshkar) seemed to have gone into oblivion—the tribal dance song, *Nain khoye khoye*; the raag Kedar-based, *Sajan bin neend na aave* (which was even left out of many prints); and the Kafi-sounding, *Ghayal hiraniya*. Surely unfortunate, as these compositions remain the toast of the connoisseur.

Subhash Mukerji recounted a rather amusing incident during the sitting sessions of *Ghayal hiraniya*.[2] 'My father wanted to inject a fear factor in one of the songs. The sequence was of a girl trapped inside a jungle, till she is rescued by the hero. Burman just couldn't appreciate the need for a song in a situation of that kind. After the song was rehearsed, my father wasn't happy. Multiple rounds of discussion failed to yield any productive results. Consequently, he asked his elder brother, Sasadhar Mukerji to intervene and counsel Burman.

'Burman went to meet Sasadhar at his office. He was slightly apprehensive as S. Mukerji was a big name (he was after all, someone who had brought him to Bombay). Sasadhar mollified him, saying that there was nothing to worry, just that Subodh wasn't getting the fear-factor in the song.

'He then said, "What if I pull your dhoti?"

'Burman was shocked at the suggestion.

'"See? I want that expression, the feeling of fear which you just experienced, in the song."

'The reflex reaction set Burman thinking, and he made changes to align it with the needs of the film.'

Paying Guest, which released a month after *Pyaasa*, did better than *Munimji*. Even today, almost sixty years hence, most of the songs from the film remain immensely popular.

By the time the film was announced, S. Mukerji had sold off most of the assets to the new owner of Filmistan, Tolaram Jalan and was only taking care of production at the studio. In the interim, he set up his own company called Filmalaya, which was formally launched by the renowned economist, Ardeshir D. Shroff at the Taj Mahal Hotel on 22 June 1955. While Subodh Mukerji also left Filmistan to start his own venture, so did Burman.

It seemed as if the music composer was entering a new phase in his career. He was in the mood to experiment like never before, which he did by using the piano accordion in what would become one of the most famous boy-woos-girl number—*Mana janab ne pukara nahin*.

'*Asa* (that is how he pronounced the first name of Asha Bhosle), if your lover were to tug at your sari, how would you react?' Burman asked the singer in order for her to get the perfect '*aah*' that was needed for the duet. *Chhod do aanchal* was possibly the first romantic Hindi film song which began with a naughty exclamation.

Although initially Burman was against using a duet for the situation, it was Majrooh Sultanpuri who was insistent that the song be composed in the question-and-answer style, and which worked wonders for the film.

Conversely, it was Burman who had influenced Majrooh to use the word, *aanchal* in the song. He recalled how his son Pancham, as a child and even during his early teens, would hold on to his aunt's *aanchal*, as told to the authors by Anuradha Gupta.[3] What was obviously a feeling of security for a child, became a plea of acceptance from a lover to his woman even as he follows her with *aanchal* in hand!

Burman continued with his experiments. For example, Asha Bhosle's intermittent humming in *O nigahen mastana*. The impishness in her voice lent a playful effect to this nightcap on a terrace. The interjection of whistling in the song was by Anoop Kumar Gangoly,[4] brother of Ashok and Kishore Kumar.

Later, Burman's son would use Asha's teasing intonation in *Ek paheli hai tu*, in yet another Dev Anand starrer, *Heera Panna* (1973).

Like the popular saying—the party isn't over unless the fat lady sings—no film of that era and even many decades later would be considered complete unless the heroine was given a soulful solo to express her innermost feelings. *Paying Guest* was no exception, and Lata sang for a lovely Nutan a stirring composition fusing ragas Bhoplai and Shuddha Kalyan. It was indeed a 'pitch-perfect' coincidence that two top music directors of the period ended up writing nearly identical melodies—*Rasik balma* by Shankar–Jaikishan in *Chori Chori* (1956) and *Chand phir nikla* by Burman. Not only was Lata a common factor in both songs, even the situations were noticeably similar.

Post *Paying Guest*, and as mentioned earlier, both Sasadhar Mukerji and his younger brother, Subodh Mukerji bade adieu to Filmistan. The latter promptly announced a film titled *Love Marriage* in 1959. According to his son, Subhash Mukerji,[5] 'My father approached Burman for the music, assuring him that he would be paid well, in line with what he was paid by Dev Anand for two films. (He had been paid 85,000 rupees for two films.) To set the ball rolling, he sent his brother Prabodh Mukerji to meet the composer to proceed with the contractual details.

'Burman was standing on the balcony of his bungalow the "Jet" when Prabodh came to meet him. For reasons unknown, Burman did not honour the verbal discussion he had with Subodh Mukerji, leaving Prabodh no option but to turn away from the gate.

'Why he did what he did isn't clear even to this day. He probably was not happy with the money offered. Subodh Mukerji took umbrage at his behaviour, and called Jaikishan to Gaylord restaurant for a story session. At Gaylord, Jai asked for a one rupee coin, which Mukerji thought was for a pack of Gold Flake cigarettes. Jai took the coin and said—"Sir, you have made *Munimji* and *Paying Guest*. How could you even think that I would need to hear the story as a pre-requisite? Consider this one rupee coin as the signing amount for your film."'

With that, S.D. Burman coldly severed his thirteen-year-old association with the Mukerjis. Although he would work with them again, but for now, it was Navketan, and only Navketan.

Refusing films because of lesser remuneration than what he deserved or desired, somehow sounds like an exaggeration. Be that as it may, S.D. Burman had willy-nilly earned the tag of 'Uncle Scrooge'. Nabendu Ghosh was known to complain how Burman wouldn't even offer him tea during day-long discussions on song situations. During *Pyaasa*'s music sessions, apparently Guru Dutt would be left to fend for himself during lunch time, while Burman would excuse himself. It was said that people were hesitant sharing a taxi with Burman, as he would never cough up his share of the fare. There is this hitherto unknown, albeit unconfirmed story about how once Burman shared a taxi with Salil Chowdhury, agreeing to split the expenses 50:50. When he got off, he coolly handed Salil fifty paise!

There is yet another story about his visit to the Ramakrishna Mission Ashram in Calcutta. As per the norm, he removed his shoes before entering the main place of worship, but kept one shoe in one corner, and the other at a distance. When asked about it, he reasoned that this would make it difficult for thieves to steal the pair. When asked what he would do if the crook managed to locate both the shoes, he said that a hard work of that level made the thief a deserving candidate for the pair!

For all the stories which justified the label of being a 'miser', there were instances of him singing for charity. He also donated liberally to causes that he believed in. His family were disciples of Dhananjay Das Kathia Babaji Maharaj. Burman, accompanied by Meera and Pancham, often travelled to Vrindavan and donated large sums of money to the ashram. However, he never spoke about it either to the media or the film fraternity, except to his 'guru bhai', Subrata Sengupta.[6]

So far as his religious beliefs were concerned, Burman was not conventional—suffice it to say that he was by no stretch either a moralist, although he drank in moderation and smoked occassionally. As an interesting aside, he would often go to a market in south Calcutta to buy animal-shaped biscuits, but would refuse to buy one which was shaped like a cow!

Navketan, Asha & Kishore

In a discussion with Sachin Ganguly, S.D. Burman had once remarked, 'I have a very close bond with Dev. It is much more than a professional relationship. Although I would have loved to, I can never ask for a raise while working with him. I have never said no to him either. It is as if we are part of the same family.

'One day, both Meera and I were out, and on returning, I found that a large crowd had assembled in front of my house. I found Dev Anand shooting in my home—with reflectors, etc. He didn't require permission to shoot inside my house.'

The film was *Nau Do Gyarah* (1957), parts of which were indeed shot inside Burman's house, the Jet, in the mid-1950s. However, it is difficult to ascertain whether Dev Anand had retained all the scenes shot in that white-and-green bungalow or used only a few for the final version.

Around this time, Guru Dutt had moved away from Navketan. Vijay Anand had a story in his bag and shared it with his brother, but presented him with a fait accompli that only he and no one else would direct the film.

As a child, Vijay Anand had a golden mop of curly hair, because of which his father began calling him Goldilocks[1]. The name stuck, albeit in a shorter form and most of his peers only knew him by that name. Goldie arrived in Bombay in 1942, and became part of the 41, Pali

125

Hill group. As a student of St. Xavier's college, he began participating in dramatics and later began assisting his brothers. His maiden foray into cinema was as the dialogue writer for *Taxi Driver* for which he was credited.

In the interim, Golide had penned another script called *Akela*, based on a story set in a coal mine, but for some reason, he scrapped it later. If one were to trace Vijay Anand's journey as a director, then it may be interesting to know that the first scene he ever directed was a song, *Aye meri topi palat ke aa* in *Funtoosh*.

In 1955–56, Alfred Hitchcock arrived in Bombay for the premiere of his film, *To Catch a Thief* (1955). One is tempted to speculate if Vijay Anand was also present on the occasion as the Hitchcockian influence reflected prominently in his work, almost till the end of his career. To begin with, there were strong shades of both, *To Catch a Thief* and *Rebecca* (1940) in *Nau Do Gyarah*. Such was the influence of Hitchcock on Goldie that during an outdoor schedule of Nasir Husain's *Teesri Manzil* (1966), members of the cast and crew began referring to him as 'Bombay's Hitchcock'! But if there was one thing which was more in evidence than his love for Hitchcock, it was his burning passion for good cinema and as time would hold testimony, he was one of the most sought-after and respected filmmakers in Bombay from the Sixties to the mid-Seventies.

Even as he was fast becoming adept at filming suspense dramas, his song picturisations would be held up as legendary for future generations of filmmakers. He created realistic images within a medium that was grossly unreal, and consequently, evolved into a master who remains unparalleled since.

His debut, *Nau Do Gyarah* was a Bollywood musical-turned-road film with Hitchcockian shades. The film begins in a tiny studio apartment in Delhi and ends in a luxurious villa in Mahabaleshwar, Maharashtra. Amongst several other aspects about the music of the film, an endearing feature ran through it like a theme—whistling in the background. For instance, in *Hum hain rahi pyaar ke,* the whistling—again by Anoop Kumar—serves as an important motif to establish the happy-go-lucky aspect of the hero's character. The song sounds extremely simple to render, which Kishore did effortlessly, but on deeper analysis, it has a tough inflection to emulate in the first line of the antara. Burman was aware of this twist and therefore replaced the shuddh *ni* with komal *ni* and simplified the return to the second line of the antara. Unperturbed by issues of negotiating difficult notes, which many a time kills a wonderful film song, *Hum hain rahi pyaar ke* became a rage and came to symbolise the carefree years of youth. In *Dil Hai Ke Manta Nahin* (1991), director Mahesh Bhatt paid a tribute to this number by making his lead pair, Aamir Khan and Pooja Bhatt dance to it and later made a movie by the same name, starring Juhi Chawla and Aamir Khan.

Running neck-to-neck in popularity with *Hum hain rahi pyaar ke* was the Kishore–Asha duet, *Aankhon mein kya ji*. A quintessential Majrooh number woven around a question-and-answer session between lovers, this Latino-sounding melody had such a momentum that radio listeners of the time vouched for how they could almost visualise Dev Anand popping out of the poster! Kishore and Asha waltz through the number in perfect synchronisation, even as Asha slips in those little *murkis* (short, brisk, ornamentations within a line) to highlight the heroine's naughtiness while teasing her man. Easy to navigate and embellished with short phrases, this song has an interlude which was probably the inspiration for *Maine dil abhi diya nahi*, Pancham's composition for *The Train* (1970). The song also has a coda, which could have led to the genesis of *Mere liye soona soona*, another Pancham composition from *Anand Aur Anand* (1984).

Initially, the opening line of the song was, *Ankhon mein kya ji, sunehra baadal*, but Goldie requested Majrooh to change *sunehra* (golden) to *rupehla* (silvery), as the song was to be sung at night.

Ankhon mein kya ji was Kishore Kumar's last song for Dev Anand in the 1950s. The reason was the singer's hectic work and personal life—Kishore was forever running from studio to studio for shoots, producing films, trying his hand at composing, singing, and handling a stressful marriage which later ended in a divorce.

With Kishore out of the reckoning, in came Mohammed Rafi and sang his first song for Dev Anand under Burman's baton—*Kali re roop mein*. In this duet with Asha, Rafi deftly modulated his voice to fill the void left by Kishore, as he also did in the romantic duet, *Aaja panchi akela hai*.

It was during the making of *Nau Do Gyarah* that Pancham began assisting his father fulltime. According to several accounts, although he did work on some scores, interludes, and codas, apart from playing the harmonica and percussion instruments, he was still in awe of his illustrious father, as was evidenced during the premiere of the film in Calcutta at New Cinema.

Pancham was enjoying the show with his friends and relatives, and animatedly narrating behind-the-screen incidents to them. Suddenly, S.D. Burman, accompanied by Dev Anand, Goldie, et al, made a grand entry into the theatre during the interval. Pancham looked up, and is said to have taken the shortest route to the exit door!

And then there was someone else who was extremely special in the *Nao Do Gyarah* crew—the son of a sub-inspector of police in Azamgarh (Uttar Pradesh), he was born as Asrar Hussain Khan. As a young man, he had pursued Dars-e-Nizami (a course in Muslim theology), and also learnt Persian and Arabic, followed by the degree of Alim. Asrar later decided to switch careers and joined Takmeel-ut-tib, a college of Unani medicine in Lucknow and established himself as a hakim in the early 1940s. It was during this period that he recited his first poem in Sultanpur, and found a patron in none other than the illustrious, Jigar Moradabadi. Six months and many poems later, he moved to Aligarh and took refuge under the tutelage of the celebrated Urdu writer, Professor Rashid Ahmed Siddiqui. In the two years that he spent in Aligarh, Asrar realised that his audiences were rarely if ever, either moved or impressed with the poetry that he recited at regular mushairas, and he began introspecting about how to make his writing more acceptable to the masses.

In 1945, he visited Bombay where a chance encounter with producer-director, A.R. Kardar landed him with a song-writing assignment for *Shahjehan* (1946). Asrar had a rare quality—he could write to tunes with peerless alacrity. For instance, for a film called *Miss Coca Cola* (1955), he wrote five songs in twenty-four hours flat! By now, Asrar had given up his original name and came to be known as Majrooh. Even at that young age, he would describe writing lyrics to tunes as 'pen-work', in contrast to writing poetry, which he said was, 'heart-work'. Majrooh Sultanpuri was just the perfect partner that Burman was seeking to fill the void left by Sahir Ludhianavi.

As mentioned earlier, after Kishore distanced himself from playback singing for other actors, Rafi became the voice of Dev. One might be tempted to infer that it was Rafi's exceptional singing in *Pyaasa* that had left Burman without an option, but then both Hemanta and Talat had a better grip on rendering for the brooding characters essayed by Dev those days. Gradually, Rafi became a regular feature in Burman's music room and the success of *Hum bekhudi mein tum* from *Kala Pani* sealed the decision.

The song's Bengali version, *Ghoom bhulechi nijhum* sung by Sachin Dev was a fabulous, albeit tough act to follow for Rafi. But far from facing a struggle to match up to the original, Rafi sounded soft, mellow and velvety, leaving the listener with a heady feeling.

The relaxed, somewhat semi-drowsy style of singing was carried over by Rafi in *Mujhe le chalo* (*Sharabi*, 1964) for Madan Mohan; for Ravi in *Sau baar janam lenge* (*Ustaadon Ke Ustaad*, 1963); or for Chitragupta, in *Jaag dil-e-diwana* (*Oonche Log*, 1965).

For *Hum bekhudi mein*, Burman did away with almost every rhythm accompaniment, except for the duggi and tabla. The use of sarangi was to suit the situation as the song was picturised in the quarters of a nautch girl, and also helped in completing the first line of the mukhda in which Rafi trails off with '*Hum....*' This soliloquy of a song with minimal instrumentation, devoid of any extra embellishment, almost sounded like a hymn.

A bit of trivia about the Bengali record, which was a deviation from standard norms—it had names of instrumentalists written on it, like Brajen Biswas who played the tabla, and Rahul Dev Burman who had played the sarod. As rarely would names of musicians adorn record labels in India, Burman had made a special request to the HMV staff, through his secretary Sachin Ganguly to get them credited.

Kala Pani was Raj Khosla's debut for Navketan. It was speculated that it was inspired by the Bengali film, *Sabaar Upare* (1955) starring Uttam Kumar and Suchitra Sen. However, Dev Anand had insisted that the inspiration was A.J. Cronin's *Beyond This Place*, which was also many said, the inspiration for the Bengali original. Finally, *Kala Pani* not only had a modest run at the box office, but it was also inferior in many ways to the original Bengali version. What resurrected it was its music, as it does even now for those who revel in Dev Anand and nostalgia. The reason being that *Kala Pani* was different from other Dev Anand films for it had two *mujras* (*Nazar laagi raja* and *Dil laga ke kadar gayi pyaare*; the second one also had Burman singing tabla *bols* or strokes); a nautanki (*Dilwale, ab teri gali*); a 'mujra-cabaret' (*Jab naam-e-mohabbat leke*); and a romantic duet (*Accha ji mein haari*).

Whether it was Sachin Dev or Rahul Dev, what made their music unique and evergreen was their constant endeavour to introduce new sounds in their compositions and in this both were extremely fortunate to have been aided by able team members. For instance, during the mid- and late-1950s, Brajen Biswas, the main percussionist in Burman's team would come up with different *thekas* (patterns) for an album and also add layers to basic taals like *keherwa* and *dadra*. If one listens carefully, the dadra in *Janey kya tunhe kahi* sounds very Western, while the keherwa in *Hum hain rahi pyaar ke* sounds almost Latino; the restrained duggi bols in *Hum bekhudi mein*, stand out fabulously in the song, as was the rolling, continuous rhythm in *Accha ji*.

Close on the heels of *Kala Pani*, yet another Burman composition for another Raj Khosla film would have a continuous rhythmic beat.

Raj Khosla came to Bombay from Punjab to become an actor and singer. Some of his forays into playback singing are documented, whereas his attempts at acting find no mention. A copy of the *The Indian Express* of September 1946 shows him modelling for a hair product called, Vaseline Pomade, and the caption mentions him as 'an actor in the film *Naen Basera* by Asha Pictures'. Although it is difficult to ascertain if the film ever got made, perhaps even under a different name, but one can safely assume that he had a penchant for acting. Maybe it was that unrealised dream which made him appear on screen intermittently—once in a cameo in *Jaal*, and next in the role of a film director in *Solva Saal* (1958). Although the movie was loosely based on Frank Capra's hit, *It Happened One Night* (1934), it somehow didn't ring the cash registers at the box office. But every time there is a discussion about Dev Anand's best films, it pops up and only because of that one song which became Burman's first top of the charts in Binaca Geetmala.

Hai apna dil toh awara was a huge hit—for the intrinsically carefree expression, the easy-to-sing tune, and for the trendy rhythm which ran through the song like a continuous thread. The beat was like hoof-trot, but sub-divided into additional notes, making it more than the standard 1-5 pattern played on the contra bass. The song also marked the emergence of Pancham as a deft harmonica player. Though he had played it previously in *Pyaasa*, the accompanying piece in this song stood out for its brilliance and is also heard during the opening title sequence.

The impact of the song overshadowed every other in *Solva Saal*. The second most popular song in the film was perhaps the sad version of it. As a singer, Hemanta's timbre in all the songs in the film was noticeably lighter than what it used to be and suited Dev Anand perfectly. So much so, that there is a sequence in the film where the heroine, Waheeda Rehman, tells Dev that he should have been named 'Hemant Kumar' (as the singer was known in Bombay sans his surname, Mukherjee).

Meanwhile, Sachin Dev Burman was on a chartbusting spree. In 1959, the Binaca Geetmala topper was yet another of his compositions. But before that, a story needs to be told, which has been narrated many times in many different ways.

In the late 1950s, S.D. Burman had a major setback in his career—a split with none other than Lata Mangeshkar. In the absence of any authentic or recorded account of the time, it is difficult to ascertain which film had driven a schism between the composer and the singer. By Lata's own admission to her biographer, Harish Bhimani, and subsequently to Nasreen Munni Kabir, the misunderstanding had occurred during *Miss India* (1957). According to a report in *Filmfare* (January 1961), *Sitaron Se Aage* was Lata's last film for S.D. Burman in the 1950s. Raju Bharatan, in an article titled, "How Asha lost Dada to Lata" in *Filmfare* (1–15 December 1985), elaborated on the incident as follows:

> It so happened that Lata, sometime in mid-1957, was to go on tour and there was a song for Burman's *Sitaron Se Aage* that she had still to dub. The song *Pag thumak thumak chalat bal khaye haai saiyyan kaise dharun dheer*—the original version of *Mohse chhal kiye jaye* from *Guide*. Lata, according to Jaidev, had agreed to dub *Pag thumak thumak* for Dada before she left on tour. But when Jaidev, as Dada's *Sitaron Se Aage* assistant, rang Lata (in the presence of Dada) to confirm the dubbing, the Melody Queen,

according to him, said she could not spare the time to do the job before she proceeded on tour. Whereupon, says Jaidev, Dada, keeping his cool, got him to enquire from Lata whether she would give his *Pag thumak thumak* first dubbing preference on her return from the tour. But Lata, says Jaidev, was prepared to make no such commitment. On hearing that, Dada, for once, as Jaidev recalls it, took courage in both hands and got his assistant to tell Lata that if she could not give him first preference on her return, she didn't need to give him preference for any song any more. The entire tangle could have been sorted out if Dada had gone to the phone to request Lata himself. That Burman demurred from doing so is, to me, a pointer that *Pag thumak* was but the culmination—and not the beginning—of the Dada-Lata feud.

Although Lata Mangeshkar didn't refute Raju Bharatan's claim, one can perhaps sew both stories to infer that the rift must have begun during *Miss India* and the parting after *Sitaron Se Aage*. As a result of the controversy, the music of *Sitaron Se Aage* was totally eclipsed. Lata's three songs from the film—the much-discussed, *Pag thumak*; *Mehfil mein aaye woh aaj dheere se*; and *Oo khilte hain gul*, as well as the Asha song, *Chanda ki chandni ka jadoo*, were testimonies of a composer's genius of mixing multiple genres with aplomb. The film, advertised as: 'She reached out for the sky...He placed her amongst the stars', was the story of a playwright (Ashok Kumar) and his protégé (Vyjayanthimala) and lent itself to several sequences of dance and music. One of the fallouts of the fracas between Lata and Burman was that the composer who was initially reluctant to rely on heavy orchestration, changed his stance. He began to use longer preludes and fillers, more instruments, longer notes, less inflections, even regularly sourcing from Western scores, like he did for *Chanda ki chandni ka jadoo* and *Dil le gaya gham de gaya* (Geeta Dutt) in this film. There also seems to be an attempt to make Asha sound like Lata in *Roye jiya aan milo morey piya* and *Aaj kal parson*. A keen enthusiast may find it interesting that Burman used the refrain of Dean Martin's *Sway* for the antara of *Roye jiya*; later, he would use the first few bars of *Aaj kal parson* as the refrain for *Ram karey babua* (*Anurag*, 1972), a song that became a huge hit when compared to the *Sitaron Se Aage* song.

With *Sitaron Se Aage*, Burman returned to the South after almost five years. The film was started in early 1956 by V.L. Narasu, the coffee magnate-turned-film producer, who had also bought the rights of Bombay Talkies' *Kismet*, and signed up its director, Gyan Mukherjee. At the time, Burman was working simultaneously with Gyan and his disciple, Guru Dutt, and this was unique in the annals of Bombay film industry.

In an interview with the authors in 2010, the late Sachin Bhowmick had recounted hitherto unknown details about *Sitaron Se Aage*, 'I had just arrived in Bombay and was working as an assistant to Gyan Mukherjee. Officially, I was assigned for *Shatranj* (1956), but unofficially I was also helping him with the continuity of *Sitaron Se Aage*. Mukherjee would suffer from bouts of headaches, and after shooting a few reels in mid-1956, he was diagnosed with brain tumour. Further investigations revealed that he was suffering from Parkinson's, and he passed away in November 1956. This resulted in the film getting stalled, and then at Ashok Kumar's insistence, Satyen Bose was summoned to do the rescue act.

'I knew S.D. Burman from Calcutta, and did the liaising between Gyanda and Sachinda. Gyanda was used to working with composers who would complete a song within a week; Sachinda took time to nurture his creations. However, Gyanda was happy with the final results.'

The film may be forgotten today, but quite a few songs from it evoke memories of a bygone era. The short title piece for example, in which one senses an element of poise which was a rarity. However, what is rather sad is that the most publicised song from the film, *Zara ruk ja pyaare ruk ja*, fails to trigger any nostalgia. A routine comic-romantic song, it was a take-off from Mohammed Rafi's songs for Johnny Walker.

As time rolled by, Asha Bhosle became Sachin Dev Burman's principal singer starting with *Lajwanti* (1958). For his shows outside Bombay, Burman would first check with Asha and then plan his trips. Pancham, who had bought his first car, a Fiat, would play the errand boy-cum-messenger between the composer and singer because his father didn't have a telephone at home.

Lajwanti was an average grosser, but earned critical acclaim. Musically, it did no wonders either, but the film was the recipient of the National Award for the Best Feature Film in Hindi, and was also India's entry at the Cannes Film Festival in 1959.

In a script that had enough scope for showcasing music, Burman's efforts somehow lacked the spontaneity of his earlier films. One finds the nat phrase repeating itself in two songs in the film—*Aaja chhaye kare badra* and *Chanda mama mere dwar*. The latter song sung by a child in the film was actually the voice of Chandbala, who was at the time married to Rais Khan, who had played the sitar for Burman in the film.

With Lata moving away from S.D. Burman and the composer's waning relationship with Geeta Dutt, Asha had come to occupy centrestage in his musical career. In *Lajwanti*, *Chanda re chupe rehna*, a soothing lullaby sung by her actually resuscitated the album, and one could extrapolate the antara to Pancham's composition, *Deewana mujhsa nahin* (*Teesri Manzil*, 1966). The song was used twice in the film, maybe more out of compulsion than design. This, along with the unforgettable, *Ga mere mann ga*, are the best songs in an otherwise indifferent album. The other Asha solo, *Ek hans ka joda*, remains popular even today.

In a script which mandated that the leading lady (Nargis) dresses like a man in order to avenge the disappearance of her husband (Pradip Kumar) on the night of their marriage, I.S. Johar's *Miss India* hardly had any room for musical interventions. Asha's *Albela mein ik dilwala* and Rafi's *Badla zamana* had little novelty, except for the O.P. Nayyaresque feel of 1-5 beat and the use of dual metering. The tune of the antara also made it to the title score, which was used by Burman a decade and a half later for *Tumre sang toh rain bitaayi* (*Sagina*, 1974). He also used dual metering for the merger song, *Yeh bheegi bheegi raaten, jaoon mein kahan*, but Manna Dey did not quite live up to the high energy levels required for the song and surprisingly, even Lata drawled through her parts. While Manna–Asha's *Thoda naseeb ki jo* sounds boringly preachy, *Malik ne hath* by the same pair was better; the tempo and the beat pattern almost forming a template for other popular songs, such as Pancham's *Chunri sambhal gori* (*Baharon Ke Sapne*, 1967). While on Pancham, it is difficult to miss his harmonica motifs which lay scattered like gems in *Miss India*, akin to what we hear in *Pyaasa*.

In the late 1950s, if someone were to ask if S.D. Burman was a successful music director, then the answer would be: yes, indeed. But with a pre-condition—due to the benevolence of a star. As success claims many fathers, Dev Anand's matinee idol charm overshadowed Burman's excellent music; as was Sahir and Guru Dutt's combined intensity which was acknowledged as major reasons for *Pyaasa's* cult status.

Furthermore, his success was in no way comparable to that of Shankar–Jaikishan, O.P. Nayyar, or Naushad. In fact, it would be unfair to include Naushad in the list because he hardly ever worked on more than a film a year and given such discipline, he ensured that the hummability quotient of his music never dipped. On the other hand, O.P. Nayyar had perfected the art of sounding trendy even with the standard matter-of-fact Punjabi music. He hardly ever deviated from a set pattern, especially when it was rhythm, preferring to go 1-5 on the double bass all the way. Compared to S.D. Burman, he certainly had a higher volume of film releases and even though several of them proved to be inconsequential at the box office, the music always succeeded in making its mark. The interesting point was that despite his limited repertoire, Nayyar always managed to sound different.

However of the lot, Shankar–Jaikishan were the most successful composers during this period, because much like Burman, they also catered to multiple genres—broadly categorised in cinema as semi-classical, folk, Western, dance, women's songs, sad songs, love songs, etc., making them acceptable to a wider audience. They also had the backing of Raj Kapoor and were therefore in constant limelight.

While his Durga Puja songs were raging hits in Bengal, a question which often came up was: can S.D. Burman compose a popular Hindi album on his own strength? Without sharing space with either Dev Anand or someone as prolific as Sahir? Even as much debate ensued over his ability to succeed on his own steam, Burman became the first Hindi film composer to be conferred with the Sangeet Natak Akademi award in 1958, which was almost like the heralding of a new phase in his life. An ecstatic Dev Anand decided to honour his 'Dada', and threw a huge party in his home, which included a qawwali recital. Sachin Dev's team was in full attendance—Pancham, Basu Chakravarty and Manohari Singh, the latter two having moved to Bombay from Calcutta at Salil Chowdhury's behest. Basu, who played the cello, joined the Hindi film industry in 1957, while Manohari, who was multi-faceted and played major wind instruments like the clarinet, alto sax, English flute, as well as the mandolin and accordion, arrived in 1958. Along with them was a young percussionist called Maruti Rao Keer, who was almost like a son to his mentor in his later years.

It was a talented team of musicians who were now getting ready to create some madness.

In 1958, Kishore Kumar turned producer with a film revolving around his father's jalopy—a 1928 model Ford T (according to the well-known photographer Aloke Dasgupta, the car was a Chrysler) which the Gangolys had bought in 1929. Kishore's father, Kunjilal, happened to be the second person in the sleepy town of Khandwa in Madhya Pradesh to own the prized model, which in itself was a rare achievement. The film was called *Chalti Ka Naam Gaadi* (henceforth referred to as *CKNG*), his second production after the Bengali hit, *Lukochuri* in 1958.

Widely acknowledged as a classic today, *CKNG* underwent a change of hands when Kamal Majumdar (who had directed *Lukochuri* as well) threw in the towel. In a repeat of the *Sitaron Se Aage* episode, Satyen Bose was roped in to complete the film.

In so far as its music was concerned, it was in *CKNG* that S.D. Burman truly displayed his panache for quirky songs. All the tracks in the film, starting with *Paanch rupaiya barah aana, Ek ladki bheegi bhaagi si, Hum ththe woh thi,* and the 1959 Binaca Geetmala topper, *Haal kaisa hai janab ka,* became instant chartbusters. The opening song, *Babu, samjho ishaare* had Burman dovetailing the antara of *Oonche sur mein gaye ja* (*House No. 44*) with the antara of this song. As was expected, the result was for everyone to both see and hear!

Soon, yet another raging debate began whether it was the brilliance of Burman, or the histrionics of Kishore Kumar which had made *CKNG* a grand success. While the debate will never reach a conclusive end, it needs to be pointed out that not all the songs in the film were originals; there were several sources of inspiration. For instance, the phrase, *Paanch rupaiya barah aana,* which sounded uncannily similar to the line, *Jibone tai aaj eto alo* from *Ei jhir batase,* which was sung by Dhananjay Bhattacharya for composer Sudhin Dasgupta around 1957.[2] That both *Ek ladki* and *Hum ththe woh thi* were based on Western songs (*Sixteen Tons* and *Watermelon Song* respectively, both by Tennessee Ernie Ford) is well documented.

There were of course murmurs about Burman borrowing heavily from elsewhere, but that was exactly what made the film and its music stay in public memory for years after its release. The film required smart and trendy tunes. If Burman realised that it was inevitable to reach out to sources beyond his own comfort zone, in all likelihood it was Kishore who propelled his music director to adapt to the need of the film. Amongst several other singers of the time, it was well known that Kishore shared a comfortable relationship with his Sachinda, and could walk up to him with any suggestions. As a result of this synergy, *CKNG* became a stepping stone for Kishore to start composing music, which he did for his subsequent productions like *Jhumroo* (1961), *Door Gagan Ki Chaon Mein* (1964), or the incomplete ones like, *Neela Aasmaan* and *Suhana Geet*. No doubt then that Kishore Kumar acknowledged Burman's immense contribution to his career and said, 'I am whatever I am because of him.'[3]

A decade later, Sachinda would elevate Kishore's career to unimaginable heights.

Sujata

Tulika Ghosh, classical vocalist and daughter of Pandit Nikhil Ghosh (younger brother of flautist Pannalal Ghosh) recounted[1] an interesting anecdote. 'This incident dates back to around 1968–69. We used to stay on 12th Road, near the telephone exchange in Khar then. My father, Pandit Nikhil Ghosh, was the ideal 'shagird' of Ahmed Jan Thirakwa Khan, the 'Mount Everest of tabliyas', one of the most influential percussionists in the country.

'One fine morning, Khansaab, who was staying with us, was resting in the garden in an armchair, engrossed within himself, and oblivious to the surroundings. Suddenly, he heard a song playing on the radio somewhere near our house. He was fascinated by the voice and asked us to play the song on our radio set. Film music was a complete no-no in our house, but we, after some effort, did manage to tune in to Vividh Bharati.

'Khansaab listened to whatever was left of the song—could be the last antara. It had such a mesmerising effect on him that he was desperate to listen to the song again. Those days, getting a 78 RPM record of an old film was not an easy job, and my father had to struggle to get a copy. Once he got hold of the shellac, Khansaab kept on listening to the song over and over again, and insisted that he wanted to meet the singer.

'Burman jethu (term of address for father's elder brother in Bengali) lived on Linking Road in Khar and would often meet my father at our place. On being told of Khansaab's desire, he was more than eager to meet father's Guruji.

'Khansaab was ecstatic, and presented him with a 10-rupee note. The amount meant a lot those days. Burman jethu touched the currency note to his forehead and said: "This is the greatest gift I have ever received; I shall treasure it for the rest of my life. I shall frame it and hang it on the wall my house."'

The song was *Sunn mere bandhu re*, a comeback song for Sachin Dev; after all, he was singing for a Hindi film after twelve long years.

Bimal Roy wanted this earthy song to be featured on an unnamed character in his film, and it was well established that except S.D. Burman, no one else had the innate quality to sing in a voice which evoked the ordinariness of a human being.

'Bimalda probably convinced Sachinda to resume singing after a long gap,' said the octogenarian, Debabrata Sengupta, a former assistant to Bimal Roy and director of *Do Dooni Char* (1968). He continued, 'Actually, a Bengali song was transformed into *Sunn mere bandhu re*. During the shooting of *Sujata*, Bimalda felt that a song was required for the sequence where Adhir meets Sujata at Gandhi Ghat. The entire set which showed Barrackpore, was actually built by Sudhendu Roy in Mohan studios. Bimalda explained the situation and the Bengali song to Majrooh Sultanpuri. Burman was ready and gave a perfect take even before Majrooh finished writing the lyrics, which he did sitting there and then.'[2]

According to Sumit Mitra[3] (who played the accordion for various composers in Bombay from the mid-1960s), Burman was extremely nervous prior to the recording of the song and kept telling his chauffeur to drive slowly during the commute from the Jet to Tardeo. However, not once did his anxiety show up during the rendition. The bhatiyali-based song, with the discerning use of komal *ni* sounded effortless. The brilliance of the song is in its quietness, although it is a plea, almost a cry of lament by a woman and therefore, the arrangement avoided the use of either the tabla or dholak. The percussion instrument which created the sound of oar on water was a wooden block, while there was a flute accompaniment all through the song. If there ever was a bhatiyali in Hindi cinema, it was this.

Much like *Devdas*, one wonders why Bimal Roy chose Sachin Dev Burman for *Sujata*, despite Salil's exceptional score for *Madhumati*. One can only attribute it to the director's intent of wanting to create a melancholic ambience for the film, like he had done for *Devdas*. For instance, during the shooting of the film, Roy would address the cast by their character names; even the songs were specifically composed for Adhir, Sujata and Rama, and not Sunil Dutt, Nutan or Shashikala.

The first song to be shot for *Sujata* was *Jalte hain jiske liye*. Debu Sen, who was working on the screenplay with Nabendu Ghosh[4] recalled,[5] 'One day, Sachinda told Bimalda, "I have a nice song for you. It is taken from *buro* (literally, old man in Bengali; but here referring to Tagore). It needs to be sung over the phone." I started laughing and said the phone would create a lot of noise. Sachinda snubbed me—"Why should there be a jarring sound?" He then sang the song to us, and later Bimalda was convinced about making the hero sing the song over the phone.'

It is worth mentioning here that Burman took inspiration from his own life to create the song situation. During his honeymoon in Darjeeling, he would get calls from friends and family members to sing for them, which he would do over the phone!

It is apparent that Burman had no qualms about accepting that he had 'taken' the song from Tagore. However the song that he was referring to was, *Ekoda tumi priye*, first made famous by Pankaj Mullick and later by Suchitra Mitra, which was devoid of any sentimentality that was so deftly woven into *Jalte hain jiske liye*. S.D. Burman's version was overtly romantic, and has a tenderness which has since been difficult to match.

This song was Talat Mahmood's favourite and despite the fact that Burman was initially reluctant to have him sing it, he must have been more than satisfied at the final output. This also raises an interesting question—Talat's most memorable songs were always those in which he sang long, straight notes with lesser inflections. With a marked vibrato which tended to jar when the notes were straight, maintaining consistent flux density must have been tough for him, and it is remarkable how Talat negotiated the long fast notes with effortless ease. At this point, one should also mention that Burman used the fillers between the lines exceedingly well, which supplemented Talat's voice.

While Burman may have revelled in the magic that he created for *Sujata*, there were rumblings of a controversy around some of the songs. For one, composer Nachiketa Ghosh[6] felt that Burman had referenced his basic Bengali composition, *Chotto pakhi Chandana*, for the lullaby, *Nanhi kali soney chali*. Of course, the most publicised controversy was around *Tum jiyo hazaaron saal*, lip-synched on screen by a junior artiste called Meena. This happy, cheery song, which became a regular feature on Radio Ceylon on the 15th of every month as a birthday celebration for listeners born in that month, was credited to Geeta Dutt. In 1987, Asha Bhosle had claimed that the credit was incorrect, and it was she and not Geeta who had sung the song. Pancham later said that his father had recorded two versions of the same song, and had given the final nod to Asha. In the compilations that followed, including the *Hindi Film Geet Kosh*, Vol III by Harmandir Singh 'Hamraaz', the song credits were changed from Geeta Dutt to Asha Bhosle.

The central character of the eponymous film, *Sujata*, had only one solo featured on her. The raga Piloo-flavoured, *Kali ghata chhaye* put over delicately by Asha. Interestingly, the song was in a near-staccato mode and rendering it in a lilting cadence was a task both creditable and enviable. There is no gainsaying the fact that much like *Devdas*, Bimal Roy's fabulous photography established the central character brilliantly and Burman's music aided the visuals with subtle yet firm inflections. While the camera often finds Sujata in a garden, almost as an extension of Mother Nature, her presence is established by cuckoo calls, strings, sitar gats, *jhalas* (fast-paced pieces) and obligatos on the flute, to capture her varied emotions.

In retrospect, the interjection of Tagore's dance drama, *Chandalika* was somehow wasted by both the director and music composer of the film, considering *Sujata* was also woven around a similar theme. *Chandalika* is a story about an 'untouchable' girl called Prakriti who offers water to a Buddhist monk called Ananda, and is enlightened when he speaks about the universal truth of all humans being equal, *'Je manob ami, shei manob o tumi, kanya,'* (The human that I am, so are you, my girl.) In the film, the sequence is treated with near indifference and both Bimal Roy and S.D. Burman seemed oblivious to its significance in enhancing the film's central theme.

That apart, there was a glaring mistake in the film's climax, where Sujata is seen donating blood to her adoptive mother. Unquestionably impracticable and not a recommended medical practice either, but the scene which actually happened thereafter does merit mention! According to Debu Sen, 'Remember, in the last scene of the film, in which Sujata, who had for her entire life heard how she is "daughter-like and not the daughter of the adopted couple", tells her adoptive mother post the transfusion, *"Nahin... beti jaisi, mujh se nahi suni jati"* (No, this daughter-like I can't accept any more)? Well, Bimalda asked, "Where is Sachinda? Go, get him." We went looking for him. Sachinda was seated on the stairs next to the bathroom in Mohan Studios. He was brought back to the set and Bimalda asked, "Sachinda, where were you?" Sachinda replied, "You filmed this scene so well that I was moved to tears. I could not bring myself to witness it."'[7]

Sujata was released on 31 March 1959, while *Madhumati* was still running to packed houses. For a film that was essentially middle of the road compared to the average Bombay fare, it had a stupendous run of thirty-six weeks. The silver jubilee of the film was celebrated with much fanfare and fireworks near Juhu beach.[8]

Burman was on a roll. In so far as his professional life was concerned, it couldn't have been better and he began to mingle with his peers a lot more. But a slice of his personal life and apropos his relationship with Tripura royalty, continued to plague him. On 6 March 1960, members of the erstwhile Tripura royal family attended the marriage ceremony of Maharaja Kirit Bikram Deb Barman with Princess Padmaraje Scindia in Bombay. Bankim Karta of the Tripura royalty accompanied by a member of the Gwalior royal family visited Sachin Dev Burman at the Jet and cordially invited him to the reception at Samudra Mahal, the palace of the Scindias. Billed as the most expensive Indian wedding in fifty years, the *Sun* of London headlined this ostentatious event as, 'Gems dazzle as Princess weds in India'. But one of the gems of the family, Sachin Karta, declined the invitation, citing ill health.

The Sixties

In June 1959, the Burman family went on vacation to the continent. They travelled to London, and other parts of the UK attending musicals and plays. One such play was *Irma la Douce* at the West End theatre.

One wonders if it was his exposure to music in England, but S.D. Burman returned to India more tolerant of Western music and during Dev Anand's birthday bash on 26 September that year, he even sang in English! This was indeed a change and as recalled by singer Subir Sen, once when a young Pancham was dancing in shorts to Western music, Burman had rued over the fact that his son preferred something ear-shattering to the sarod in which he was given training.[1]

Gautam Choudhury (a Salil Chowdhury aficionado and musician, also owner of the site on the maestro, *salilda.com*) mentioned to the authors how Salilda once told him of an anecdote which underscored Burman's simplicity. After his return from the UK, Sachinda had an animated discussion with him about the international music scene and said that he was particularly impressed by the music of a composer called *Batch*. Salilda figured it was Bach that Burman was referring to.[2]

But soon thereafter, S.D. Burman had to focus on things in hand as the film industry was gearing up for the release of the first indigenously made cinemascope film called, *Kaagaz Ke Phool*.

Flashback—Kaagaz Ke Phool

Over the years, much has been written about *Kaagaz Ke Phool*. The discerning ones called it a classic; many branded it futuristic. But for a common cinegoer, the movie was unfortunately a crushing bore. Guru Dutt's part-autobiographical story failed badly, and he once said, 'It was good in patches. It was too slow and it went over the head of the audiences.'

The film dragged under the weight of Guru Dutt's repeated attempts to make the audience understand his story—of a supremely talented filmmaker who faces failure due to the pressures of a marketplace which has no understanding of art and artists. As a result, even the film's music failed to coalesce, and it was apparent that the director's sole intent was to establish the theme song of the film, *Dekhi zamaane ki yaari, bichde sabhi baari baari*. It was as if he was trying to drown his audiences in bucketsful of self-pity.

No wonder that the multi-layered composition—based on Burman's little known, *Phire gechi bare bare*, where the essence was similar as well—was written almost like an opera, keeping count of every rejection that the failed director faces until his piteous and unsung death.

Burman brought out the mellowness in Rafi's voice yet again. The fabulous singer warbled through Kaifi Azmi's lines in a metre-less narration, totally in control of the pathos that was expected of him.

147

At a couple of places, Rafi almost *sighs*, his intonation blending both resignation and sarcasm displayed by a cruel and unrelenting world.

As the camera follows the old Mr. Sinha (played by Guru Dutt) and creates a vignette of his life—his days of glorious success, the autograph hunters, the waiting fans with garlands and the photographers, the deferential salutes on every street corner—the orchestra chimes in. The chorus with a deep cello, innumerable violins, fleeting notes of *A Christmas Carol* etc., morphs the number into a song within a song. The music suddenly becomes imperial, worthy of a grand ballroom.

But it does not end well. Although *Udd ja, udd ja, pyaase bhanware*, the concluding part of the song was even released as a separate song in the original shellac version. The entire song without this portion sounds tranquil, the waltz-like cadence defining the contemplative nature of the theme, before the introduction of high notes, which makes it overly melodramatic. A song like *Dekhi zamaane ki yaari* needed to be simple yet polyphonic and one can only speculate that Burman was perhaps not very convinced of the song situation.

Be that as it may, there was another song in the film about which he had no doubts whatsoever. In an interview with Nasreen Munni Kabir[1], poet Kaifi Azmi mentioned that S.D. Burman had first composed a tune for which a situation was created later. Kaifi began writing the lyrics to suit the tune, but unfortunately, the first two iterations were rejected. Thereafter Azmi literally turned his back and wrote *Waqt ne kiya kya haseen sitam* facing a wall!

The song was recorded in March 1959 and for most part, Burman layered the entire song on the string section, punctuated by piano notes with an organ for support. For a change, Sebastian D'Souza, who mostly worked with Shankar–Jaikishan, O.P. Nayyar and Salil Chowdhury, was brought in as the arranger for this song. Once while relaxing in his ancestral house at Reis Magos, Goa, the late maestro had confessed to musicologist and fellow Goan, Dr. Chandrasekhar Rao how *Waqt ne kiya* was like cherry on the cake of his twenty-five-year-long career.[2]

At a time when Hindi film music was focussed on romantic ballads, this song challenged the conventional norms. Paradoxically, *Waqt ne kiya* not only became *the* iconic sad song in Geeta Dutt's career, but also mirrored some of the tragedies in her life.

Musicals, Noir & Family Planning

Despite the brilliance and wide acceptance of *Waqt ne kiya*, Geeta Dutt was fast receding from S.D. Burman's life. Asha Bhosle had already become his favoured voice after the fracas with Lata Mangeshkar over *Sitaron Se Aage*.

However, in his second film for Vijay Anand, the ladies took a back seat. Post 1950, Dev Anand was well established as the quintessential romantic hero and had gotten over the image of a brooding lover which had reigned strong during the early part of his career. Hence, when he signed *Kala Bazar* (1960), Burman decided to choose Rafi as his voice, and the result was *Khoya khoya chand* which became one of the breeziest songs in Burman's career. In all probability, *Khoya khoya chand* must have been the first song composed for the film and the last that Burman finalised before his trip to Europe. Dev Anand had already completed the outdoor shoot in Ooty in June 1959, even as Burman was savouring the English summer.

What made *Khoya khoya chand* evergreen? The reverb-backed loud call out at the start of the number, for one. Secondly, the recall value of its antara which in any case happens to be one of the parameters for measuring the longevity of a song. Not only was *Khoya khoya chand* a simple melody to remember, it was easy to hum along, further underlining why a classical-based number never finds its way into the hearts of the masses.

The song was structured on the notes—not the progression—of raga Dhani, and followed an interesting arrangement pattern. It had four interludes and all were different. The first used the flute/piccolo and guitar; the second was mostly built on the mandolin and accordion; the third interlude had only Rafi's voice bridging the stanzas; and the final one started with a E-seventh chord strummed on the guitar, which was also used as the prelude, followed swiftly by the violin, mandolin and the flute.

As the energetic E-seventh chord kickstarts the number, one could almost visualise Dev Anand skipping along the hilly terrain in Ooty, ecstatic in the discovery of a new love. It is believed that Burman with his impending Europe trip had run out of patience with the poet-lyricist Shailendra and had given him an ultimatum. Finally one night, Shailendra sat on Juhu beach and delivered the lyrics at one go, with the moon providing him inspiration.

The song remains the centrepiece of *Kala Bazar*, blurring other brilliant compositions like the silky-smooth *Apni to har aah; Teri dhoom har kahin;* or *Sach hue sapne tere.*

Apni to har aah was yet another example of how judiciously Burman had used the mellow tone of Rafi's voice, which sounded velvety soft even at high octaves. That it was a 'train song' didn't even need viewing, as the bamboo flute-whistle was woven inextricably into the refrain. The song was shot in a customised train compartment at Guru Dutt Studios.

Teri dhoom har kahin was a cocktail of romanticism and noir, punctuated with the sound of coins clinking. The song's progression was almost in the manner of jazz, with a surfeit of brass in the interludes.

Although it is difficult to establish, this raga Kafi-based Asha Bhosle solo, *Sach hue sapne tere* may have been inspired by more than one Tagore song—*Epare mukhar holo keka oi* and *Nyay anyaye janine janine janine.* Asha hit the pivotal notes with a fluency that was reminiscent of Geeta Dutt's renditions in the early 1950s.

Burman was not done with the album yet. Two more sugar-sweet duets—*Rim jhim ke tarane leke aayi barsaat* (Geeta–Rafi) and *Saanjh dhali* (Asha–Manna) added significant layers to the unusual love story. In the former, Burman displayed how a simple piece of arrangement could create a visual effect—the build up was especially spectacular, with the sitar-flute jugalbandi establishing a poignant contrast.

It is often a topic of discussion amongst music lovers whether Burman had suggested the song picturisation of *Sanjh dhali* to Goldie, the director of the film. The reason being that it was one of those force-fitted duets so typical of Indian cinema. Here was a couple who were not yet in a relationship, but were comfortable singing a duet together. Manna, as on so many other occasions, was the second voice of the hero after Rafi or Mukesh (and later Kishore). But in *Sanjh dhali*, which is a naughty number, Burman plumbed Manna's light, romantic trait, which was so under-utilised in Hindi cinema. The metre of *Sanjh dhali* might have inspired him later for *Dil ka bhanwar* in *Tere Ghar ke Samne* (1963).

Although there is no recorded evidence of this, but one of the main musicians in S.D. Burman's group, Manohari Singh had once said that the only bhajan in the film, *Na main dhan chahun* was composed by Jaidev, under Burman's supervision. The 'transpose', wherein the *sa* of the scale keeps on changing was a Jaidev speciality, and the template would be used later even by Pancham in *Aa khuda hai faisla* (*Abdullah*, 1980).

Not only did *Kala Bazar* stand the test of time, it was the only film to feature the three Anand brothers, Chetan, Vijay and Dev. Yet another lesser known, albeit interesting piece of information is that this was also Vijay Anand's first double role—one as the second hero, and another as a cameo, accompanying Dilip Kumar (some reports say this was unintentional) to the premiere of *Mother India* at Liberty theatre. But the bigger story was how Burman managed to pull off such a fabulous album without two of his most trusted singers—Lata Mangeshkar and Kishore Kumar.

However, it wouldn't be unfair to mention that there were weak links in this otherwise brilliant score. For example, the cabaret, *Sambhalo* did little justice to the genre, and apart from what was in later years to become Rahul Dev Burman's signature, the huffing and puffing, it was a mediocre song. Also, the use of flutes, especially treble flutes, was not something one associates with the Western Ghats, as shown in the film.

Set in pre-Independent India, roughly around 1929–1932,[1] *Manzil* was partly financed by Dev Anand. The story of an aspiring musician—sans the love angle—the film *was* probably influenced by the initial struggles faced by S.D. Burman. Only the locations shifted—from Comilla to Simla, and from Calcutta to Bombay.

Given the familiarity of the story, the music of the film was unfortunately insipid. After all, not only did Burman know the minutest details of the struggles faced by an upcoming musician, he was also well versed with the music of the period. The early days of the Indian talkies used deep, sonorous, but nasal male voices, and strong female voices. The accompanying orchestra was mostly limited to string instruments, like the organ and piano. But these elements were somehow missing from *Manzil*'s music. As a result, all the songs featured on Dev Anand, except for *Yaad aa gayi woh nashili nigahen* sung by Hemanta Kumar (which was also used in the climax), have low recall value. The intricacies in the romantic songs, which were set in the hills, were driven more by the locale than the period, something which was fine in isolation, but failed to evoke the period.

Talking of singers, Burman used Hemanta, Rafi and Manna as the voice of Dev. The use of three singers whose voices had minimal overlap, proved to be the Achilles heel of the film. Also, although both Manna and Rafi did a laudable job, especially in *Ai kaash chalte milke* and *Chupke se mile pyaase* respectively, the female counterparts—Asha Bhosle and Geeta Dutt, respectively—stole the thunder in these songs.

One of the reasons for an indifferent score could possibly have been the delay—*Manzil* went on the floor in 1958, but was postponed as Dev Anand was preoccupied with multiple assignments, including travelling to Jharia for *Sharabi* (1964), and to Madras (now Chennai) for *Amar Deep* (1960). Burman was known to deliver a score at a stretch, and the frequent changes in schedule might have disrupted his thought process.

However, not all was lost. Burman referenced a *bandish* (a fixed phrase in Hindustani classical music) by Faiyaz Khan for the comic, *Hatho kahe ko jhoothi* (sung by Manna Dey), which was featured on the most popular comedian of the time, Mahmood. In an interview to Rajnikumar Pandya for the book, *Aapki Parchaiyan*, Manna spoke about the making of the song, as follows:

> This was, as you know, a thumri by Faiyaz Khan. But Burmanda said, Manna, we need to give it some other effect. Envisage that a stylish paanwala and not an ustad is singing this song. Hence we need to make the song lighter. It should sound interesting. We worked on the song for ten days to make it sound different. That is how this song became evergreen.[2]

Manzil however stood out for its remarkable background music, including a mandolin-harmonica duet within fourteen minutes into the film (most probably played by Laxmikant and Pancham, respectively) which sounded like a take-off from the 'Meena theme' of *Pyaasa*.

The sequence which captures the protagonist, Raju's (Dev) ascent as a composer is rather interesting; one hears *Mera sundar sapna* as part of the tunes which are played in sequence. This was probably used with an intention to chronicle S.D. Burman's career in Bombay. One could have accused Sachinda with inaccuracy here—as *Mera sundar sapna* was released in 1947, which was many years later than the period shown in *Manzil*, but Burman was perhaps referring to the original Tagore song, *Rodon bhora e bosonto* which was composed in 1892.

Like several other Dev Anand films, *Manzil* was received well at the box office, but failed to leverage its initial momentum. As mentioned earlier, the hummability of any song is a major factor in the success of an album, and unfortunately for *Manzil*, except for *Kahe ko jhoothi*, no other song fit the bill.

However, waiting in the wings was a noir-musical by Raj Khosla, which brought Sachin Dev back into the reckoning yet again.

❧

Bombai Ka Babu (1960) was an adaptation of O. Henry's *A Double-eyed Deceiver*, with a major interpolation in the form of an incestuous relationship. While any discussion on the film often leads one to talk about its fabulous music, it is prudent to call out the early signs of change in Burman's style of designing the background score. For instance, the well thought out emphasis on wind and brass, so much so that the first note in the film was a high one on the trumpet. That the film was noir is established within the first seven minutes, with songs from *Taxi Driver*—*Dilse milake dil pyaar kijiye* and *Dil jale toh jale* playing in the background. If there was one film which used music as a tool to create drama, it was this. When the backdrop shifts from Bombay to the beauteous valley of Kulu in Himachal Pradesh, a potpourri of flute, chimes, and mallet-based instruments is used to indicate the locale. One also hears the intermittent use of a sax riff which is used to build up the tension between lead characters—acting almost as a forewarning, reminding viewers that all was not well.

Despite the language handicap, Burman merged the mukhda of the Telugu song, *Eruvaka sagaro ranno chinnanna*—which had Waheeda Rehman debuting as a dancer in Tapi Chakanya's 1955 Telugu film, *Rojulu Marayi*—with 'balle balle' in Punjabi and so was born, *Dekhne mein bhola hai, dil ka salona*. He repeated the experiment by blending Bengali with Punjabi folk, in *Tak dum tak dum*.

On the one hand, if Burman was mounting an ambitious background score, he was well aware that the masses seldom bothered about subtleties. Therefore, he went back to the basics and composed three

155

songs which were easy on the lips and the larynx. The first was *Deewana mastana*, in which Asha at her playful best, mocks her partner while singing the opening notes, *pa ma ga, ma re ga, pa ma ga ma,* while Rafi's voice has this echo-like tonal feel, a deliberate recording technique, which was used to match the pictorial brilliance of the undulating hills in the sequence.

Interestingly, Madhubala was to play the lead in the film and *Deewana mastana* was one of the first songs composed, perhaps keeping her in mind which alas never came to fruition owing to her ill-health. The song had become extremely popular even before the release of the film via record sales, and Burman milked it abundantly by cherry-picking refrains of it to play out in the background throughout the film. Burman also used the same notes in the antara of the Punjabi folk-based, *Aise me kachu kaha nahi jaye,* merely by shifting the second line a note lower.

Finally, about the two songs which were swathed in sadness—the kind of sentimentality which hovers over you for a long time for its sheer beauty. *Saathi na koi manzil* had a feathery-light cadence and was devoid of any percussion support, except for Chinese blocks. Rafi's rendition bordered on divinity and even as the hero walks alone looking forlorn, he reaches out to touch those who grapple with the burden of loneliness.

As did *Chal ri sajni* by Mukesh. The song had originally been composed for Kishore Kumar in another film, but the singer-actor apparently wasn't enthused by it and had rejected it on grounds that it sounded too 'Indian'. After the producer and S.D. Burman had failed to persuade him, Raj Khosla who was present in the recording room, immediately grabbed the song for *Bombai Ka Babu.* Burman made Mukesh negotiate two octaves in the song—both the mukhda and antara starting on a common note, *sa.* The male–female overlapping in the chorus created the perfect pitch for the poignant *bidai* (when a girl leaves for her husband's house at the conclusion of a wedding) ceremony. With the human voices replacing the typical mandatory instruments—except the obligatory violin, sarangi, taar shehnai, etc—the effect was maudlin. The bride wept copious tears, as did the audience.

Traditionally speaking, children are considered to be the natural corollary of a marriage. Although this can be challenged in today's times, in the Sixties' India this thought found universal acceptance. However, in what could be termed as revolutionary for the times, *Ek Ke Baad Ek* challenged the idea of procreation, while encouraging the benefits of family planning. A good thought for a country which battled and continues to battle population explosion, but as a film, it wasn't.

In all probability, it was Dev Anand who made Burman accept Raj Rishi's disastrous film and it was said that he regretted the decision. However, its music was a shade better when compared to the disastrous film!

The only song which merits mention was, *Na tel na bati*, sung with great passion by Manna Dey featuring a sequence when the debutant, Tarla Mehta, a mother of six, dies during labour in the film. One finds a lot of similarity between *Na tel na bati* and Jaidev's *Chale ja rahe hain* (*Kinare Kinare*, 1963). The reason might have been that both films were started around the same time, and Burman and his erstwhile assistant, may have exchanged notes.

Meanwhile, on 24 December 1958, Burman signed another film starring Dev Anand, called *Pilot*. The film was slated to be one of the most ambitious projects of its time, to be shot in multiple locations, including France, Switzerland, Hong Kong and the US. But alas, *Pilot* vanished in thin air and failed to make a landing!

The other three films that Burman signed during 1958–59 were for his trusted lieutenants—Mohan Segal, I.S. Johar, and Mahesh Kaul. Unfortunately, *Apna Haath Jagannath* (1960); *Bewakoof* (1960); and

Miya Bibi Razi (1960); ended up slowing down his career which had got great momentum post *Sujata*.

One wonders if Burman was singled out for such disasters considering the movies in themselves were rather unbearable! Nevertheless, even these terrible films had some interesting takeaways. While in Mohan Segal's *Apna Haath Jagannath*, the audience rejected Kishore Kumar as a humble washerman-turned-business magnate, his singing was unquestionable even as he soared by hitting the flat seventh note in *Chhayi ghata bijli kadki*. (Kishore would later re-use this particular yodel in other songs.) It is quite likely that a Punjabi folk tune was playing in a loop in Burman's mind as he was working on *Bambai Ka Babu* simultaneously, and the short piece of Heer (a traditional Punjabi folk song) in *Tum jahan jahan* blended rather well with the main melody.

The background score of the film also made one sit up and take notice. Like the nat strain which Burman had used multiple times in many songs, made a comeback in this film, but in the avatar of a sitar piece. In the climactic scene, where Kishore and Sayeeda Khan—who debuted in this film—reunite, much like Cary Grant and Deborah Kerr in *An Affair to Remember* (1957), the antara of *Door kon porobashe* (the original of *Wahan kaun hai tera* from *Guide*, 1965) was used. Burman incidentally would record this basic song the same year (along with *Baanshi shune aar kaaj nai*), and perhaps the tune was on his mind while composing for *Apna Haath Jagannath*.

One is rather flummoxed why Burman even accepted to work on I.S. Johar's comic thriller, *Bewakoof*, which was a watered-down and terrible version of Agatha Christie's *Witness for the Prosecution*. After all, Johar wasn't known for this directorial prowess yet; his *Miss India*, for which Burman was the music director, had floundered badly at the box office. But fresh from a BAFTA nomination for *Harry Black and the Tiger* (1958), I.S. Johar had signed up the French writer-cum-actress Francoise Dorin for a role in *Bewakoof*, and was contemplating shooting parts of the film in Italy. Burman was also supposed to join him, which finally did not happen, and neither did Dorin!

Subsequently, Johar planned a series of musical plays and invited S.D. Burman to collaborate both as a composer and actor. The press announcement came as a bit of a surprise because not only was Burman terribly stage-shy, he had had a couple of not-so-happy experiences in the past. However, he did have a whacky sense of humour and may have seriously contemplated acting out the parts as proposed by the director! Bhanu Gupta, the guitarist and harmonica player who was later a regular with Pancham, recalled a sample of Burman's tongue-in-cheek humour to the authors, 'This happened during one of our music recordings for a film I cannot remember. After the rehearsal, Burman clapped and shouted, "Sixty minutes break," hearing which the producer came running in. Even as he was expecting to be confronted by the hapless gent who was at his wits' end, since studio time (and cost) was precious, Burman winked and said—"Six *tea* minutes," which relieved the producer greatly!'[1]

The first in the series of musical-plays planned by Johar was to have a cricket test match as its backdrop, in which Burman was supposed to play the role of a 'singing paanwala'. However, the idea fell through. But I.S. Johar was relentless and tried another stunt—of organising an All India Conference of Fools to coincide with the release of *Bewakoof*, in August 1960. While the ridiculous conference came to naught, the film fooled nobody, because despite the moderate reviews, it was given a wide berth by the masses.

If I.S. Johar got lucky in one department of what was otherwise a futile exercise, it was in the music of the film which was both fresh and contemporary. Therefore it remains a mystery why *Tumhi piya chikara* (Kishore–Asha), or *Aankhon se aankhon ka* (Kishore–Manna) failed to register with the audiences, because they continue to be popular amongst film music lovers till date. Kishore's uninhibited yodelling in *Sach sach sach* was later used by him in the title song of *Jhumroo* (1961). One wouldn't be wrong in assuming that Burman may have taken it easy once Kishore was at his freakish best, but it did little to help. The songs of *Bewakoof* were relegated to the back-burner.

While on the subject of making wrong choices, it was also intriguing why Burman chose to compose for Mahesh Kaul's *Miya Bibi Razi* (1960). The preachy story directed by Jyoti Swaroop whose better days lay ahead, made worse in the way the evils of the dowry system were highlighted in a quasi-comical manner, was absurd, to say the least.

However, as mentioned earlier, even the least known albums of Burman had certain redeeming features. For instance, *Miya Bibi Razi* remains one of the rare films in which he tested three new voices. Though he was not contractually obliged to sign-up Mahendra Kapoor (winner of the Metro Murphy singing competition, 1957, he had won himself a chance to sing in films. Burman had refused an offer to be one of the judges and hence was not obligated to use Kapoor, unlike Naushad Ali or Anil Biswas, among others), he used him for the title song. Suman Kalyanpur, who till then was somewhat ignored and only recognised for sounding 'so much' like Lata Mangeshkar, got to sing the dazzling *Chhodo chhodo mori baiyaan, saanware.* This song was used twice in the film, and has been popular ever since.

The third singer whom he used in the film was a relatively unknown entity. Burman had discovered Kamla Sista during the annual function of St. Xavier's college, Bombay in August 1959, where he had been invited as the chief guest for the launch of their music club called Sangeet Mahal, and had promptly signed her on for the film. It needs to be mentioned here that Kamla had done a decent job of the duet, *Pani hota doob hi jaate* along with Rafi. Unlike the Mangeshkars or Suman Kalyanpur, Kamla Sista had a husky voice which could have lent Hindi film music more variety. However, due to reasons unknown, her career failed to progress any further after that one song.

S.D. Burman was known to be very selective about using new voices. Subir Sen, who arrived in Bombay at the behest of Guru Dutt, was rejected even without a trial by Burman, as he had marketed himself as a Hemanta clone. That had left a deep scar on the singer.

Nirmalendu Chowdhury, the iconic folk singer from Bengal, who had once shared the stage with Burman, wanted a foothold in Bombay. But Burman had advised him to first rise to the level of playback singers in Bombay! But the tragi-comic encounter would happen with one of Bengal's most gifted singers ever, Manabendra Mukhopadhyay.[2] He had met Burman during a show in Calcutta, and was invited by the composer to accompany him to Bombay. On the day of the journey, Mukhopadhyay waited at the agreed spot at Howrah station, only to learn that Burman had left earlier. After a year, when the two met again in Calcutta, Burman, in his trademark style asked, 'Manab, how is life?' Manab, with a sarcastic smile on his lips, replied: 'You know, I am better than I was in Bombay.'

With several films flopping around him, there came a time when S.D. Burman started refusing work with new directors and lyricists. But his relationship with Shakti Samanta, which he had cemented prior to *Miya Bibi Razi*, would however bear fruit, albeit a few years later. Samanta's *Insaan Jaag Utha*, which was cleared in April 1959 and released a few months later, with the blurb, 'Amidst the clatter of men and machines, a romance so tender, a love so warm'—was a film Burman thoroughly enjoyed working on, although it did not see commercial success. During a conversation with the authors at his Mumbai residence, Shakti Samanta's son, Asim recounted what he had heard from his father about the genesis of a particular song. 'Our association with Sachinda was from *Insaan Jaag Utha* in 1958, when I was three or maybe four years old (He was born in 1954). He was like an elder brother to my father. He once told me about an incident which proved how dedicated Sachinda was about his work. For the song, *Janu janu re*, Baba (father) told Sachinda that he would be shooting with a crew of girls moving around at the Nagarjuna Sagar dam which had huge earthmoving vehicles, the wheels of which were as wide as ten feet. (It was originally planned to be shot at the construction site of Gandhi Sagar dam on the Chambal river.)

'Sachinda liked the idea. He composed the song, but asked my father to come the next day as he was planning to play him the music pieces. My father went to Sachinda's house at the appointed hour. The door to the room in his house was slightly ajar. My father peeped in and saw Sachinda with his eyes shut, moving back and forth from one side of the hall to another. He also noticed that Sachinda had placed one *chappal* (slipper) on one end of the room and the other on another end. The distance between the two was around 15-18 feet.

'After a few seconds, Sachinda opened his eyes and said, "Hey, Shakti, when did you arrive?" Father said, "Dada, a few minutes back." Sachinda said, "Why didn't you tell me?" Dad replied how he didn't want to disturb him.

'"But what exactly were you doing?" Father asked him. Sachinda replied, "You recall I had called you yesterday asking for the distance between the two wheels and you said that it would be around 15-18 feet? Hence, I'd kept two slippers 15-18 feet apart and was trying to compose the music," replied Sachinda.

'He actually went from one slipper to the other, and at the end of the imagined wheel on location, when he turned back, he introduced the sound of bangles clinking. This was later adapted by my father in the film with Minoo Mumtaz and Madhubala moving around the wheels and clinking their bangles at strategic intervals.'[3]

By running or rather manoeuvring across slippers positioned at two ends of the room, Burman was actually finalising the points where the rhythm was to be emphasised by using ghungroos or percussions to sound like the clinking of bangles. Often, discussions amongst music enthusiasts about this Asha–Geeta duet is limited to this factoid alone. The fact of the matter being that in this dazzling composition, both Asha (singing for Madhubala) and Geeta (singing for Minoo Mumtaz)

A wedding picture of S.D. Burman and Meera Dev Burman, 10 February 1938

A newly-married S.D. Burman (third from left) during his honeymoon in Darjeeling, February 1938

The legends of Hindi film music—S.D. Burman flanked by C. Ramchandra (first from left) and Naushad Ali

Aditya Dasgupta

S.D. Burman (on the left) with his wife, Meera Dev Burman, and the renowned lyricist, Sahir Ludhianvi (third from left)

The famous duo—Dev Anand with S.D. Burman

A young R.D. Burman aka Pancham with his father, S.D. Burman

Holi celebrations in the Burman family. In front, Meera Dev Burman, wife of S.D. Burman with a camera around her neck, and S.D. Burman (fourth from left)

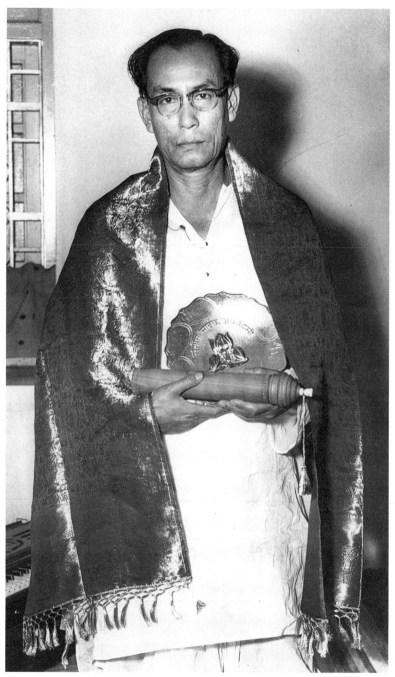

S.D. Burman holding the plaque after receiving the Sangeet Natak Akademi award, 1958

The Burman men on a fishing expedition. A young R.D. Burman aka Pancham (first from left) with his father (in the middle), S.D. Burman

S.D. Burman receiving the National Film Award for Best Male Playback Singer (*Aradhana*, 1969) from Dr S. Radhakrishnan. Smiling in the background is actor-director, Prithviraj Kapoor

Abhijit Dasgupta

S.D. Burman receiving the Padma Shri from President Zakir Hussain, 26 January 1969

S.D. Burman (third from left), with friends and family during a picnic

S.D. Burman during a music session with his son, R.D. Burman aka Pancham

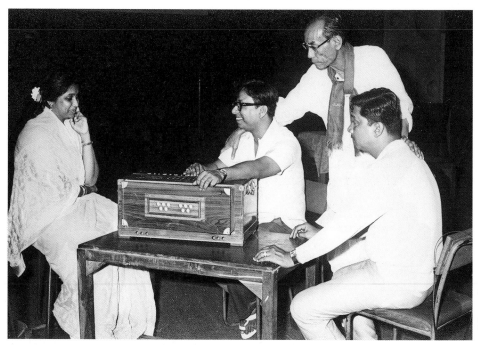

During a rehearsal, Asha Bhosle (on the left), R.D. Burman aka Pancham (second from left), and with his hand on his son's shoulder, S.D. Burman

Abhijit Dasgupta

S.D. Burman in conversation with one of his favourite male playback singers, Mohammed Rafi

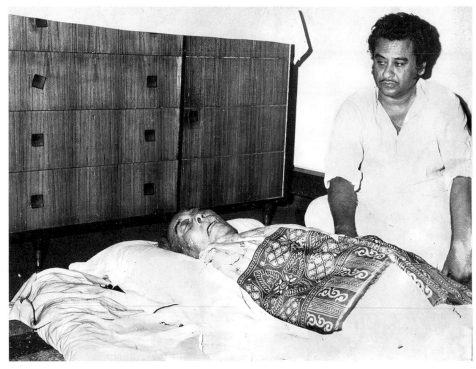

A pensive Kishore Kumar mourning the death of S.D. Burman, 31 October 1975

are engaged in a healthy competition, negotiating short, convoluted notes in the Dadra-based metre.

If working on more than one film, however bad they ended up, had a silver lining, then it did show up in the film's best known song, *Chand sa mukhda kyun sharmaya* (Rafi and Asha), a delicate romantic melody which had the refrain of *Dho le tu aaj apne dil ke daag* (*Apna Haath Jagannath*), in one of the interludes.

Furthermore, the drama of the film was elevated several notches by a strong background score. For instance, a poignant flute piece in the dream sequence where Sunil Dutt and Madhubala are seen raising a happy family, and living an ideal life; or the sax and wind pieces during the initial part of the film which created a spooky ambience, particularly when the hero is in jail.

S.D. Burman, who was generally reluctant to talk about his music, did speak about the songs in the film, as follows.[4]

> Keeping in mind the locale, in this case Orissa, I had used two folk songs as the base for the tunes of *Janu janu re* and *Mehnat kash insaan jag utha*. I also tried to colour the tunes with experimental music in order to match the visual sequences in the film. For the song *Chand sa mukhda kyon sharmaya*, I used a new instrument, a ponga (a woodwind instrument, somewhat like the flute), and the huge success of the song gave me satisfaction in my experimentation.

A year after *Insaan Jag Utha* was declared a flop, Burman would again engage with woodwind instruments. The backdrop of this film also happened to be a jail.

Bandini

'The roots of the song were sown when Bimal Roy was explaining the scene to S.D. Burman. Kalyani had secretly begun to long for Bikash. One night, after completing her household chores, she is seen leaving the house, and humming to herself.

'Bimal Roy stopped the narration, saying that Kalyani would never behave in such a fashion—never hum while she is outdoors.

'Burman argued with the director, "How could she sing indoors when her father was present in the house?"

'Bimalda said that she had heard Vaishnav poetry from her father, and it would not be surprising if she, for once, switched sides.

'"This is not a recitation, but a song!"

'"So turn it into a poem; she'll sing a poem."

'"The song will lose its charm if sung in the confines of a house."

'"Then take her out to the garden or porch, but she'll not leave the compound!"

'"If she can't leave, then I won't compose the song," said Sachinda.'

This riveting story on the making of one of the most beautiful songs in *Bandini* was narrated by Debu Sen to me (Gulzar). 'Bimalda explained that as it was a night scene, Kalyani would be hesitant to step out as the moonlight would have bared her face to people. Hence, she needed to be confined to the courtyard,' continued Debu.

'Sachinda called me home and explained—"She is aware of the risk of being spotted in moonlight; however, she does cross the courtyard, but keeps constant vigil."

'Actually, when I heard both Bimalda and Sachinda, I understood the full import of Kalyani's true mental state.

'Sachinda called me to his place the next day and hummed the tune: *LLL La LLL La*. These were the original lines of the song. Rahul (R.D. Burman) modified it as: *DDD Da DaDa DDa Da*.

'Sachinda hummed it again with corrections: *LLL La DDa Da LLa La*...

'The first lines of the song were ready—a little *LaLa* and some *Dada*. I was baffled and kept staring at the two. I felt like singing my own version—*Tata tata ta*....

'Sachinda played the tune on the harmonium for some time and I tried humming along. Little by little, the words started forming: *Do char... do char... dui char pug pe angna; dui char pug... bairi kangna chanak na*.

'Some words were formed as a result of my confusion—*Bairi kangna chanak na. Mohse koso door laage. Dui char pug pe angna*.

'Sachinda tested the words by singing in tune, and suddenly, I could understand the flow. I came back home, humming all the way along. I kept thinking about Kalyani's mood. What would she be thinking? How would she have felt? Then it struck me, what if she were to tell the moon, speak to it? *Mein piya ko dekh aaoon; zara munh phira le, chanda* (Let me go sight my lover, O moon. Turn your face away).

'It immediately struck me that Shailendra had already woven these feelings beautifully in a song: *Dum bhar jo udhar munh phere, O chanda; mein unsey pyaar kar loongi; batein hazaar kar loongi* (Only if you would look the other way, O moon. I would speak to my lover; look at him for a bit).

'Kalyani was looking at the moon till now. The moon was peeping from between the clouds, smiling, as if asking, where she was headed? "How can you walk in the dark? I'll illuminate the way. You'll be spotted by all." Kalyani is riled and conveys her irritation through the line: *Tohe rahu laage bairi; muskaye jee jalai ke* (May the Rahu envelop you; you smile while I suffer).

'She sits down in a fit of rage and thinks of retracing her steps home. She is tempted to go out, but is also shy to step out. Bewildered, she asks herself: *Kahan le chala hai manwa, mohe bawri banai ke* (Where is my heart taking me? It is as if I am in a trance).

'Kalyani continues sitting, and thinks—what if moonlight didn't exist? Or if she wasn't born fair, then she could have blended into the darkness and met her lover. A hapless Kalyani returns home, singing:

Mora gora ang lai le
Mohe shyam rang dai de

And a lyricist-poet was thus born in the Hindi film industry—Gulzar.

The genesis of this historically significant Lata solo was thus described by Gulzar in the preface of his book called, *Mera Kuch Samaan*.[1] The song was historically significant because it brought Lata Mangeshkar and S.D. Burman together after a gap of nearly three years.

Sampooran Singh Kalra aka Gulzar had previously written a couple of inconspicuous songs for low budget films like *Diler Hasina* (1960), *Choron ki Baraat* (1960) and *Sreeman Satyavadi* (1960).[2] The *Bandini* song was his stepping stone to the world of good, meaningful cinema.

To quote Gulzar from Nasreen Munni Kabir's *In the Company of a Poet*[3]:

S.D. Burman and Shailendra had a tiff and Bimalda needed a lyricist for *Bandini*. Shailendra told Debu Sen to ask me to write the songs for the film. I refused at first, saying, 'I don't want to work in films and definitely don't want to write songs.'

Debu Sen repeated my comment to Shailendra. He was older to me and when he heard my reaction, he ticked me off saying, 'You're a great advocate of literature, but do you think all film people are illiterate? People are dying to work with Bimalda. Go and see him!'

The scolding had the desired effect and I promptly accompanied Debu Sen to meet Bimal Roy. That's how I got to write *Mora gora ang lai le*.

Shailendra and S.D. Burman then made up and Dada told Bimalda he did not want to work with the new writer and wanted Shailendra back. Bimalda asked, 'Dada, weren't you happy with the song? Why not continue working with Gulzar?'

'I worked with a new writer in *Apna Haath Jagannath* and the film flopped. I won't work with a new writer,' was Dada's reply.

Although Burman was often reluctant to encourage new talent, despite having given one of the greatest poet-lyricists, Sahir Ludhianvi a foothold in *Baazi*, he made an exception for Gulzar. As a norm, Burman would ask the lyricist to sing his verses and if feasible, also accompanied by the harmonium. The reason being that at the time, most lyricists in Bombay could manage to sing decently. But as Gulzar couldn't, Burman saved him the embarrassment and sang his lines for Bimal Roy. But as fate would have it, this was the only song that Gulzar ever wrote to Burman's music because, Shailendra was soon back in the reckoning.

Sujata was a success. But Bimal Roy was unable to rest on his laurels. His *Parakh* (1960) failed the box office test despite Salil Chowdhury's ethereal music. To begin with, *Parakh* was not the usual Bombay masala film—Bimal Roy had made the film with a little known cast, as a result of which the film had languished in the cans for a long time. Meanwhile, his next production in the same year, *Usne Kaha Tha*, which was nearing completion, was also made with stark newcomers, Sunil Dutt and Nanda. Bimal Roy was also directing *Prem Patra* (1962), starring Shashi Kapoor and Sadhana, both barely a film old at that time.

Therefore, even as the future looked rather bleak for Bimal Roy, *Bandini* happened to him in September 1960, with Ashok Kumar and Nutan who were well established in the industry.

Debu Sen told the authors how Bimal Roy had zeroed in on *Bandini*. 'Bimalda wanted to make Jarasandha's (nom de plume of the retired jailor-turned-writer, Charuchandra Chakrabarti) *Louhakapat*. But before that, Phani Majumdar was interested in making the film, which didn't happen. Finally in 1958, Tapan Sinha made the film in Bengali which inspired Bimal Roy to take up another "prison-based" story by the same writer.'

Eventually, Bimal Roy invited Jarasandha for the Filmfare Awards function in April 1960 and finalised *Bandini*, which was based on his Bengali story titled, *Tamoshi*.

S.D. Burman geared up to work with one of his favourite directors yet again. After all, his music for Bimal Roy's *Sujata* had been well received and this despite the fact that he had no Lata Mangeshkar for support. In an interview, Rahul Dev Burman recounted how Lata and his father had patched up just before *Bandini*:

I got an assignment to do a film and went to Didi (Lata Mangeshkar), requesting her to sing my first song. She agreed. In those days, we used to have rehearsals. She came to our house for the rehearsal, blessed me after hearing my composition (the song was *Ghar aaja ghir aaye* from *Chhote Nawab*, 1961), and then wished to meet my father. Father was in the adjacent room, eager to meet us, and it needed just a nod from Lata to get him out of his self-imposed exile. He came, and in his simple, inimitable style, asked—'Lata, how many dates can you give me?' Lata said—'As many dates as you want, Dada.'

This was the point from which father and Lata bai started working together again.

Lata's version of the story was almost the same, except that it was embellished with nuggets such as, how Burman had proudly showed her around his quaint little new bungalow, the Jet, and also offered her samosas, which she had refused on account of a sore throat.[4,5,6]

Nutan, who played the lead role in *Bandini* had been married for around a year when she accepted the film. It was well known that she was contemplating quitting films until her husband, Rajnish Bahl, who was directing her in *Soorat Aur Seerat* (1962), persuaded her to accept the title role of *Bandini*. But within two months of accepting the film, she became pregnant. In an article titled, "Working with Dada",[7] she mentioned how the shooting was concluded before her delivery.[8] However, her version didn't match with the actual release date of the film, which was two years later, in 1963.

Be that as it may, Burman wrote some phenomenal music for *Bandini*. In the halo surrounding the celebrated, *Mera gora ang lai le*, another Lata song, *Jogi jab se tu aaya mere dwaare* played second fiddle, despite being more popular during its time. On repeated hearing, this improvised Bengali kirtan does come across as a far more fluid composition than *Mora gora ang lai le* because despite the strong presence of traditional elements, it sounded fast-paced and breezy, while retaining the soul of the kirtan and underscoring the intricate vocal nuances that only Lata could manage. The prominent use of the sitar and tar-shehnai phrases, representative of a woman in love, somehow evoked memories of *Kali ghata chaye* from *Sujata*, and apart from Nutan, who was the common factor in both, it was also the perfect ambience which the director and composer were able to create for both films.

Did this mega re-union between Lata Mangeshkar and S.D. Burman (in Lata's own words, 'reunion songs with Dada') push the other musical gems of *Bandini* into the background? Thankfully not. Burman shrewdly engaged the sisters in a battle for the best—Asha Bhosle's two songs in the film featuring a little known actress called Leela Agha (who had changed her name to Meenakshi[9]) were in no way less than those by her illustrious elder sister.

Ab ke baras bhej bhaiya (based on *Nimbua tale dola rakh de musafir*, a folk song from Uttar Pradesh which Burman had heard from Shailendra) was about separation from one's loved ones—a brother, father and childhood friends; reminisences of carefree days by women-inmates who have no hope for freedom. The flow of the song was thus dramatic, with long-phrased notes (in contrast to Burman's characteristic short notes), and the mood was that of lost enchantment. The first short interlude fleetingly references to the prelude of *Chal ri sajni* (*Bombai Ka Babu*), as if carrying over the angst of separation. Burman's fascination for 7/4 rhythm comes into play, and the leisurely gait of the *deepchandi* taal (a rhythm cycle of fourteen beats) lends a sinuous flow to the song.

The song also happens to be one of Asha Bhosle's favourites, and she has on a number of occasions spoken about how while rendering the song she was reminded of her brother, Hridayanath Mangeshkar, which had made her cry.

If *Ab ke baras* evoked pangs of separation, *O panchi pyaare* symbolised liberation. A cheerful number on perfunctory hearing, it is a finely-disguised love-poem in the question-and-answer mould. Burman and Shailendra used the mukhda as the question, and the antaras as responses. While Shailendra wrote in metaphors using words like *pinjre* (a cage), *pankh* (wings), *sagar gehra* (the depth of a sea symbolising separation), *phagun* (the spring), Bimal Roy used stellar visual references to expand on it—the prison bars, its walls, and the solitary tree with a 'tricoloured munia'[10]. Interestingly, while the recorded version of the song has two additional lines in the form of a *sher* (a couplet), the film version starts directly with the line, *O panchi pyaare*.

As the subject of the film centred around a woman, the majority of songs were obviously in female voices—all by Mangeshkar sisters. It was perhaps for this reason that *Mat ro mata* by Manna Dey, a song with bold tones, didn't find resonance with listeners. However, Bimal Roy's continuing romance with the river resulted in the immensely popular, *O jane wale ho sake toh laut ke aana* and *O re majhi*.

The late Pandit Ravi Shankar had once described the voice of Mukesh as so straight and linear that the sporadic use of *alankaars* (subtle variations) magnified the beauty of his singing manifold. Burman used Mukesh's deep bass and the natural pathos in his voice to great advantage. Dr Ratna Mukherjee, the daughter of late singer-composer Arun Kumar Mukherjee, who was present during the recording of *O jane wale ho sake toh laut ke aana* at Bombay Labs recalled to the authors that initially Mukesh had some difficulty in getting the correct nuances. Apparently, Burman had led him to a separate room on the first floor and coached him to such an extent that it elevated an otherwise plain melody.[11]

Shailendra's lyrics for the song were based on Rabindranath Tagore's *Jokhon porbe na mor payer chinho ei baate*. His choice of words was especially brilliant—both the mukhda and antara terminating with the vowel '*a*', thereby creating a drawn out and sonorous effect. Sachin Dev Burman enhanced the resonance further by using an all-female choral harmony. Not once did it sound contrived; instead, it made the feeling linger on for moments thereafter.

At this point, it is necessary to recall an oft-discussed detail about the recording of the song. Apparently, R.D. Burman, then an energetic young man of twenty-two, had wanted to use the alto sax during the interludes. Sachin Dev paid little heed to his son's request, and subsequently stomped out of the studio when Pancham insisted that he had already re-recorded the song with Manohari Singh. When the senior Burman returned to the recording room after a while, he was reassured by his recordist, B.N. Sharma that the final take was sans the alto sax, as suggested by him.

One does hear the saxophone in the film, albeit in the background in fits and starts, for instance in a scene involving Devendra (Dharmendra) and Kalyani (Nutan). The alto sax is heard yet again in the scene between Devendra and his mother (played by Sulochana Chatterjee) leading up to the song, *Ab ke baras bhej,* and also during the climax at the Sahibgunj Ferry Ghat. The repeated use of woodwind in a setting which was based in pre-Independent India and therefore a little out of place wasn't surprising either, given Manohari Singh was by then a regular in the Burman camp. Also, by now S.D. Burman had developed an uncanny ear for 'sound', and was not opposed to experimentation. This was evidenced in the rhythm he'd so skillfully developed for *O panchi pyaare*—the shaking of the winnowing basket, supported by tabla and the duggi.

If one hears the sound of conch shells at Kalyani's village home at dusk, quietude was used to portray gloom in the sequence of Kalyani's father's (played by Raja Paranjpe) death. For this scene, the flute was blown from the rear end to generate a sound resembling a hushed silence in the background, while the Vaishnav *padavali* recitation is heard in the foreground.

It was unusual of Burman to refer to his own songs; a rare example was the opening line of *Sunn mere bandhu re* (*Sujata*) which is heard during a flashback sequence showing Kalyani standing on the banks of the Ganga (shot at Bhagalpur where the river was rather expansive those days). Burman returned to singing in Hindi with *O re majhi* in the film. Tulika Ghosh, the classical vocalist recalled Burman's voice in this song as being particularly full-bodied and powerful. 'Burman jethu would often visit us at our residence in Khar. We used to stay on the ground floor. He never rang the bell or knocked at the door. He used to come near our window and call for my father, "Nikhil!" and the window panes would reverberate.'[12]

In the history of film music, *O re majhi* shall always be evoked to reiterate the eternal conundrum faced by human beings—the situation in which Kalyani finds herself, torn between the temptations of a regular life and the call of duty. Interestingly, her options were not limited to choosing her lover; Kalyani was in love with both men at different points in time. It was in choosing responsibility and commitment over a protected existence. This was skillfully drawn out by Burman, who insisted that the lights be dimmed in the recording room to create the suitable ambience for the song. 'D.M. Tagore, Mike Machado, Laxmikant, and Maruti Rao Keer were among the handful of musicians present; while Kamal Mitra and Sumant Raj played a variety of flutes,' said Sumit Mitra who was present in the studio during the recording of this unforgettable melody.[13]

The Unsure Years

A Village Tale

*B*andini was arguably the best from the Bimal Roy–S.D. Burman stable. One could go even further to say that it was the best that Burman had done so far.

In the meantime, India was changing and with it the Bombay film industry. The advent of colour had transformed the dynamics of filmmaking—big budgets became routine and gradually, altruism gave way to escapism in subjects and themes.

By now, Sachin Dev Burman had earned the reputation of a composer who had an eye for meaningful scripts. However, it was also said that he chose to work only with a select few and faced failures each time he stepped out to experiment with unknown evils. It was perhaps this reason why he refused *Chhote Nawab* (1961), which ultimately went to his son and the rest as they say is history.

The other and more important reason for his reluctance to take on more work during the period was his failing health. In 1961, Burman suffered from a heart condition and was advised rest. Coincidentally, Lata Mangeshkar was also suffering from severe bouts of sinusitis and asthma and had stopped singing till 13 June 1961, until she came back with a bang with *Kahin deep jale kahin dil* for *Bees Saal Baad* (1962).

The beginning of the Sixties was hence tough on Sachin Dev Burman.

In so far as his work was concerned, while it would be unfair to be dismissive of all that he was doing, much of it paled in comparison to *Bandini*. However, the films he signed were more of episodic in nature, and gave him a wider canvas for experimenting with voices and genres. An example was Rajendra Bhatia's *Padi Likhi Bibi* which was later renamed as *Dr. Vidya* (1962). In a deviation from the regular fare of kirtan and Bengali folk, Burman created rhythm-based melodies for the film in synch with the script revolving the leading lady (Vyjayanthimala) and her anglicised friend (Helen). The song, *Pawan diwani* based on *Alo chhaya dola* which Burman had sung under the baton of Himangshu Dutta, is still recalled for its sheer beauty.

In an interview with the authors, the late Kersi Lord recounted that *Pappa jamarlo*, the song which plays out when Helen and Vyjayanthimala compete as dancers, was one in which his brother Burjor, and their father, Cawas Lord played the rhythm. It was one of the biggest orchestral arrangements to be used by S.D. Burman in his entire musical career.[1]

However surprisingly, the only male solo in the film had little to do with orchestra. Mukesh's *Ae dil-e-awara chal* which was devoid of any fancy ornamentation, picturised on Manoj Kumar riding a bicycle in the manner of carefree leading men, became the most popular song from the film.

Dr. Vidya was the only film in which Lata Mangeshkar sang the Hindi version of a Bengali tandem by Geeta Dutt and S.D. Burman. *Ami jani, bhomra keno, katha koyena* was sung by Geeta in the mid-1950s for Guru Dutt's incomplete film called, *Gouri*. Later, Burman also recorded the same song in 1957. The music scholar and scribe, Sudhir Chakraborty in a conversation with Debasis Mukhopadhyay of the periodical *Aajkaal*, had pointed out that this was probably the first Bengali song that began with an exclamation.[2] The Hindi version of the same was penned by Majrooh as *Jani, tum toh dole daga daike*.

Guru Dutt's *Gouri* had another song in Geeta's voice—*Baanshi shune aar kaaj nai*. Having recorded *Ami jani*, Burman wanted to record this song as well in his own voice. Sachin Ganguly narrated that particular incident to the authors, as follows. 'Sachinda decided to seek Guru Dutt's permission for the song after *Gouri* was shelved. Guru Dutt was in Calcutta at the time, and was staying at the Grand hotel. We went there, only to be directed to the Lighthouse theatre and found Guru watching *Alibaba and 40 Thieves* at the miniature hall inside Lighthouse (only Roxy, Jyoti and Lighthouse had miniatures). Burman asked him in his native Bengali, "What are you planning to do with *Gouri*?" Guru also replied in proper Bengali, "No, Sachinda, I have decided to shelve it." Sachinda then asked for permission to sing the song, *Baanshi shune aar kaaj nai* for a Bengali basic album, and Guru had no objection.'[3]

It Happened One Night

In the early 1960s, the only Indian actor to have earned a diploma in ballroom dancing was Chandrasekhar. Or so screamed the publicity campaign for a Rafi–Lata duet, *Sheeshe ka ho ya pathar ka dil,* for a dance drama sequence featuring the actor and Waheeda Rehman in *Baat Ek Raat Ki* (1962), a customised version of Alfred Hitchcock's *The Paradine Case* (1947). This was also the first *released* song by Lata Mangeshkar for Sachin Dev Burman after their famous split.

However, neither was Chandrasekhar's skill lauded despite the formal training, nor did the song become popular. Perhaps of some importance was the prelude to the song—*One two cha cha cha,* which was featured on actor Bela Bose. Pancham, who was assisting his father in almost all the films, later used this phrase in Krishna Shah's *Shalimaar* (1978). Further, the metre of *Sheeshe ka ho ya pathar ka dil* was also used in the form of *Kuch tum karo, kuch hum karen* in Umesh Mehra's *Hamare Tumhare* (1979).

The song which made great waves in the film was by the 'one-song-a-year singer', Hemanta Mukherjee, *Na tum hamen jaano.* Yet another of Burman's tandems, this song was used as a bait in the script when the criminal lawyer, Rajeshwar (Dev Anand) tries to infuse sound waves into his client's subconscious in order to unlock her mind and rid her of the inhibitions in vocalising her innermost thoughts.

In the duet version, Hemanta sings the entire song, while one eagerly awaits for Neela (Waheeda) to respond in a Pavlovian fashion. Suman Kalyanpur, who sang the counter melody in the first antara and the refrain in the last lap of the song, is best remembered for one of the best obligatos in the history of Hindi film songs.

Alankar Chitra's *Baat Ek Raat Ki*, which was started with the working title *Main Akela*, was launched by Dev Anand to help Shankar Mukherjee tide over the disaster called, *Pilot*. The story of the film was written by the well-known lyricist and scriptwriter, Pranab Roy, who was one of Kazi Nazrul Islam's disciples. The working title, which was derived from Dev Anand's signature song with a fishing rod, *Akela hoon mein* was retained for some time, until it was changed to *Baat Ek Raat Ki*. While Dev's 'cool' matinee idol image was established right in the beginning with a Rafi song delivered in a devil-may-care style, it is the Hemant–Suman tandem which remains the musical high point of the film.

The song is also historically significant. For one, it was one of Suman Kalyanpur's last songs for S.D. Burman. As was widely speculated, it may have been because of Lata's return to the Burman camp. The authors made a few abortive attempts to contact Suman Kalyanpur to know the real reason, but drew no response from her on the issue.

And the second and rather intriguing reason was that this song also happened to be Hemanta's last one for Sachinda.

Apart from his own compositions, the one composer for whom Hemanta sang the maximum number of hit songs in Hindi films was none other than S.D. Burman. There is no gainsaying the fact that Hemanta was grossly under-utilised in the Bombay film industry, and it was said that even composers like Shankar–Jaikishan who initially appreciated his singing, later became reluctant to use him as he was viewed as a competitor, considering he was an extremely good music director.

Therefore, for Hemanta, Burman was like a saviour in the rough-and-tumble of Bombay and he signed a song-a-year pact with him.

But subsequently, things soured between them. Sachin Ganguly went back in time to recall the circumstances, 'The Bengali film, *Saheb Bibi Golam* (1956) was produced by my maternal uncle, Haru babu. Sachinda was in Calcutta when it was being shot (he was working on *Pyaasa* then), and would frequent the studios at Tollygunj. The film was being directed by Kartick Chattopadhyay and had music by Rabin Chattopadhyay. Sachinda felt that this was an excellent subject matter for a Hindi film and took the idea to Guru Dutt, who was interested.

'I was asked to meet *Saheb Bibi Golam's* director, Bimal Mitra—who used to stay near Chetla Bridge—and invited him for a meeting with Guru Dutt at Sachinda's Dhakuria home. After discussions, it was finalised that the Hindi version of *Saheb Bibi Golam* would be directed by Guru Dutt. Sachinda was very happy and began composing some tunes for the situations that he had in mind, using dummy words. My uncle's film was screened in Bombay, but Sachinda could not see it in a theatre due to time constraints.

'In end-September/early-October1961 when the film was under production, Sachinda went off to the erstwhile USSR as part of an Indian delegation for cultural exchange. He was flying directly from Bombay and didn't have adequate winter clothing for the trip. He had one coat in Calcutta and wrote to his mother-in-law to send it through Hemanta, who was in Calcutta for a recording. He also called Hemanta and requested him to bring the coat. I went to deliver the coat to Hemanta, who carried it with him to Bombay.

'When Sachinda returned to India, he learnt that he had been replaced in *Sahib Bibi Aur Ghulam* by Hemanta. He was very, very upset.'[1]

In this entire episode, what was most puzzling was Guru Dutt not waiting for Sachin Dev Burman! The most plausible reason could have been the composer's illness—he was bedridden in the first half of 1961, as a result of which some of his films were delayed. Additionally, a few that he had signed on in 1959–60 were also shelved. Two such films were by producer-director Rishi Raj. One about children stricken with the dreaded polio, starring Sudesh Kumar and Sharda, and the other was in Eastmancolor (the details of which are unknown).

Anyway, after Burman had recuperated, he proceeded to Russia and returned home to resume work. His prolonged absence from Bombay may have made Guru Dutt restive; patience was certainly not one of his virtues. It seemed as if Guru Dutt was in a tearing hurry—he had started shooting for *Sahib Bibi Aur Ghulam* on 1 January 1961, when S.D. Burman was ill. Almost all the scenes, except the songs and parts involving the lead actress, were also canned. Exactly a year later, on 1 January 1962, Meena Kumari began shooting for the film, and the song sequences followed thereafter.

Burman was extremely hurt by the turn of events. He felt as if Hemanta had capitalised on an opportunity which was originally his brainchild. After all, Burman had begun composing the tunes even before he had a written contract in hand. He is said to have expressed his disappointment to Sachin Ganguly—how could Hemanta accept the offer? He knew I was doing the film.

S.D. Burman's visit to the erstwhile Soviet Union was the result of a general agreement signed between India and the USSR on 10 September 1960. This opened up several opportunities between the two countries. Sasadhar Mukerji had even closed a deal for a co-production film in colour, although it was shelved later. During his trip to Russia in 1961, Burman met many people, including journalist Subhomoy Ghosh and his wife Supriya Ghosh, who were posted there. One of the many songs that he sang in Russia was *Allah megh de pani de*.

Gradually, the distance between Sachinda and Hemanta widened even further. Sachin Ganguly recalled a particular incident to highlight the misunderstanding between the composer and singer. 'Sachinda would often sing gratis in support of causes. The centenary celebrations of the dailies, *Jugantar* and *Amrita Bazar Patrika* in 1968 was one such occasion, which was held at the Rabindra Sarovar Stadium. Apart from Sachinda, Chabi Banerjee and Hemanta Mukherjee were also the other two main performers. Sachinda's session was to follow Hemanta's. I was with Sachinda all along because he would often forget the lines of his songs. It is then that I noticed Sachinda requesting Hemanta to stay back for his session. However, Hemanta left, without informing him.'

Unfortunately, although his relationship with Hemanta was strained, an episode during the making of *Baat Ek Raat Ki* strengthened his relationship with another singer who had worked with him closely for many years—Manna Dey. It so happened that Burman had composed *Kisne chilman se mara* strictly with Manna in mind, to be picturised on Johnny Walker. When the actor-comedian was told about it, he threw a fit and demanded that Rafi be used as his voice. Burman was resolute and refused to accede to the actor's demand. Johnny Walker then raised the issue with Shankar Mukherjee. The director was aware that Rafi had not only sung for Walker many times, but rather successfully, and he therefore tried influencing the composer to give in. Burman's response was matter-of-fact—'You are at liberty to get the song recorded by Rafi. Just get the music composed by someone else.'

The Endless Night

As mentioned earlier, the early Sixties, and particularly 1962, wasn't an eventful year for S.D. Burman. *Baat Ek Raat Ki* and *Dr. Vidya* weren't great money-spinners. His next film was *Naughty Boy* starring Kishore Kumar and Kalpana (who had stepped in to replace Madhubala, who was battling a terminal illness), his second assignment with Shakti Samanta, after *Insaan Jaag Utha*.

Unfortunately, the film which was supposed to be a rom-com turned out to be a miserable failure and even its music was lacklustre. It seemed as if Burman had tried too hard and the songs, despite their high hummability quotient, fell by the wayside. The hero of the film, Kishore Kumar, was also preoccupied at the time, so much so that *Ho gayee sham*, arguably the best song in the film and which was shot in colour, had to be finally dubbed by Manna Dey. Two other songs from the same film were also shot in colour—*Jahan bhi gaye hum* (the YouTube version is in B&W) and *Tum mere pehchane*. Despite this so-called colour technique and the fabulous production values, Kishore Kumar and S.D. Burman never worked together as an actor-music director duo ever since.

With Hemanta and Talat exiting and Kishore cutting back on work, Burman's options were now severely limited. Mukesh anyway did not fit the bill when it came to delivering on Burman's technique which required manoeuvring short notes with multiple inflections. Gradually, the choice boiled down to Mohammed Rafi and Manna Dey—the market demanded Rafi, while classical compositions were best suited for the latter, and it was to Burman's credit that he maintained a near perfect balance.

For instance, in Rafiq Ali Khan's *Meri Surat Teri Ankhen* (1963), Burman brought out the best in both Rafi and Manna. In the jingoistic war which had broken out between rival fan-groups of these two singers, it was conveniently forgotten that Lata, Mukesh, and Suman also performed fabulously in the album.

Meri Surat Teri Ankhen was based on a Bengali novel called *Ulka* by Dr. Nihar Ranjan Gupta. The story was first adapted for a Bengali film in 1957 by Naresh Mitra, and introduced one of Bengal's best known modern composers called Sudhin Dasgupta to the world. Later, the rights to the novel, which had previously also been adapted successfully as a long-running play in Calcutta, were bought over by Ashok Kumar.

Like *Devdas*, the tenor of *Meri Surat Teri Ankhen* was established right at the outset—the manner in which the opening scene, with a boy staring into the horizon and waves crashing on the rocks, was merged with a tune in raga Bhairav. When Manna Dey connects the three notes, *sa, ni* and komal *dha*, along with humming which sounds like a hymn, the effect is that of a landscape in painting—simple, yet enveloping multiple elements in its expanse.

Burman moved from Bhairav to Ahir Bhairav (though the Ahir Bharav composition predated the Bhairav composition) with a song which is arguably the most representative of Manna Dey in Hindi film music. *Poocho na kaise maine rain bitayi* was like the musical outpouring of a man who had suffered neglect and rejection from birth.

A widespread story in Burman's native Bengal was that the song was based on Kazi Nazrul Islam's *Aruna kanti ke go jogi bhikari*. In an interview with the authors, Nazrul's daughter-in-law, Kalyani Kazi, spoke of yet another angle, 'People said that Nazrul had copied *Aruna kanti* from *Poocho na kaise*. I had to tell them that *Aruna kanti* had been composed decades earlier.'

Once during a radio programme, S.D. Burman had diffused any further argument on the subject. To quote from music enthusiast Ritu Chandra's website, sdburman.net:

> It is widely perceived that *"Poocho na kaise"* is an adaptation of Nazrul Geeti *"Aruna kanti ke go jogi bhikari"*. However, S.D. Burman gave an interesting insight in his radio programme *Jaimala* where he attributed the original tune to a traditional bandish in Raag Ahir Bhairav by Ustad Mushtaq Hussein Khan.

That the compositions by Nazrul and Sachin Dev sounded similar could easily be attributed to both taking recourse to the classical bandish by Ustad Mushtaq Hussein Khan. Many composers are known to have used bandishes as inspiration time and again, but very few songs scaled the heights that *Poocho na kaise* did. S.D. Burman's handling of the tune, both in the duet version between S.D. Batish and Manna Dey (with additional lines by Asha Bhosle[1]) and the solo by Manna Dey, left its counterparts way behind.

The song also happened to be one of Burman's personal favourites. During the Filmfare Award nominations of 1963, Burman was in hospital for an eye operation. When Manna Dey came to visit him one day and let him know that his song was not in the list, tears had rolled down Burman's cheeks from under his eye-patch. The story would repeat itself three years later, with *Guide* in 1967.

While *Poocho na kaise* continues to mesmerise listeners even half a century later, one needs to appreciate that the other songs in the film were no pushovers. Like *Tere bin soone*, the Rafi–Lata duet in raga Piloo, which had Burman's rephrasing his own solo, *Ami chinu eka* (1940). Sung by Rafi in a voice which was intentionally made to sound frail and dulcet, even better was the moment when Lata makes her entry. The original Bengali version might have had a reference point in K.L. Saigal's *Lag gayi chot karejwa* (the singer's first hit for New Theatres), composed by Pankaj Mullick for *Yahudi Ki Ladki* (1933). The tune can be further extrapolated to fit in with the Nazrul geeti, *Saawan aashilo phire*, the first known recorded version of which was done by Dhiren Mitra in 1943. Whatever the inspirations might have been, *Tere bin soone* was distinctly different from many other similar sounding songs.

Both, *Poocho na kaise* and *Tere bin soone* sound as if they have a life of their own. There is a somnolent, dream-like quality about them, conjuring up a mystical world, sans the harsh realities of life. Along with Burman, the credit for the songs goes to Shailendra's magnificent poetry. In his autobiography, Burman spoke about this great poet-lyricist as follows:

> I miss Shailendra. The loss to my music caused by his absence cannot be fathomed. We collaborated on many films. He had a great quality, the gift of expressing the deepest thoughts in the simplest of words. This helped the average listener to grasp the essence and remember the song.

Burman also wrote about the inspiration for the song, *Nache mann mora magan* in his autobiography, as follows:

> The idea for the tune came from the use of the *bol, tigda dhigi dighi,* which were used by the Kathak maestro, Bindadin Maharaj while training his nephews. I was close to Acchan Maharaj (son of Bindadin Maharaj) and I fell in love with the *bol.* Shailendra wrote the line, *Nache man mora magan,* and I added the phrase *tigda dhigi dhigi.* To enunciate the *bol,* I sought the services of Pandit Samta Prasad of Banaras who played (the tabla) in this song.

For once, Burman had erred in the choice of the singer. Rafi's strength was soft and dreamy soliloquies, not thumri. *Nache mann mora magan* could never reach the heights of a *Laga chunri mein daag* (released the same year from the film, *Dil Hi To Hai,* composed by Roshan and sung by Manna Dey).

Amongst the other songs from the film, the Suman–Mukesh duet, *Yeh kisne geet cheda* which was used in a dream sequence, was a kirtan turned into a taut, breezy romantic song. Burman beautified this song with a prelude which sounded like a duet between the guitar and mandolin, with horns ruling the interludes. Suman was ultra-sweet, and Mukesh with his linear notes, sounded just so matter-of-fact. An amazing creation which deserved a better sequence, this was also the first song in which classical maestros, Pandit Shiv Kumar Sharma and Pandit Hari Prasad Chaurasia played for S.D. Burman.

On 14 August 1961, *Meri Surat Teri Ankhen* had a modest muhurat at Shree Sound studio. In what was otherwise a fabulous story, the film ended up like a regular fare with large doses of romance, crime, and melodrama. In the face of such torture, Burman's role as the composer was critical because a terrible background score would have further added to the woes of the viewer! It must be mentioned here that it was perhaps prescient of him to have understood the limitations of the script and therefore, the minimal background music, which was a rarity in Hindi films.

Meri Surat Teri Ankhen and *Bandini*, released within three months of each other (February and May 1963 respectively), had contrasting box office returns. The former sunk with no trace, while *Bandini* despite negative reviews by a section of the media which rued over the fact that the film was way too intense, had a huge first week collection, almost sixty per cent more than Bimal Roy's own, *Sujata*.

Meanwhile Burman was also working simultaneously with Hasrat Jaipuri, Shailendra's partner in almost all Shankar–Jaikishan's films in Vijay Anand's *Tere Ghar Ke Samne* (released in April 1963), which also happened to be the last Nutan–Dev Anand film.

Hasrat

Shot mostly in Delhi and Simla, and partly based on Ayn Rand's *The Fountainhead*, *Tere Ghar Ke Samne* was a rom-com musical. According to veteran film critic Raju Bharatan[1] in *Filmfare*, its music was panned by critics—'noisy' was used as a dysphemism for anything 'Western' by the so-called connoisseurs of film music. That attitude, however faulty, was strongly endorsed by certain music composers as well.

To S.D. Burman 'labelling' meant little. No wonder then that the title track of the film was representative of a 'Westernised' Burman. So was the club song, *Dil ki manzil*. Inspired by Can-can, with brass notes, English flute solos, Cha-cha-cha, bongo beats, huffing, grunting, long coda, etc., it belonged to a modern era. The Spanish-sounding 'scatting' was perhaps used by Pancham later in *Rang rangiley* (*Gardish*, 1993). The sequence, featured on Edwina and Helga, was replete with crane shots, something which Goldie would fine-tune in *Teesri Manzil* (1966).

Contrast this with the other tracks that are distinctly traditional and simplistic in arrangement. *Dil ka bhanwar karey pukar*, shot in a set replicating the interiors of the Qutub Minar (which also showed Goldie in a cameo for a few seconds) will forever remain one of the most iconic Dev–Rafi solos. Burman designed the number in staccato metres—using dadra taal in such a way that one felt a beat skipping every half a cycle—it seemed to so wonderfully synchronise with Dev's skipping down the steps of the monument while wooing his love.

Tu kahan yeh batah was a melody which did not conform to any established norm. It was a product of wild imagination coupled with Rafi's soothing rendition. The arrangement had novelty; for example, the flute which was used for obligatos at times set up a duet with the first line of the antaras. Like *Khoya khoya chand,* this song also had four antaras which was unusual for a Hindi film song. The reverb was used with caution, emphasising the pivotal points, and creating an air of mystery, as Dev looks for Nutan in the mist-laden lanes of Simla.

Goldie's innovative song picturisation in the title track (showing Nutan 'inside' a glass and an inebriated Dev singing to her), was somehow overshadowed by the sheer beauty of the song. Despite a score which is hugely popular even today, Hasrat Jaipuri and Burman worked in only two films, the second of which followed immediately.

Pramod Chakraborty, known in the Bombay film industry as Chakida, began his career as an assistant director in the 1950s. His acquaintance with Raj Khosla introduced him to Guru Dutt's family and he later married Geeta Dutt's sister, Lakshmi Roy. During his initial years in Bombay, Chakida used to make short films on celebrities such as, Ashok Kumar and S.D. Burman.

Like several others, he had to struggle for many years before he found a foothold in the film industry. Post and past his debut in the murder mystery, *12'O Clock* (1958) and failures like, *Passport* (1961) and *Gangu* (1962), he went to Sachin Bhowmick for help, who developed an idea into a film called *Ziddi* (1964). Chakida was now rearing to go and signed up S.D. Burman as the music director. This was also Burman's first foray into Eastmancolor.

In an interview with the authors in 2010[2], Sachin Bhowmick conceded that he never had a fixed script while working with most directors. In films like *Ziddi* (1964) and *Love in Tokyo* (1966), both he and Chakida kept improvising the script till the very end. Fortunately for Chakida, these films did well, and his career took off.

Work for *Ziddi* started in 1963. Till then, as mentioned earlier, Chakida was branded as a flop director. Sasadhar Mukerji stepped in and agreed to finance the film on the condition that his son, Joy Mukerji, be made to look like Marlon Brando![3] Sadhana, one of the two heroines recommended by Mukerji, refused the film, and Asha Parekh, who was the second choice, accepted but on condition that her remuneration be doubled.

One wonders what made Sachin Dev Burman accept the assignment. Maybe it was his love for East Bengal…

The Bengali writer and documentary filmmaker, Rabin Sengupta recalled an incident which took place in Helsinki, where S.D. Burman had been invited as a jury member for a music festival.[4]

'I was part of the team from India in July 1962 for the Youth Festival[5] which was held in Helsinki. One morning, Salil Chowdhury and V. Balsara told us about a proposed visit by S.D. Burman. I, along with Sudha Malhotra, Amar Sheikh, Salil Chowdhury, Purna Das Baul and others, was eager to meet him. When I was introduced to him, I bowed down and touched his knees, which was typical of the royal family of Tripura. Startled for a split second, he asked me in an accent specific to East Bengal where I was from. I said, "Agartala". His surprise knew no bounds when I further told him that I was Prafulla Sen's (polymath, a man of medicine and magic who P. C. Sorcar Senior considered his mentor) son. He was ecstatic and embraced me in front of the group and told his wife, Meera Devi, "Look, we have someone from back home."

'He then started enquiring about almost everyone—from Rabi Nag, Pulin Thakur to Lalu Karta, and the conversation went on to the tall trees in front of his old house in Agartala. The other members thought I was a VIP. I realised that a man who had spent his childhood and adolescence savouring the fragrance of the earth and wild flowers, can never be indifferent to the common man.'

Ziddi took a while to complete, mainly due to Burman's illness, and adversely affected the film. Its music sounded severely disjointed— while *Raat ka sama* was vintage Burman, *Teri surat se nahin milti*, *Pyaar ki manzil*, or *Champakali dekho* sound hurried. One particular number, *Janu kya mera dil* sounded more like the work of an amateur! Although Lata's *Yeh meri zindagi* is a fabulous song, it was clearly lifted from the Hebrew wedding song, *Hevenu shalom alechem*.

If there was one takeaway from the film, it was the re-establishing of Manna Dey as the best voice for actor-comedian, Mahmood Ali— *Pyaar ki aag mein tan badan jal gaya* was based on a raga as sombre as Darbari, but it was the sheer genius of the composer that he so subtly turned it into a song which evoked mirth. The other light duet, *Mein tere pyaar mein kya kya na bana dilbar* was Geeta Dutt's swan song for S.D. Burman. A pale shadow of her glorious past, she may have been included at the insistence of her brother-in-law, Chakida. Be that as it may, it was a sad exit for Geeta, who had sung around seventy songs for S.D. Burman in her illustrious career.

Shakeel

All good things come to an end. Like the Bimal Roy–S.D. Burman combination did with the failure of *Benazir* (1964).

For one, the story was indifferent; the casting, a gross mistake—Meena Kumari was not known for her dancing skills. To top it all, she had put on weight and looked older; Ashok Kumar, who was past fifty, was most unconvincing as the lover. The director of the film, Syed Khalil, who had previously directed *Bhaijaan* (1945)—the film on which *Benazir* was based (incidentally, *Benazir* too had the same working title), did not have the right credentials to handle a film for Bimal Roy Productions.

The music failed to inspire, given that the film had eleven songs, one of the highest ever by S.D. Burman. To put it simply, it was patchy. Even within a song, for example, *Mil ja jane jana* sung by Lata, the mukhda with a touch of raga Kedar was brilliant, while the antara fell flat in comparison. It is difficult to fathom why for a mukhda so high on melody and inflections, the antara was so linear with needless emphasis on high notes. The most recalled number from the film, *Dil mein ek jane tamanna*, was built round a simple melody, but somewhere it lacked in spontaneity which was least expected of a Burman song. For someone who avoided signing films indiscriminately fearing repetition, Burman resorted to recycling the melody of the phrase, *Saiyaan, kaise dharun dheer* (from his earlier, *Sitaron Se Aage*) in *Husn ki baharen liye aaye ththe sanam*.

The rest of the album—*Baharon ki mehfil suhani; Ai mere dilruba;*

Hum unko dekhte hain; *Le gai ek hasina* or *Ya Gafoor Rahim ya Allah* have little or no recall today.

When things begin to go wrong, nothing stems the descent. *Alvida jane wafa*, a delectable melody composed in raga Todi with an Arabic flavour to be featured on Meena Kumari during the climax, was left out in favour of the more trendy, *Gham nahin gar zindagi*.

For trivia lovers, *Mubarak hai woh dil* can be said to be the precursor for Pancham's *Dulhan maike chali* (*Manoranjan*, 1974), in the sense that both songs had all the three Mangeshkar singers singing—Lata, Asha, and Usha. Both Suman Kalyanpur and Mubarak Begum sang their last songs for Burman—*Ai mere dilruba* and *Hum unko dekhte hain*, respectively.

In the final analysis, *Benazir* failed to impress. Burman did learn music from some great Muslim musicians, but composing for a Muslim social was not his cup of tea, as was evidenced in the film. On the other hand, some of his contemporaries like Naushad, Roshan or even Ravi's work in this genre remains unparalleled. Unlike his comfort levels with either Shailendra or Majrooh, Burman's chemistry with lyricist Shakeel Badayuni who was the de facto song writer for most Muslim socials, failed to generate the expected results.

Bimal Roy never recovered from the loss of *Benazir*. He fell sick at the time of the film's release, and died a year and a half later. His daughter, Rinki Roy Bhattacharya spoke to the authors, as follows[1], 'A chain-smoker, whose favourite brand was American Lucky Strike, Baba often smoked all night. He was detected with cancer around 1964 and was treated by the best oncologist of that time, Dr. Borges[2], who was attached to Tata Memorial. He also went to the UK for treatment in 1965, but to no avail. He died in January 1966. On the day of his *shraddh*, there were several guests at home. I remember S.D. Burman was present too, and he broke down while trying to sing.'

Bimal Roy's death was an irrepairable loss for S.D. Burman. His friend-cum-colleague had also left a few incomplete projects behind—one of which was a comedy, which was to star Guru Dutt in the lead, but had to be abandoned post Guru's death in October 1964. Based on a Bengali story which had already been made in a film in 1952, it was later picked up by Mahmood and made into Hindi as *Padosan* (1968).

Even before Burman could come to terms with Guru's sudden and shocking demise, news came of Bimal Roy's sickness, followed by his demise. It was almost the end of an era for him. But life, just like showbiz, had to somehow go on.

A few months prior to that, Guru Dutt's brother, Atmaram had approached Burman for his debut film, *Kaise Kahoon* (1964). Biswajeet, who was first chosen and later dropped by Guru Dutt for *Saheb Bibi Aur Ghulam*, was signed up to play the hero in the film, the story of which had an uncanny resemblance to the life of Beethoven.

Therefore, the script was ideal for any music director—a singer-hero who encounters temporary deafness, even as the love of his life happens to be his music teacher's daughter. But somehow, despite music being the kernel of the film, the script fell short of expectations. *Zindagi tu jhoom le zara*, the most popular song from the film, was later packaged as one of the songs in the 'Rare Gems of Mohammed Rafi' in the late 1980s by HMV. As the name suggests, even the most popular song had to be termed 'rare'.

One also wonders what may have prompted Burman to recast his tune, *Mein kal phir milungi* (*Dr. Vidya*) as *Kisi ki mohabbat mein*, which was a duet between Rafi and Asha. For trivia enthusiasts, the most interesting *musical* part of the album was a cameo played by veteran singer G.M. Durrani, as a composer-musician in the film.

Meanwhile, in the real world, cometh 1966, and S.D. Burman's market value suddenly quadrupled.

Dev Anand—Phase II

Guide—The Uncut Version

In August 1962, Dev Anand returned from an extensive tour of Berlin, Paris, London and the US, and hinted about pursuing an ambitious venture.

'I am at the turning point of my career. I don't want to disclose anything until the deal is signed, sealed and delivered. But I may assure you, my fans that big things are shortly going to happen.' The press had gauged his intentions correctly. Dev Anand was planning to go international.

Thus, began a long and interesting story. One which was embroiled in controversy, personality clashes, envy, volte-face, political intervention, rigging, debacle, and triumph. The genesis of *Guide*, the exquisite musical album, and the Filmfare Awards, make for a story which is no less unique than the film itself.

All this gains more relevance in the context of S.D. Burman, as the music of *Guide*, which was its strongest point, was the worst impacted.

There are many versions about how *Guide* was conceived. The one which had gained credence in the early 1960s went something like this. After the Berlin Film Festival in 1962, Dev and his wife travelled to London and later, at the invitation of the Nobel laureate, Pearl S. Buck and the Polish–American TV film director, Tad Danielewski of Stratton Productions, went to the Waldorf Astoria in New York. Pearl and Tad had been to India earlier and had met filmmakers for an Indo-American project. Their trip to India also took them to Calcutta where they had approached Satyajit Ray. In Bombay, they got in touch with Dev for starring in an American film based on a story by an Indian author. According to Pearl S. Buck, Dev Anand was the only hero who was acceptable to the American audience.

However, nothing much came out of the meetings.

There was probably one more reason for Dev to go to America— to meet Irving Stone and Irving Mass, the head of Motion Pictures Association of America (MPAA). He had left the English version of *Hum Dono* with Irving Mass to explore the possibility of a release in the US.

However, Dev's trip to America had started off badly. In LA, he received news of Marilyn Monroe's death and like several others the world over, Dev Anand must have also been in shock over the suicide of one of the most iconic stars of the time.

But first things first...

According to a report in *Filmfare*, when the Anands were in New York, Pearl S. Buck and Tad had taken them to Greenwich Village near Lower Manhattan. It was while eating a dish called 'scorpion' at a restaurant in 'The Village' (as Greenwich Village is commonly referred to), that Dev presented Pearl S. Buck with a copy of R. K. Narayan's *The Guide*. While both Pearl and Tad were impressed by the possibilities of a cinematic adaptation of the novel, they had doubts whether Narayan would be willing to part with the film rights of his novel. Secondly, the book had been adapted into a Broadway play starring Pakistani actor, Zia Mohyeddin as the guide.

Dev lost no time and immediately sought an appointment with

R.K. Narayan and signed a contract with him. In *Cinema Modern: The Navketan Story*, Sidharth Bhatia mentions that someone who knew Narayan wrote a letter of introduction, even as Dev dashed off a telegram to the writer from the US. That 'someone' was none other than Natwar Singh, Indian diplomat and later Union Minister, who was based in New York at the time.

There are however different versions of this story. In his autobiography, *Romancing With Life*[1], Dev wrote that he'd stayed back in London after the Berlin Film Festival, while his wife, Mona returned to Bombay to be with their kids. He also said that he'd stayed at a hotel called the Pearl in New York (not the Waldorf Astoria) and that he had telephoned (and not sent a telegram) to R. K. Narayan who said that he had only given a verbal nod for the Broadway play and expressed interest in Dev Anand's proposal.

On the other hand, R.K. Narayan's article titled, "Misguided Guide", which was published in *Life* magazine in 1966 said that he had received a letter (neither a phone call nor a telegram) from Dev Anand.

Be that as it may, with R.K. Narayan's consent, work began on the screenplay for *The Guide*, and it was submitted in late December 1962. There was also a broad consensus that the film be made in both English and Hindi. Dev Anand floated yet another company called, Navketan International, and while Tad was de facto director of the English version, for the Hindi, it was a tossup between Chetan Anand and Raj Khosla, who had had an amicable working relationship with Dev, having directed him previously in *C.I.D.* (1956), *Kala Pani* (1958), *Solva Saal* (1958) and *Bombai Ka Babu* (1960). The selection of Raj Khosla, and Fali Mistry as Director of Photography, may have come to fruition during the shooting of the unfinished, *Sajan ki Galiyan* that Mistry was producing, and Raj Khosla was directing, with Dev in the lead.[2]

The search for Rosie, the leading lady, had also begun. While Tad preferred the English-speaking actress, Leela Naidu, Dev Anand always had Waheeda Rehman in mind. But according to Vijay Anand's biographer, Anita Padhye in *Ek Hota Goldie*,[3] Vyjayanthimala, who was initially suggested by Dev, was turned down by Tad with the explanation that the American audience did not fancy buxom women! Therefore, Waheeda not only became the choice on the rebound, but was also recommended for her dancing skills, as it was mandatory for Rosie's character. However, Waheeda was reluctant to act under Raj Khosla's baton and thus was summoned Chetan Anand, to take over the project. The story wasn't over as yet, as Chetan Anand came with his own set of demands, one of which was Priya Rajvansh for the role of Rosie. Chetan's contention was that Priya, courtesy her upbringing and lineage, knew better English than Waheeda. This request was however turned down by Dev—he would have none except Waheeda play Rosie.

That year, after the Christmas and New Year break, the American crew arrived in India for location scouting and went from Mysore in the South to Rajasthan in the North-west. Meanwhile, the author of *The Guide* was miffed by the entire episode, which he would make apparent later and rather forcefully. Meanwhile, Dev Anand was building his team for both versions—Ram Yedkar was on-boarded for art direction and S.D. Burman was to be the music director. For the Hindi version, Vijay Anand, Vrajendra Gaur and M.A. Latif were to write the script based on the English version, while Hasrat Jaipuri, in continuation from *Tere Ghar Ke Saamne*, was chosen as the film's lyricist.

Finally, the shooting for *Guide* commenced in January 1963. However, as mentioned before, Chetan Anand came with his own set of ideas about filmmaking, and by the time the shooting progressed at Mehboob Studios and in Rajasthan, Dev Anand had given up on the idea of shooting the bilingual versions simultaneously. When the crew returned from the Udaipur schedule, Chetan Anand received news that the Punjab government had finally granted financial assistance for his magnum opus, *Haqeeqat* (1964), and he soon got busy with it.

With Chetan retreating, Dev's next choice was an obvious one—

his younger brother, Vijay. However, it wasn't as if Goldie had jumped at the offer—he told Dev that he would shoot only after the English version was complete, and in the meantime, he re-wrote the Hindi script in eighteen days flat—much like *Deewar* (1975) which was also written in eighteen days by Salim–Javed.

By June 1963, the shooting of the film's English version was completed and Pearl S. Buck who viewed the rushes, found it up to the mark. Meanwhile, Dev was on his way to the US as a guest of the American government under their Cultural and Educational exchange programme. But he had to return soon as his music composer had suffered a heart attack. Incidentally, Sachin Dev Burman had also signed Guru Dutt Productions' next film, *Baharen Phir Bhi Aayengi* around the same time, but was replaced by O.P. Nayyar, owing to his heart ailment.

Although Burman was severely indisposed and realised that he may not be able to finish the work on hand, the past came back to haunt him yet again. He began losing out on films, and prominent among them were Pramod Chakraborty's *Love in Tokyo* (1966) and Raja Nawathe's *Gumnam* (1965). The thorough professional that he was, Burman advised Dev Anand to sign on a new composer for *Guide*, but Dev put his foot down and insisted that he should first get well and then take over. The Hindi script demanded quite a few number of songs, some to synchronise with the dance sequences, and Dev Anand was unwilling to risk it with anyone else. The background score for the English version was done by R.D. Burman, Manohari Singh, Basu Chakravarty and Maruti Rao (Pancham and Manohari were credited as assistants for *The Guide*) in S.D. Burman's absence.

Meanwhile in distant Mysore, R.K. Narayan was seething with anger, as Tad, apart from adding his own interpretations to the story, had shifted its location from the fictional town of Malgudi to the colourful Udaipur and other parts of Rajasthan. However, when Narayan saw the English version in January 1964, he wrote to Dev, labelling the film profound, artistic, and exquisite. He further added that he was completely fascinated by the picture, and electrified by Dev's on-screen presence. 'Personally I feel very hopeful that this picture is going to make a mark and perhaps the beginning of a tremendous name for Indian movies and for you,' he said, adding that Waheeda Rehman was 'the sweetest Rosie I have set my eyes upon.'

In 1964, Dev began promoting *The Guide* in the US as he had managed an invitational show for it from the UN. The premiere elicited encouraging responses from a cross section of viewers. Actress Greer Garson, who met Dev at the premiere, said, 'We found the film most absorbing, not only for its picturesque hero and the great beauty of the settings, but also for its philosophical and satiric elements. What a wonderful role for an actor—such range and variety—and you were graciously equal to every demand.'

Back home, the filming of *Guide* was progressing at a snail's pace. Dev Anand was travelling and Goldie was busy with his first directorial venture outside Navketan, *Teesri Manzil* (1966). The brothers were distanced in more ways than one—Dev Anand who was initially signed on to play the lead in *Teesri Manzil*, had later walked out. Goldie had also shifted to his own flat at Pali Hill in early 1964.

Meanwhile, Dev went ahead and sold the worldwide marketing rights of the still-to-be-completed *Guide* to Ashoka Company Ltd in Tehran, even as the English version premiered at the Lincoln Art theatre in New York in February 1965.

Somehow the mainstream press in America didn't take a liking to *The Guide*. Although the most talked about review by Bosley Crowther in the *New York Times* (dated 10 February 1965) lauded the quality of staging and colour photography, but it raised questions about the narrative elements in the film, almost rubbishing the flow and theatrics. Not one to lag behind, even the *Time* magazine was unsparing in its criticism.[4]

The film was however showcased in several theatres in America—it was also one of the official entries at the Chicago International Film Festival in its inaugural year (1965), and the best news was Waheeda Rehman bagging the Silver Hugo for the Best Actress[5]. But overall, the market response for the film was lukewarm and made worse by the difficulties faced during its release. Some groups amongst the film fraternity influenced by certain political forces wanted the film banned for its theme which they found adulterous and hence objectionable. Matters came to a head and the film went up to the then Information and Broadcasting Minister, Indira Gandhi for her intervention to obtain the release certificate.[6]

Although the English version had evinced a lukewarm response, shooting for the Hindi version resumed at a frenetic pace at Mehboob Studios, and in locations such as, Udaipur and Chittor in Rajasthan, and at Limdi in Gujarat, where the climax was to be shot. But before that, it was decided that the Hindi version needed some cosmetic surgery. For one, a motive had to be established for Rosie's estrangement from her husband. Hence, her husband, Marco, was shown to be an alcoholic, a womaniser, and overall, a violent, insensitive man. Secondly, with the female protagonist Rosie essaying the role of a dancer, the song-and-dance elements had to be first-rate and for that, S.D. Burman was required to be in good shape. In a few days, work began on giving a final shape to this crucial aspect of the Hindi version. The noted choreographer, Hiralal began teaching Waheeda the dance steps, and S.D. Burman slowly began inching towards the best album of his career.

Waheeda's practice sessions for *Guide* were extremely rigorous, so much so that according to some news reports of the time, she was forced to wear a surgical collar to prevent the pain from spreading down to her entire body. The film had three dance sequences, which were used as metaphors to take the story forward. The legendary radio presenter, Ameen Sayani once mentioned how Burman had himself demonstrated a few dance steps to Waheeda, although it wasn't clear which ones!

While Dev was busy marketing the English version, most of the music had been composed for *Guide*. Meanwhile, two other important changes had also occurred—Hasrat Jaipuri had been replaced by Shailendra. (It is puzzling why Majrooh Sultanpuri, a regular with Navketan, was left out), and Rahul Dev Burman was given more space to operate, although he was working as his father's assistant in the film. Sachin Ganguly recounted why this had happened. 'Sachinda had bought an ash-coloured Austin and would drive it around himself. Once when he was driving on a wet road accompanied by his wife, the car skidded and almost hit a buffalo. This near-fatal accident shook him up so badly that it impacted his eye. His retina was detached, and he had to be subsequently hospitalised for a long duration.'[7]

There is confusion regarding which song was first recorded for *Guide*. In to an interview to the Marathi magazine, *Rasrang* (Diwali issue, 1966), S.D. Burman had said that in the absence of Kishore Kumar, he had opted for Mohammad Rafi as the lead voice for Dev Anand:

> *Guide* had a Kishore Kumar–Lata Mangeshkar milestone duet, *Gaata rahe mera dil*. Director Vijay Anand showed perceptible understanding of the medium and picturised it immaculately. Dev and Waheeda too complemented each other beautifully in the song. Everybody contributed in making this song a masterpiece in the genre of romantic love songs.

> Seeing Dev on screen, lip-synching *Gaata rahe mera dil*, made people feel that he was actually singing the song. It goes without saying that this feeling keeps recurring whenever Kishore sings for Dev. The voice of Kishore Kumar fits the persona of Dev like the proverbial glove. Hence, whenever I have composed for Dev, I have had only Kishore in mind. Only when Kishore couldn't make himself available that I have gone ahead with Rafi. Kishore was available for only one song in *Guide*—*Gaata rahe mera dil*, and his unavailability made me record the other three songs— *Tere mere sapne*, *Din dhal jaye* and *Kya se kya* with Rafi.[8]

According to *Ek Hota Goldie*, the Anand brothers had also wanted Kishore Kumar to sing all the songs for Dev Anand. However, Kishore was away in the US (probably for the medical treatment of his wife, Madhubala) and the songs were composed keeping Rafi in mind. After Kishore's return, the Anands made him sing *Gaata rahe mera dil*.

Logically speaking though, the first song to be finalised for *Guide* would have to be the one with Shailendra—as recounted by Dev and Goldie in multiple interviews, it was *Din dhal jaye*.

In a story by Nalin Uchil in *Star & Style* (dated 11–24 October 1985), Dev Anand had mentioned that the original song was written by a Pakistani poet. However, H.Q. Chowdhury in his book, *Incomparable S.D. Burman*, sets the record right:

> For *Din dhal jaye*, Dev Anand and Vijay Anand politely told Dada that while the song was good it did not quite carry the mood of the sequence. "This is fine," said Dada over the phone, and hung up. A little later he called Dev Anand that he was coming over and a harmonium should be arranged. Upon arrival, within minutes, he composed the tune we hear today. It is also said that *Din dhal jaye* was originally not in the film at all. There was another song, *Hum hi mein thi na koi baat, yaad na tumko aa sake, Tumne hamein bhula diya, Hum na tumhe bhula sake* by Hafiz Jalandhari which was composed differently, and yet another one by Hasrat Jaipuri.[9]

Dinesh Shailendra, son of the late Shailendra, recalled that Hasrat had written two songs before his father was asked to join the team.[10]

The Anands were somehow not satisfied with the songs written either by Hasrat or Hafiz. Accompanied by S.D. Burman, they decided to meet Shailendra at his bungalow, Rim Jhim in Khar, where the poet is supposed to have downed a peg and written *Din dhal jaye* sitting in a corner. Later, Shailendra asked for an additional one hundred thousand rupees over and above what was offered to Hasrat. In 1964, that was quite an amount, but the Anands agreed. Kishwari Jaipuri, daughter of Hasrat, told the authors that the Anands were so magnanimous that Dev Anand never asked her father about returning the signing amount.[11]

In one of his interviews, Vijay Anand confirmed that *Din dhal jaye* was recorded late at night, around 11 p.m., which was odd because by then an ailing S.D. Burman would insist on winding up early. But what was also true was that he had started giving a free hand to his assistants. Manohari Singh recalled to the authors how the assistants were deeply involved in the music sessions of *Guide* as it mandated heavy orchestration. Most of the preludes, interludes and fillers were composed by them, and one of these, the alto sax filler in *Din dhal jaye* was later used as the first line of the Asha Bhosle–Mahendra Kapoor duet, *Mera kya sanam* in O.P. Ralhan's *Talash* (1969).[12]

Nilu N. Gavankar in her book, *The Desai Trio* wrote about the noted recordist, Mangesh Desai being impressed about a particular song from *Guide*, as follows:

> One morning, during one of his daily visits to our place, he (Mangesh Desai) entered singing *Gaata rahe mera dil*. He had a wonderful singing voice. I asked him whether it was a new song. He said, "I recorded this song yesterday and it is going to be a mega hit. Tell your big brother Pushpya (Pete) in America that his friend Rahul is a genius. Finally his father is allowing him to run the show for the upcoming movie *Guide*. I think his father Dada Burman is going to give Rahul the credit that he deserves in this movie."[13]

In a TV interview, Dev Anand had also acknowledged that it was Pancham who had composed the mukhda of the song. Then there were of course several other discussions about how Jaidev's tune was referenced for *Tere mere sapne*.

However, *Guide* for all the contribution from the team, was essentially S.D. Burman's brainchild. The metres, the light-heartedness, the use of short and simple notes, the occasional glimpse of melancholy, were all quintessentially S.D. Burman. For example, even in the mukhda of *Gaata rahe mera dil*, which was attributed to Pancham, the delicate inflection at *"beete na"* was so senior Burmanish.

Another important aspect of Burman's composing principle was reusing the well-defined but less successful metres, something which he did with great success in the song, *Mohse chhal kiye jaye*. In this, he used the metre of *Saiyyan, kaise dharun dheer* from *Sitaron Se Aage* (1958). *Mohse chhal* was the only film song where the santoor player and maestro, Pandit Shiv Kumar Sharma played the tabla upon the insistence of his friend, Rahul Dev Burman.

Shailendra's lyrics conveyed the soul of the film—the longing, desire, and futility of love when faced with life's realities, which is best manifested in the title song, *Wahan kaun hai tera*. Burman remodelled his own Bengali song, *Door kon porobashe* in his second solo for Shailendra, breaking the antaras of the original into short, manageable melodic phrases, while keeping the mukhda intact. The song which is heard during the opening titles (a rather lengthy one; albeit pleasurable), shows Raju, the guide walking from Udaipur jail to an unknown destination. Burman's pathos-laden rendition, strong yet soulful, with delectable inflections and voice-breaks adding to the overall Sufi feel, is almost an ode to the mysteries of life. Shailendra layered the simple lyrics with such deep philosophy that it ceased to be just another road ballad. S.D. Burman had once acknowledged Shailendra's immense contribution to his music and said that only he could have elevated his music to the level that it deserved.

The dubbing for *Guide* commenced at Mehboob Studios in mid-1965. *Piya tose naina lage re* was probably recorded right at the end. Meanwhile, the background score happened almost simultaneously. For the longish snake dance sequence in the film, Burman moulded the lines, *Kahin beete na ye raatein, kahin beete na ye din* from *Gaata rahe mera dil* to go along with Waheeda's dance. On the topic of the snake dance, the central melody of it was the same as in *The Guide* in bits and pieces during the titles, and sounded like an offshoot of Pancham's harmonica filler in *Rahi manwa dukh ki chinta* (*Dosti*, 1964, composed by Laxmikant–Pyarelal). The clavioline, the principal instrument used to simulate the sound of a snake charmer's *been*, was played by Vipin Reshammiya, the father of Himesh Reshammiya.

In November 1965, *Guide* was sent to the US for processing, and Dev Anand travelled to New York on the night of 20 November to obtain the final print of the film. He had plans to release the film by the end of the year, but suddenly, he was faced with a barrage of protests from some quarters who strongly recommended that the film be banned on grounds that it promoted infidelity, that too by a woman! Dev Anand, who was then the President of the Actors guild, tried his best to work around it, but to no avail.

In February 1966, Dev spoke to the press. He said that *Guide* had been called a 'reckless misadventure' by a section of the media. Rumours had been spread about both versions—how the English version would never be released and that the Hindi version would never be made, and if made, it woulldn't 'sell'. Dev reacted to the rumours as follows: 'For the most ignorant of the educated masses realise that the project of an earnest movie-maker does not have to be sold. It is sold the day it is planned.'[14]

He also mentioned how a set of 'new clothing' had been given to Narayan's theme, and the clothing included music. Finally, *Guide* released on 8 April 1966. It had a shaky start, for here was a film which didn't present Dev Anand as the quintessential lover boy. The audience was flummoxed—their favourite hero in a sanyasi's ochre robes and finally dead? One is guessing that the entire premise would've not only sounded incredulous, but also offensive!

Gradually, good reviews started pouring in. Even the usually acerbic, Baburao Patel had good things to say about it—'It is worth travelling a hundred miles to see it.' *Filmfare* gave it four stars, perhaps the only film to get such a high rating in the previous two–three years. The Marathi newspaper, *Loksatta* praised it as, 'among the best films produced in India so far.' However, the black marketers held their heads in despair.

With *Guide* eliciting an initial lukewarm response, the music sales were also sluggish. Raju Bharatan, while talking about the tepid response to the songs of *Guide*, mentioned how Burman was going around asking all and sundry to listen to his latest work.[15] Gradually, realisation dawned upon the public, and the penny dropped.

In *Star & Style*, Vijay Anand once commented about S.D. Burman's understanding of the film medium, as follows:

> There have been so many music directors who were talented but who did not understand the difference between composing for films and composing otherwise—like Madan Mohan.

> Take this: *Jiya le gayo ji mora sanwariya*—here the line, *O papihe*, is repeated in so many different ways that it becomes very difficult for the director to cut.

> Burman understood or at least was aware of the technicalities of the film medium. He had a definitive idea of what a song would finally look like on the screen.

Guide was a feast of colours. The music was more like an impressionist's response to a plethora of hues around him. All the songs, even the sombre ones, and the dance sequences including the snake dance, have several layers of colourful undertones. The varied palette of the melody, rhythm and instruments, the vibrancy in the voices of Lata and Kishore; Rafi's melancholic tone, and the bard-like resonance of Burman, finds the best parallel in Claude Monet's landscapes. The S.D. Burman of *Guide* was like Monet at Argenteuil, playing with the changing tones of the Seine and its surroundings.

Once the music was appreciated by the public, the marketing strategy for *Guide* was swiftly altered. Blurbs in newspapers started with lines from a song—*Gaata rahe mera dil, tu hee meri manzil* on the first day; the next blurb which appeared a few days later, started with, *Kya se kya ho gaya bewafa tere pyaar mein*. Gradually, even the distributors realised that the music stood out in a film that the average filmgoer found difficult to fathom. Despite a recommendation by the then President of India, Dr. S. Radhakrishnan, along with a number of articles citing *Guide* as heralding the rebirth of Hindi cinema, it did moderately well only in metros, except Gujarat, where it celebrated a silver jubilee. To mark the occasion, there was a big party at Dev's house in September 1966 and the guests included Raj Kapoor, Rajendra Kumar, K.N. Singh, Sardar Akhtar, Nasir Husain, Shakti Samanta, Yash Chopra, Saira Banu, Nanda, Asha Parekh, Jairaj, and Jaikishan, among others.

Not one to rest so easily on his laurels, Dev Anand immediately got down to his next film. Meanwhile, S.D. Burman was resolute in his professional principle of sticking to one or two films per year.

The story of *Guide* does not end here. That and the Filmfare Awards is a story in itself.

Filmfare Awards: Myth & Reality

From its inception, the Clares, later renamed as Filmfare Awards, was set up as a benchmark for the best in Hindi cinema. For a number of years, when awards were still based on merit and not on a recipient's ability to influence the system, the Filmfare Awards were considered next best to the coveted State Awards (later renamed as the National Awards). A voting system which was extended to the buyers of *Filmfare*, formed the basis of shortlisting the nominations, post which a jury would select the final names from the list.

Gradually, in the face of charges that the awards had become too commercial for comfort, the sheen wore off. Further, as it is today, even then there were allegations that the awards were fixed by a select group of contenders in the most ingenious manner! Bombay's Dadar station was supposedly the hub from where the magazine would be distributed to retailers, and there were rumours of potential candidates having people on their payroll pick up as many copies of the issue containing the nomination forms, and then have them filled and mailed to the *Filmfare* office. The same copies would then be resold at pavements at throwaway prices.

In the years that rolled by, one sensed a feeling of great discontent, especially in the music category of the awards. For instance, Naushad was extremely disturbed when *Mughal-e-Azam* (1960) had lost out to *Dil Apna Aur Preet Parayi* (1960). The jury apparently considered his compositions too classy for the medium of cinema. There were also widespread rumours of the awards being manipulated by touts.

In early 1963, the office-bearers of *Filmfare* decided that the awards process mandated an amendment and the 8 February 1963 issue of *Filmfare* carried a letter by its then editor, B.K. Karanjia:

In response to repeated requests made by you, requests reiterated by men who matter in the industry, *Filmfare* has made a change in the voting system for its annual awards.

The system so far was to publish the polling form in *Filmfare* itself. This will not now be done. Now, to make the Readers' Poll fool proof, you will have to fill in, sign and post to us the coupon published below. On receipt of this coupon bearing your signature, we shall mail to you the actual polling form to enable you to indicate your preferences.

In order that you may not have to spend on postage twice, we shall, when sending the polling form to you, enclose an envelope, postage guaranteed, for its return to us after being filled by you. We hope you will not mind this little extra trouble which is necessary in your own interest that your vote may carry the weight that it deserves and merit may get its just desserts.

It is our passionate conviction that you who pay to see films should get your views heard. Cinegoers who are the patrons of this industry should logically constitute the final judges of its products.

You will no doubt appreciate, dear reader, that this imposes on you a dual responsibility. Each one of you has, first, to cast your vote, for the more of you do so, the more representative will be the selection of these awards. Secondly, you have to make your selections after careful consideration and thus give a resounding retort to those producers who say that your deteriorating taste has been responsible for lowering the standard of our films.

We, at *Filmfare* anxiously await your selections for this year's awards.[1]

On 5 April 1963, the changes proposed by Karanjia made it to the magazine. The key points highlighted in it were:

1. To make the casting of bogus votes insuperably difficult

2. To make it possible to discover and disqualify the few bogus votes that might still be cast

3. Third, to place these findings and the pattern of voting before the panel of judges to enable them to finally decide

The Editor's Note also mentioned that the change in the polling pattern had actually resulted in higher readers participation. This move was welcomed with congratulatory letters from eminent film personalities in the magazine's issue dated 19 April 1963. The list included, B.R. Chopra, J.B.H. Wadia, Vasant Joglekar, Dev Anand, Mohan Segal, Vijaya Chowdhury, Balraj Sahni, Pandit Mukhuram Sharma, Nanda, Nana Palsikar, and Johnny Walker.

The latest results were published in the same issue, but stirred up a fresh and fierce debate yet again. *Sahib Bibi Aur Ghulam*, the winner in the category of Best Film, was not even nominated for its music. However, the film's composer, Hemanta Mukherjee was nominated for his score for *Bees Saal Baad* as was Madan Mohan for *Anpadh*. But the winner that year was *Professor*, which in retrospect must have even surprised its composers, the talented duo of Shankar and Jaikishan.

The controversy reached a flashpoint in 1965, when the awards for the previous year were announced. The nominations included, *Sangam*, *Dosti* and *Woh Kaun Thi?* When *Dosti* edged out the others, there was an avalanche of debates.

Many years later, composer Pyarelal admitted to having shelled out money to secure the award for *Dosti*.

Come 1967 and *Guide* featured in the Filmfare Awards' nomination list along with *Do Badan* and *Suraj*, which received the coveted trophy that year. While this broke many hearts, there is a logical explanation of what could have actually happened.

To begin with, *Suraj* was a more popular film than *Guide*. Released on 3 June 1966, precisely two months after *Guide*, its recall value was impressive during the readers' voting phase, which took place in January 1967. However, one wonders if Shankar and Jaikishan would have termed *Suraj*'s score as one which was not only amongst their best, but also deserving of an award? Be that as it may, *Suraj* collected all the major awards in the music category that year—Best Music Director, Best Singer (Rafi), and Best Lyricist (Hasrat Jaipuri) for *Baharon phool barsao mera mehboob aaya hai*.

Going by the current trend in the film and music industry, where the success of a film or a score is dependent on clever marketing strategies, one often hears how things were above board in the good old days and so on and so forth. Although the degrees may differ, the PR machinery of respective filmmakers and composers was active even then and it was overtly manifest in 1965–66 in the way *Suraj*'s music was promoted on different platforms. Rafi would be called upon to sing *Baharon phool barsao* at several functions ad nauseum. In May 1966, when Shankar–Jaikishan held a reception at Natraj Hotel to celebrate twenty-five years of Mohammed Rafi's career, he once again sang a few lines of *Baharon phool barsao*.

Yet another factor which mattered and still does to a great extent involves maintaining relationships in the fraternity. As mentioned earlier, S.D. Burman hardly ever socialised. At the Silver Jubilee celebrations of *Guide* at Dev Anand's home, actor Jairaj was heard discussing loudly the forthcoming Shankar–Jaikishan Night at Ahmedabad. Although this may be construed as the personal opinion of an individual and therefore natural, it did seem out of place considering the evening was about *Guide*.

As was well known, Burman was reclusive by nature, and didn't attend the Shankar–Jaikishan Night in Ahmedabad in October 1966. However, there were other composers in attendance, including Naushad,

C. Ramchandra, S.N. Tripathi, Kalyanji–Anandji, Roshan and Avinash Vyas. Rafi once again sang *Baharon phool barsao* at the function.

Prior to the announcement of the Filmfare Awards that year, S.D. Burman was excluded from the contingent that flew to Delhi for a charity show called, 'An Evening with Stars', in aid of PM's Bihar Relief Fund at the National Stadium in April 1967. The 150-something group had amongst others, Naushad, Kalyanji–Anandji, C. Ramchandra, Shankar–Jaikishan, as also singers like, Rafi and Sharda. Yet again, Rafi was made to sing *Baharon phool barsao*, while the relatively new Sharda sang *Titli udi* from the same film.

All said and done, even as questions were being raised about the achievements of Shankar–Jaikishan and Mohammad Rafi, three men who had a fabulous body of work to their credit, what was most puzzling was Sharda receiving a special award for her rendition of *Titli udi!* Adding insult to injury, this song was cited as 'the reason' to have separate categories for male and female playback singers from the following year. This raises a valid question—with due respect to Sharda, what was so special about her singing which mandated the need to bend rules and create a separate category in 1968? Surely the jury could have thought of revising the rules earlier if they had so wanted. After all, Lata Mangeshkar, Asha Bhosle, Geeta Dutt, Talat Mahmood, Manna Dey, Rafi, Hemanta, Kishore Kumar and Mukesh, had all been competing against each other for a fairly long time. If the intent was to encourage new talent, there were not only several before Sharda, but way more versatile than her—Suman Kalyanpur, Sudha Malhotra, Mubarak Begum, Meena Kapoor, Subir Sen, Arati Mukherjee, Dwijen Mukherjee et al. Surely, the jury could have been a little more judicious?

The jury for the Filmfare Awards in 1966 included the well-known businessman (also a member of the Bombay board of film censors), Ramnath Kapoor, Vijay Bhatt, Roshanlal Malhotra (President, IMPPA), Gajanand Jagirdar, Thrity H. Taleyarkhan (prominent social worker) and P.K. Roy. The panel was presided over by Justice K.K. Desai.

Apart from Vijay Bhatt, not a single name amongst the list had any association with music, let alone judge it for its merits.

But the worst was still to come. The 1967 edition of the Cine Music Directors' Association (CMDA) awards to promote the best film song (and not the most popular one) handed out the award to *Baharon phool barsao*. On 19 May, a reception was held at the Ritz hotel to honour Shankar–Jaikishan for the song. The evening saw the presence of familiar faces yet again—Naushad, C. Ramchandra, Roshan, Kalyanji–Anandji, Laxmikant–Pyarelal, G.P. Sippy, and F.C. Mehra. Those who were absent included the Burmans, Salil Chowdhury, Hemanta Kumar, the Mangeshkars, the Gangolys and the Anands.

When rival groups are formed in politics, it is acceptable, for that is the norm in the cesspool of power play. But somehow, when lines are drawn in the world of art and culture, it often seems out of place, for authority or rank has little or negligible role to play in such a field. As it turned out, there was deep fragmentation within the CMDA—and two separate groups, the 'Bengali CMDA' and the 'Non-Bengali CMDA' groups were subsequently formed. Naushad Ali once went on record to say that when he was heading the 'Non-Bengali CMDA', his colleague, Salil Chowdhury was heading the Bengal wing of the association, and they did not share the best of relationships. It would not be incorrect to infer that the open biases in the organisation must have definitely influenced the decisions in a particular year.

Coming back to Filmfare Awards, there is hardly any written documentation on the issue, except one. In Goldie Anand's biography, *Ek Hota Goldie*, Anita Padhye wrote, 'Goldie told me the story, which was unbelievable. How come *Guide* got seven awards and Sachinda did not get one?'

The story, as narrated by Goldie to his biographer is summarised as follows:

One day before the announcement of the nominations, the Filmfare award committee members (*names were not mentioned*) met S.D. Burman, promised him the Best Music Director award for *Guide* and demanded a sum of Rupees 50,000 in return. An indifferent Burman refused to entertain their request, and literally drove them out of his house. The members then went to Goldie and extended the offer for the film and direction. Goldie not only refused them point blank, he took it upon himself to call all the directors, the names of whom were mentioned by the people who came to meet him. The nail had been hammered— the word spread in the industry after Goldie's call to the other directors. The committee then thought that it would be a shame if *Guide* was deprived of the major awards. Fearing that this could ultimately result in great harm to their reputation, the committee acted fast and gave seven awards to *Guide*.

However, *Guide* did not receive a single award for music. This rude fact pained the Anands no end, and Goldie hit back by referring to the music of *Guide* as "beyond the confines of any award".

The above-mentioned passage seals all controversies surrounding the music of the film.

The staff of *Filmfare* was probably inundated with letters from readers, one of which was published on 12 May 1967. P. Sambasivrao, from Parasia, West Bengal, wrote:

I do not agree with your awards for Best Music, Best Lyrics and Best Singer. (He mentioned Burman and Shailendra for *Guide* and Lata for *Kaaton se kheench ke yeh aanchal*).

I hope there are other FF readers who feel like myself.

On 19 January 1968, *Filmfare* issued a disclaimer:

It has been brought to our notice that during and after the polling, certain individuals go about claiming that they are in a position to influence the giving of Filmfare Awards. These individuals are not in any way connected with *Filmfare*, have no authority whatsoever to speak on its behalf and their claims are palpably absurd and false. Stars, music directors, and all other ranks of film industry are requested in their own interest to ignore them.

This disclaimer was however a few years too late.

In 2006, in a nation-wide poll in *Outlook* magazine, in which only select personalities connected with music and cinema were invited to list their ten favourite Hindi film songs, two songs from *Guide*, *Din dhal jaye* and *Tere mere sapne* vied with *Kuch toh log kahenge* (*Amar Prem*, 1971) for the second position. Another song from *Guide*, *Piya tose naina laage re* was tied at number four. One may however argue that even this does not qualify as conclusive evidence, for any poll has certain intrinsic flaws. However, it did reflect what had stayed in the collective conscious of a jury constituted forty years after the release of *Guide*, which unlike the one appointed by *Filmfare*, knew its music rather well. The *Outlook* poll concluded *Guide* as the most popular musical film ever.

Teen Deviyan

In his autobiography, Dev Anand claimed (perhaps a bit unkindly) that he had ghost-directed *Teen Deviyan*—the story of a young musician-poet caught in the vortex of three stunning women. The film was mostly shot at Mehboob Studios, and there were a few shots of Calcutta (however, erroneous), and this despite the fact that there wasn't a single Bengali character in the film, barring a junior artiste! Despite such obvious discrepancies, it had, true to what was expected from a Dev Anand film, six glimmering songs, all fitting pleasingly into the framework of the film, which was *officially* directed by Amarjeet.

The years 1964, '65 and '66 saw a dip in the number of films signed by S.D. Burman. He was battling several health problems—a heart ailment, retinal detachment and other minor irritants. No filmmaker had the patience to wait for him endlessly, and with Dev Anand backing him as always, Burman only had *Guide* and later *Teen Deviyan* (1965) in his kitty.

Although *Teen Deviyan* was classified as B grade by critics for lack of seriousness in its approach, the music of the film was proof that Burman was moving with the times. Looking back in time, one is tempted to say that he had actually forged way ahead of his peers. At least, most of them.

While the subjects of *Guide* and *Teen Deviyan* were diverse, their coinciding timelines led to overlapping of sentiments, as one is tempted

215

to infer that *Tere mere sapne* (*Guide*) and *Aise toh na dekho* (*Teen Deviyan*) may have originated from a common kernel of thought—apart from the fact that both had Rafi singing in his silky, smooth voice.

According to music director Anil Biswas[1], Buman had based *Aise toh na dekho* on Tagore's *Ami tomaye joto, shuniyechilem gaan*. The mukhda (asthayi) does sound similar, but Burman improvised and employed a special cadence, lending a lilt to the taal that made it sound modern. The absence of the prolonged, recurring tabla beat also added to the uncluttered feel. The song was essentially a slow, romantic number, but had a pace bordering on gay abandon. The other Rafi solo, *Kahin bekhayal hokar* is touted to be based on a tune originally created by Jaidev, but there are no records to validate this claim. However, the tune in contrast to Burman's principles which determined a film song, may have sounded complex, but turned out to be extremely hummable.

That Burman chose Kishore Kumar and not Rafi for four songs proved that the composer not only had the knack of making the correct assumption, but respected Kishore for his immense talent. Three out of the four songs—duets, *Likha hai teri ankhon mein*, *Arrey yaar meri*, and the solo, *Khwab ho tum* continue to grow in stature both in terms of popularity and critical applause. 'You're absolutely right. The music lives on even today,' agreed Simi Grewal the veteran actress who acted in the film.[2]

Teen Deviyan was also one of the first films where the orchestral arrangement, to use a cliché, was more 'modern' compared to Burman's previous films. One heard longer preludes, robust interludes, strong back-up vocals and varied instrumentation. The background score with a heady mix of musical forms such as, jazz, R&B, swing, etc., and a heavy dependence on instruments such as chimes, sax, trumpet, and piano stood out, unlike his earlier films. It sounded like a film which belonged to the decade of the Seventies. As in the case of *Guide*, Burman had relied heavily on his team of assistants—his son, Pancham, Manohari Singh, Maruti Rao and Basu Chakravarty. The late Badal

Bhattacharya, one of Pancham's closest friends, had put it quite bluntly to the authors—'Teen Deviyan was mostly Pancham. S.D. Burman was either ill or occupied with Guide.'[3]

Probir Mukherjea, who was in Bombay during that time trying his hand at music direction, recounted an interesting story about the Kishore–Asha duet, Arrey yaar meri tum bhi ho gazab: 'I was assisting Roshan for a month during the background music recording of Chitralekha (1964). During that phase, I had gone to Karta's place one day accompanied by the director of Air India, Sabyasachi Ghosh. Karta wasn't well, and I found Rahul playing a duggi, and singing, Arrey yaar meri tum bhi ho gazab. He was deeply involved in the singing, so much so that his physical movements were in synch with the tala of the song. I also saw Maruti Rao there, sitting with the tabla.

'It was clear that Rahul had composed it, although it was later released in his father's name.

'The next day, we went to the recording at Mehboob Studio. Dev Anand, who was advised not to smoke, was constantly borrowing cigarettes from Mr. Ghosh. We were also shown some rushes of Guide. During the rehearsal of the song, the ending was changed by Kishore. Dev wasn't also satisfied with the arrangement and remarked—"Something is missing."

'I said to Dev Anand, "Is it the accordion?"

'He said, "Yes, the accordion." Rahul did not like my intervening in this fashion one bit, and accosted me: "Did you say something about the accordion?"

'Finally, the accordion was excluded from the song.'

On the flip side, one gets to hear the mukhda and the first interlude of Pancham's acclaimed, Aja piya tohe pyaar doon (Baharon Ke Sapne, 1967) in the form of a santoor-flute duet in the background score of Teen Deviyan. Pandit Hariprasad Chaurasia, who played the flute in the background piece, recalled that the song had already been composed when he and Pandit Shiv Kumar Sharma were asked to play the tune. Although it is difficult, rather impossible to confirm whether the song was composed for *Teen Deviyan* or *Baharon Ke Sapne*, the use of short, intricate phrases indicated that it could have been the handiwork of senior Burman.

Classical musicians, Shiv Kumar Sharma and Hari Prasad Chaurasia were regulars with the Burmans. Apart from playing for songs, there are multiple instances of them playing strains of a song/s either on the flute or santoor in the background scores of many films. While Sachinda was rather secretive about his tunes, Pancham had no such issues. He used them frequently, examples being the tune of *Aaj unse pehli mulaquat hogi* (*Paraya Dhan*, 1971), played by Shiv Kumar Sharma in *Pyar Ka Mausam* (1969), or Hari Prasad Chaurasia playing a slow version of *Bahon mein chale aao* (*Anamika*, 1973), in *Caravan* (1971).

The film used the real names of a few actors—I.S. Johar, Nanda, and Kalpana (who played herself in the film). Dev Anand was named Dev Dutt Anand. In real life, Dev Anand was Dharam Dev Anand (Dharam Dev was later used in the film, *Bullet*, 1976). Somehow, several journalists began labelling Dev Dutt as his original name and it stuck. Dev Anand did write to quite a few scribes, but in vain, and had to clarify this in writing in his autobiography which was published in 2007.

A case of misplaced identity....which was also the subject of the next Dev–Burman film.

Jewel Thief

Throughout the mid-1960s and well into the 1970s, S.D. Burman was one of the few composers who'd succeeded in adding several layers to his oeuvre. He obviously had the talent, but it was his ability to adapt to the changing times which was most admirable, considering he was offering stiff competition to composers half his age, including his son.

After the release of *Bhoot Bangla* in April 1965, Pancham went on a vacation to Darjeeling, where he met his future wife, and the two got engaged and later had a civil marriage. Dev Anand was summoned to break the news to Pancham's parents and although they would have preferred a middle class Bengali girl, Rita found ready acceptance into the Burman household. She moved in to Lino Minar on 15th Cross road, where Pancham would stay occasionally.

The Burmans decided to celebrate their son's marriage and held a lavish party at the Turf Club, which was well attended by prominent members of the Bombay film industry. Meera was not only a gracious hostess, but also a loving mother-in-law who gifted almost all the jewellery that she had received from the royal family of Tripura to her daughter-in-law, Rita.

Pancham began his new life at Lino Minar. By mid-1966 with *Teesri Manzil*, Pancham's career had taken wings. S.D. Burman, who had previously asked Goldie to avail of Pacham's services for Navketan's next film, *Jewel Thief*, started work on the film himself. Pancham was busy with other assignments, but he continued to assist his father.

The first song to be composed for *Jewel Thief* was *Rulake gaya sapna mera*. Shailendra, fresh from his success with the Anands in *Guide*, was the lyricist by default. Initially, he had written the lines as *Rulake gaya sapna tera*. Vijay Anand suggested the change from the word '*tera*' to '*mera*', to indicate how Shalini (Vyjayanthimala), through her lament was actually attracting the attention of Vinay (Dev Anand). Burman used a melancholic tune with a touch of mystery to add body to it.

This major scale composition was one of his classiest ever. The ending on the ninth/second signified a kind of abruptness, as if the lyrics were waiting in the wings. The antara had six lines, separated by a sigh, '*hai*', after two. The first couplet expressed a deep sense of depression, which spiralled into resignation in the third line. The next two lines were based on high notes, enouncing torment and helplessness. Burman used his trademark komal *ni* as the first note of the fourth line, which was remarkable as the song was in a major scale with the sporadic application of teevra *ma*.

The next song was none other than, *Hothon mein aisi baat*. Vijay Anand would often arrive at Shailendra's home to get him to write to the tune composed by Burman, but he would be told that the poet wasn't in. It was only later when Goldie discovered that Shailendra was actually badly stuck with *Teesri Kasam* (1966). Dinesh Chandra Shailendra in an interview with the authors, said that his 'father was cheated by some people and lost a lot of money in the process of making the film. Everyone except my father made money from *Teesri Kasam*. My father was a creative person and did not know a thing about business. He had no clue about producing a film. Whatever he knew was what he had seen. So, when it actually came down to shooting, everyone—the production controller, the production manager, etc., were skimming off money. Even a simple thing like the bulls that were used for the cart— he was advised to buy a pair and put them in a *tabela* because getting a pair of bulls for every shot created a problem of continuity. He bought the bulls and within a week, the owner of the *tabela* was sitting outside our house saying that both his bulls were dead! Everyone was making money and my father was footing the bill.'

Goldie remembered how Shailendra would be extremely depressed, and gradually began drinking heavily. Once, after being told that Shailendra was not at home, Goldie sent in a chit saying that the poet shouldn't get caught up in depression and should get a hold of himself. It was then that Shailendra had walked out to meet him.

Alas, Shailendra was unable to finish writing *Hothon mein aisi baat* and the Anands went to Majrooh Sultanpuri for help. The song had to be shot in a strict time-frame—only in the month of October, and time was running out. Although Goldie acknowledged Majrooh as a competent poet-lyricist, he was of the opinion that unlike Shailendra, Majrooh lacked the ability to express profound thoughts in simple, straightforward words. But then, Goldie also felt that a film like *Jewel Thief* did not mandate songs with a high dependency on lyrics. After all, *Jewel Thief* was no *Guide*.

Within three or four months of Majrooh replacing Shailendra, the latter, distraught with the world and its ways, died of cirrhosis of the liver on Raj Kapoor's birthday, 14 December. His son Dinesh said, 'Financially *Teesri Kasam* was not much of a setback because, according to people I knew, the kind of money he was charging to write songs, he could have easily recovered the money in six months. But it wasn't his financial investment that had gone wrong—it was his investment in people. It was more of a heart-break than monetary loss. When he saw that people very close to him had let him down at this critical juncture in life, that's when he lost interest in living.'

Shailendra's loss was not only a big loss for the industry, it was a personal loss for S.D. Burman, as the duo had created some of the best songs together. Although for most part of his career, Shailendra was largely associated with Shankar–Jaikishan and Salil Chowdhury among mainstream composers, his association with S.D. Burman in *Kala Bazaar*, *Bandini* and *Guide* was unforgettable. Burman recalled him in his autobiography, saying: 'Shailendra's memory haunts me. Losing him has led to a great loss in my creativity.'

If Dev romanced three women in *Teen Deviyan*, in *Jewel Thief*, he increased the number to five. Except Anju Mahendru, all the others knew how to dance, and the film had one dance for each. *Hothon mein aisi baat* was the climactic dance, and despite being an accomplished Bharatanatyam dancer, it was alleged that Vyjanthimala had found the complicated steps so difficult that she had to be coached by Saroj Khan, who was then assisting the veteran dance director, Sohanlal.

The song used a plethora of drums—the tabla tarang, the Burmese drum, including a drum specific to Sikkim which was brought at the special insistence of Sachin Dev Burman. Pancham, who partly supervised the rhythm section, used his 'chapki beat' (typically associated with the Burmans), which was played on the khol by Sudarshan Adhikari.[1] It was a mammoth affair, recalled percussionist Amrut Rao, who was one of the tabla players and had to also play the gong with his fist as the mallet was missing.[2]

Yet another dance item, this time performed by Faryal, only had instrumental music, in a mix of Indian melody, jazz, with the bossa nova creeping in almost silently, and tapering off with Arabic belly dance music. However the dance paled in comparison to the song featuring Helen (who was also called so in the film), *Baithe hain kya unke paas*, which used the twin-track recording, like Pancham had done for *Kya janu sajan* in *Baharon Ke Sapne*, in 1967. This was followed by a rendezvous, set up with the 'imaginary' 'Jewel Thief', and had one of the most spectacular pieces of the Blues music in the background.

A Dev Anand film had to have romantic duets, and Burman gave two—one sugar-coated and the other, impish. The saccharine sweet, *Dil pukare* (Rafi–Lata) was probably the first song to be shot in Sikkim, after Dev had received the go-ahead from the Chogyal in January 1967. A throwback to simple melody, Burman remodelled one of his lesser known songs, *Tasveeren banti hai*, especially for the last three lines of the antara of *Dil pukare* (which also happened to be the first Lata–Rafi duet post their patch up, which happened a few years after they had a tiff about royalties and decided not to sing together).

The playful Kishore–Lata duet, *Aasmaan ke neeche* displayed an interesting Burman trait; the mukhda was on a minor scale, while the antara hinged on major. Prior to the beginning of the song, Dev in response to Lata's humming of the tune, sings '*Pyaar ka jahan, banake chalen...*' in the style of a qawwali. Come to think of it, with a different percussion arrangement, the metre could well have fitted a qawwali!

Kishore Kumar's flamboyant, *Yeh dil na hota bechara* was composed following a viewing of *The Bridge On The River Kwai* (1957) by S.D. Burman and Pancham, who attempted to remodel the marching track of the film. The lyrical inspiration was probably from Majrooh's own lines in *Likha hai teri aankhon mein* (*Teen Deviyan*)—*Abhi talak yeh dil hai bechara*. Composed originally as the title song for Guru Dutt's *Baharen Phir Bhi Aayengi* (according to Raju Bharatan), this remains an iconic number most befitting for the carefree, freewheeling character that Dev Anand was in the film. The use of the fishing rod was a throwback to the song, *Akela hoon mein* (*Baat Ek Raat Ki*). Dev Anand's funny act of walking down the road right in front of Tanuja's car, with the actual intent of getting to know her, finally bears fruit as she falls for his charms, albeit after a few more encounters. Later in the film, she boldly decides to seduce her lover, and one should doff one's hat to the Anands for making a statement at a time when India was not only reluctant, but extremely conservative when it came to women's sexuality.

Filmed indoors with an interesting use of colours and billowing curtains, *Raat akeli hai*, like *Hothon mein aisi baat*, is among the most popular songs in the film. Burman complimented Asha Bhosle on her spectacular breath control, especially in the line where she had to sing in a high pitch and then hold the tune. Asha mentioned how while teaching her the song, Sachinda had suggested that she recalls a childhood game, where one starts speaking softly in the ear, as if whispering a secret, and then screams suddenly! In his autobiography, Burman recalled this song as follows:

There was a requirement for a new type of score in Navketan's *Jewel Thief*. The film had two heroines. Tanuja, one of them, was of spirited character, uninhibited and bubbly. Vijay Anand needed a special song for her. Normally, the Hindi song follows the asthyai-antara-asthayi pattern. For Tanuja, I took a different approach, and scored the music for a blank verse. I tried to relate to the character through the tune. The song sequence finds the impetuous heroine singing—'*Raat akeli hai, bujh gaye diye, aake mere paas, kaano mein mere, jo bhi chahe kahiye*'. My tune had the heroine crooning the first few words before suddenly going very loud and high in the line, *Jo bhi chahe kahiye*.

Raat akeli hai went on to become a benchmark for 'seduction' songs in the industry. Three years down the line, when Goldie was directing *Johnny Mera Naam* (1970), he advised the film's composers, Kalyanji–Anandji to base the score for *Husn ke laakhon rang* on *Raat akeli hai*. The brothers did a good job, using the standard progression in Indian classical music—*sa-re-ga, re-ga-ma, ga-ma-pa* for the soft start, to suddenly reach a crescendo at *pa-dh-ni*, and then return to *ga*. The antara however failed to live up to the promise of the mukhda and the song would have fallen by the wayside had it not been for Padma Khanna's fabulous dancing.

This point begs a significant intervention to highlight the style of composing for Hindi cinema—the importance of antara in the overall scheme of a song. Generally speaking, producers and directors were and are perhaps still prone to laying maximum emphasis on a hummable mukhda. This was reiterated by the late Manmohan Desai while discussing his working relationship with composers Laxmikant–Pyarelal, and could be taken as an industry standard for an average Hindi film. The standard mind-set is that the public does not remember the antara; the mukhda is what one normally remembers.[3]

S.D. Burman was a composer who refused to be slotted in the mukhda stereotype. He used to accept limited assignments in order to avoid sounding repetitive, and this also helped him focus on his work. On most occasions, at least till the mid-Fifties, he would compose alone, and even his wife, Meera Dev Burman wasn't allowed to intervene. Later, if needed, he would also put his assistants to work, as confirmed by Rahul Dev Burman in the interview, "My God, That's My Tune", in the *Filmfare* magazine, dated June 16–30, 1984:

> He had a habit of composing the mukhda and passing on the antara to his two assistants (Jaidev Verma, Suhrid Kar) and me. A sort of healthy competition prevailed while we tried to outdo each other. My father would choose the best and sometimes I scored too.

For *Jewel Thief* however, Dev Anand went on record[4] to say that it was Pancham who had composed most of the mukhdas, while Burman completed the antaras. Manohari Singh added in an interview to the authors, 'Dada would not interfere in the orchestration process, though he could have placed restrictions on the length of the music pieces and the use of instruments.'[5] The film credits both Basu Chakravarty and Manohari Singh as arrangers.

The music of *Jewel Thief* was representative of Brand Burman: a wondrous mix of east and west, of experience and youth. Not only was the film shot at multiple locations, from the outskirts of Bombay to the hills of Sikkim, the storyline was not the run-of-the-mill kind—its complexities needed careful handling. It therefore took more time than usual and added to that were other issues as well. Raj Kumar, who was originally selected to play the character of the jewel thief, refused, and the role went to Ashok Kumar who had just recovered from a heart ailment and was obviously very strict about following his daily routine. The film began in mid-1966 and received the censor certificate on 27 October 1967, and during these one-and-a-half years, S.D. Burman did not have a single release. The press wasn't paying any heed to this long hiatus, but several of his fans did wonder why Burman was out of circulation despite his marvellous musical score for *Guide*.

But alas that was exactly the reason for his temporary oblivion—after *Guide* was ignored by *Filmfare*, he almost bowed out of limelight. But even this phase was temporary, and thanks to Lata Mangeshkar who announced a show to celebrate her twenty-five years in playback singing. The show was organised by the Lata Mangeshkar Satkar Samiti, and was held at the Rang Bhawan in Mumbai on 25 April 1967, and when Lata requested Burman to conduct the orchestra, he did it with élan.

Several male playback singers, except Rafi, Talat and Kishore were present at the show. Mukesh, Manna Dey, Hemanta, Bhupinder, Asha Bhosle and Lata—all of them sang Burman's melodies. The composer stepped in as well and sang *Wahan kaun hai tera*.

Four days later, S.D. Burman was yet again called upon to conduct the orchestra for a show where he was the main guest of honour. It was 29 April, and the Bharati Kala Manram had organised an S.D. Burman evening at the Rang Bhawan; the singers included Rafi and Talat as well. There was a huge demand for Burman's *Wahan kaun hai tera*, which he was forced to sing halfway through the show. Manna Dey sang *Poocho na kaise*; *Pyaar ki aag mein*; and *Kisne chilman se maara*. Lata had to do a repeat of *Aaj phir jeene ki tamanna hai*. Rafi, who was conspicuous by his absence at the Lata Silver Jubilee show, garlanded her on stage and complimented her for completing twenty-five years in the industry.

The Lata wave continued—she was a guest presenter on *Jaimala*, the popular show on AIR, and played her sixteen favourite songs. Four out of the list—*Poocho na kaise, O jane wale ho sake toh, Teri duniya mein jeene se,* and *Wahan kaun hai tera,* were from the Burman collection. Therefore, despite less work, Sachin Dev remained in circulation through shows, and his songs which were repeatedly played on radio.

The year however ended on a low note for him. His good friend and fellow musician, Roshan with whom he'd shared many evenings, died suddenly. On 16 November 1967, Roshan and his wife Ira had plans to attend the premiere of a film. However, on receiving news from his friend, Hari Walia that his film *Latt Saheb* (1967) had opened to a good reception in Indore, Roshan gave the premiere passes to his two sons, Rakesh and Rajesh, and proceeded to meet his friend. Walia returned to his flat after an outing in an upbeat mood, greeted Roshan who was in the drawing room and poured him a drink. He cracked a joke, which made Ira giggle from ear to ear! Roshan, who was in a jovial mood, got up to greet his friend, and sat down immediately, without having spoken a word. Within a few seconds, he was dead.

Rajesh and Rakesh were at the premiere of *Jewel Thief.*

SD

In his mid-Sixties, Sachin Dev Burman had become adept at changing trends in film music. Rahul Dev Burman, whose identity as 'RD' was in synch with his music, defined his father as, 'More modern than me.' No wonder S.D. Burman came to be referred as just, 'SD'.

The Watershed Years

1969

In the 1960s, C. Mohan was a famous art designer in the Hindi film industry. His expertise lay in creating logos for publicity material. In October 1967, while *Jewel Thief* was in its final stages of completion, Mohan decided to produce a film starring Siv Kumar and Zeb Rehman, and signed up the music director duo, Sonik–Omi.

But little did he know that he was about to make a significant contribution to the history of Hindi cinema.

The late Sachin Bhowmick in several interviews with the authors between April–December 2010, spoke about the genesis of another film. 'This was just after I had completed writing *Anuradha* (1960), which was directed by Hrishikesh Mukherjee. Pancham and I went to see *To Each His Own* (1948), starring Olivia de Havilland. It struck me that the story could be easily adapted into Hindi as it was a woman-oriented script. I wrote the basic plot and took it to Hrishida. He found it interesting and suggested we look for a leading lady. Suchitra Sen was our first choice, but many of her films had bombed at the box office. Hrishida didn't want to risk taking an actress who was not accepted by the Hindi-speaking audience. He then suggested Nutan, who at that time was in the family way. We also thought of some other actresses like, Nargis and Mala Sinha, but somehow nothing came to fruition. Meanwhile, the story was lying with me.

'Around six–seven years later, when we were shooting *An Evening in Paris* (1967), I narrated the story to Shakti Samanta, who seemed to like it. He said that the story reminded him of his mother and her struggles. After *An Evening in Paris*, Shaktida was planning to make a quickie, as his grand plan was to ultimately shoot a film in the US, which would've taken time.

'Meanwhile, he had signed a new hero who had made it through a talent contest where Shaktida was a judge and hence, he was legally bound to offer him a film at a pre-negotiated rate of 35,000 rupees. Shaktida was also scouting for a new actress to play the leading lady. I remember, I had also met Aparna Sen at that time, but nothing worked out.

'Next, Shaktida asked Rinku (Sharmila Tagore), who accepted the film without any preconditions.

'Shankar and Jaikishan, who had scored the music for Shaktida's *An Evening in Paris* were expensive and it was then that Shaktida suggested we go to S.D. Burman. Sachinda told Shaktida that he had increased his price as well. "Last time (*Insaan Jag Utha*) you paid me 75,000 rupees. That won't do." Shaktida said that he was willing to shell out a lakh. Sachinda jumped. "What, one lakh? Just see what music I give for your film."

'Actually, Burmanda had thought that he would ask for 80,000, just 5,000 more than the last time. He was that simple a person. With him, money was never a question. If he found a script which had the potential for music, he would accept readily.

'Now came the task of narrating the story. I sat with Sachinda and gave him an outline of the plot. "What is the film called?" he asked. The working title at the time was, *Subah Pyar Ki*, which was derived from the last line of the mukhda of *Raat ke humsafar*, a song written by Shailendra for *An Evening in Paris*.

'"*Cholbe na*" (Won't do), said Sachinda.

'A few days later at Natraj Studios, Shaktida met C. Mohan for the publicity design. Mohan also suggested using a simple, non-Urdu sounding name.

'Shaktida remembered that Mohan was also producing a film. He asked him about it and Mohan said that he was yet to start work on it. Shaktida then asked him what he was planning to call it. *Aradhana*, said Mohan.

'The title was already registered and after some persuasion, Shaktida bought it from C. Mohan.'

Aradhana was reborn with a new story, a new director, two new actors and a new composer. However, the publicity designer remained the same—C. Mohan stretched the letters *d* and *h* in *Aradhana* to create the shape of a lotus.

But *Aradhana* had more hurdles to cross....

The monumental success of *Jewel Thief* saw SD getting back into the social circuit. He wasn't in any case a party person, but that year he made an exception and even attended a New Year party, dressed in his traditional Tripura attire. His new-found enthusiasm would translate into vibrant music in the years to come.

Meanwhile, the Bombay film industry was facing some turbulence. In early 1968, an 'Action Committee' was formed by a group of small-time producers with the intent of controlling the production cost of films. The group laid down a set of rules for producers, distributors, theatre owners and other allied bodies related to film production, including the CMDA. However, when producers and theatre owners protested against the diktat, yet another group was formed by the set of small producers who also roped in technicians, actors and several other people related to the profession. This they named as the 'Film Sena'.

In March 1968, the Film Sena along with the Action Committee took a firm decision—the production and delivery of prints to cinema halls in Bombay was to be discontinued. The theatre owners tried opposing this, but had to eventually concede by stopping the exhibition of films from 5 April 1968.

Many meetings later, there rose conflicts within the Film Federation of India (FFI), an apex body which had members from various other bodies as well. The difference of opinion within its constituent members in turn led to the resignation of the Indian Motion Pictures Producers Association (IMPPA) and the Film Producers Guild of India from the FFI. The movement was finally called off on 24 April.

Owing to this series of meetings and the consternation expressed by several members thereof, the industry suffered terrible losses. For instance, in contrast to 104 films certified by the Censor Board in 1967, only eighty-nine were granted certification in 1968. Amongst several others, Shakti Samanta bore a severe brunt as *An Evening in Paris* had no screenings for almost a month, and led to massive losses. This in turn had a cascading effect and delayed his schedule for *Aradhana*. The muhurat was finally held on 1 June 1968 at the Famous Studios, months after the film was planned.

After the terrible impasse in the industry, the first film to go on floors was O.P. Ralhan's *Talash*. SD was chosen to compose its music, which had Ralhan's brother-in-law, actor Rajendra Kumar in the lead.

The story narration of *Talash* was held at the Jet. RD, who was assisting his father in the film, was in attendance taking notes. Even as the story was gradually unfolding, Pancham felt uneasy. The reason being that he was doing a film called *Anokha Pyar* for Hrishikesh Mukherjee, which had the same storyline! Ralhan and SD pacified him, and the father and son decided not to be influenced by each other.

SD and Pancham met almost everyday even when the latter was living with his wife at Lino Minar. SD would take his car along to Juhu during his morning walk and would stop at his son's place for tea on his way back[1].

Meera Dev Burman knew that the son and father met frequently; it was the daughter-in-law who was the problem. Cliched as it may sound and a theme which has routinely obsessed filmmakers and TV shows, there was a problem between Rita the *bahu* or daughter-in-law and Meera, the *saas* or mother-in-law. The father and son were aware of the strain between the two women, but devised ways to keep their relationship going.

At the time, Meera had also expressed her desire to relaunch her career and get back to singing. In the 1950s, she had asked her mother to play mediator, who conveyed the message to her husband.

'Why? Do you feel I am not taking good care of her?' was how SD reacted to his mother-in-law. One of the main reasons for Meera wanting to revive her career was because of the empty nest syndrome—Pancham had moved out and was on his own, and her husband was anyway preoccupied with work. In 1965, Meera wrote a few songs in Bengali expecting her husband to compose them. However, the renowned lyricist, Pulak Bandyopadhyay, also wanted to write lyrics for SD's Puja songs. SD suggested that Pancham compose tunes for Bandyopadhyay. RD composed eight tunes and offered Bandyopadhyay to choose any two. *Amar malati lata* and *Ami boli tomaye*, sung by Lata, were selected and heralded RD's entry into the world of Durga Puja songs. On his part, if SD facilitated his son's initiation into the world of Puja songs, Meera also had her desire fulfilled a few years later[2].

However till much of 1968, SD somehow never found the time for his wife's songs. According to music collector, Sanjay Sengupta[3], the first published songs were only released in September 1968, *Bhongite tobo nesha* and *Nitol payer rinik jhinik* as part of record number, 7 EPE 1071. While the second song was immensely popular, two songs written by Meera in 1969, *Shono go dokhin o hawa* (later remade into *Khayi hai re humne kasam, Talash,* 1969) and *Borne gondhe chhonde geetitey* (also remade as *Phoolon ke rang se, Prem Pujari,* 1969) were monumental successes. Meera continued to write for her husband till 1973, after which SD stopped recording in Bengali, closing the chapter with, *Shey ki amar dushman dushman* and *Ki kori ami ki kori.*

On Republic Day in 1969, SD was awarded the Padmashri by the Government of India. While this was heartening news for him and his family, there was a storm of protest in Bengal that he deserved a higher award. Amongst many, Sachin Ganguly also voiced his protest at what was being viewed as the government's lackadaisical attitude towards one of the most accomplished artists of Bengal. Even as the rumour mills worked overtime, it was felt that he had been punished for disassociating himself from AIR after the harmonium was banned at radio stations by Jawaharlal Nehru. SD, not to be swayed by emotional outbursts, handled it with dignity and tacit disapproval. In his response to Ganguly, he wrote:

> I understand you all love me too much, and agree that this act
> might have pained you no end. It is but natural. However, I
> wish to remain beyond petty protests based on, "What I have
> received; what I should have received; or if I have been deprived
> of genuine awards". I have received immense love, respect and
> adoration throughout, and have spent my life in a very simple

manner serving the purpose of music. I wish to continue in this manner for the rest of my life. Please do not feel hurt by the fact that I have been deprived of legitimate recognition....[4]

Although his response was carefully worded, there was no doubt that he was hurt. Years of struggle, often neglect, unrealised dreams and a sense of resentment finally made him pour his heart out in his autobiography titled *Sargamer Nikhad*. In the Indian classical music tradition, *nikhad* is the seventh note, and by ascribing the note to himself, SD was pointing towards having lived an incomplete life. A man who was striving to complete the 'sargam' or the seven notes, but had only succeeded in reaching the penultimate note, as it were.

A few weeks after the Padmashri, SD threw a party for the media at the Jet. He was in a good mood and deviating from usual practice, even sang a few numbers from his yet-to-be-released films. He was known to be secretive about his compositions and never sang them before their release, fearing pilferage of tunes. But this time around, he gave a sample of his future work to the media and it was as if he was readying himself for a spectacular innings in the coming months.

The first release came four months later, and was called *Jyoti*. Niranjan Pal (son of freedom fighter, Bipin Chandra Pal), who worked as a script writer for Bombay Talkies, had written a story called *Faith of a child*, which highlighted the conflict between atheism and belief. London's Lotus film company had already made it into a three-reel film in 1915. The film was later made in Hindi as *Jyoti*, partly in black and white and the rest in colour.

However, the movie was a disaster and even a competent actor like Sanjeev Kumar failed to save it. The plot was bizarre, the acting even worse, despite a senior and rather accomplished actor like Abhi

Bhattacharya, who was ridiculously shown to be reincarnated as Sarika (who was credited under her chosen name when she played a boy—"Moppet Suraj"). The lead actress of the film, Libi Rana aka Nivedita, was probably one of the most beautiful women of her times, but that was her only claim to fame.

Jyoti's music was however luminous. The most celebrated song, *Sunn munne mere* by Lata Mangeshkar, is probably the simplest, yet arguably the most exquisite lullaby in the history of Hindi film music. Traces of Chaplin's *Limelight* theme notwithstanding, the song was as original as one could expect from SD at his best.

The *Limelight* theme had multiple adaptations in Hindi cinema, but none among them, including Salil Chowdhury's *Zindagi hai kya* (*Maya*, 1962) and Pancham's *Tum meri zindagi mein* (*Bombay to Goa*, 1972) had as delectable a mukhda as the one from *Jyoti*. The antara of *Sunn munne mere* was later reused by Pancham in Kishore–Lata's *Kali palak teri gori* in *Do Chor* (1972).

But the song which hit directly at the solar plexus was *Soch ke yeh gagan jhume*. Among the best of Manna–Lata duets of all times, it is comparable with *Yeh raat bheegi bheegi* (*Chori Chori*, 1956); *Bheegi chandni* (*Suhagan*, 1964); or *Kanha bole na* (*Sangat*, 1976), amongst others. In this, Manna and Lata are engaged in a healthy competition, and Lata's poise is matched note for note by Manna's subtlety and uncanny inflections. SD allowed both singers enough latitude to express their emotions, which they did with consummate ease.

The song was about a childless couple who are seen lying in a park under a moonlit evening sky. The woman looks ecstatic for she has just been told that she is pregnant. Apparently, SD was struggling with the tune for days when one day he got an early morning brainwave—from Himangshu Dutta's raga Pushpachandrika—and rang up the film's director, Dulal Guha. After listening to the tune, Guha returned home a few hours later, and told his family how Sachinda had created a cracker of a tune.[5]

Anand Bakshi wrote the lyrics for *Jyoti*, his second film with SD. The first assignment was in 1964 for an untitled film which was shelved after two songs had been recorded.[6]

Jyoti's score had two SD songs in the background—*Wahan kaun hai tera* (*Guide*) and *Baaje na baanshi go* (basic Bengali song, 1949), probably the only instance of a composer using two of his own songs as short motifs in a film.

A few months after *Jyoti's* release, SD received his first National Award for playback singing. It was for *Aradhana.*

Aradhana was slated for an all-India release on 24 October 1969. It had a few special screenings before that, including one for Mohammad Hidayatullah, who was then the acting President post V.V. Giri's resignation. However, it was ultimately released in November 1969 in some circuits, and in January 1970 in Bengal.

The impact of the film was seismic. It gave birth to Hindi cinema's first superstar—Rajesh Khanna. Kishore Kumar, in his new avatar of an independent, standalone playback singer, became his voice.

The music of the film has been discussed threadbare so many times, that there is hardly anything new to add to its brilliance. *Aradhana* was HMV's first Golden Disc in the 1970s and later celebrated several Golden Jubilees across the country. SD came to Calcutta for its premiere and visited every theatre, starting with Menoka near Rabindra Sarobar, and received a thunderous ovation. There were viewers who sought his autograph on 100 rupee notes, but SD being the man he was, refused to oblige his fans! He was then asked to sing a song by the delirious crowd, and he did oblige this time by singing two lines of *Kahe ko roye*. Next, the manager of Lotus cinema took him to Chaya cinema at Maniktala in north Calcutta where audiences had queued up with records and record covers of *Aradhana* to have them autographed by him[7]. Similar to *Guide*, publicity managers capitalised majorly on *Aradhana*'s songs—advertisements began appearing with the line of a song. For instance[8]:

January 24 – *Roop tera mastana*
January 25 – *Safal hogi teri Aradhana*
January 26 – (no papers were printed, it being Republic Day)
January 27 – *Mere sapno ki rani*
January 28 – *Baagon mein bahaar hai*
January 29 – *Chanda hai tu*
January 30 – *Kora kagaz tha yeh mann mera*

The winter of 1969 and early 1970 became even more memorable for SD, because on Christmas Eve that year, East Bengal drubbed Mohun Bagan 3–0 in the finals of the Rovers Cup at the Cooperage stadium in Bombay.

While there was crazy appreciation for the music of the film, there were also several controversies about the exact contribution of the Burman duo in *Aradhana*. There were also stories about how SD had first recorded the songs with Rafi, after which the singer had gone off for a pilgrimage to Mecca. Some more stories were added to the construct, and it was said that as SD had fallen sick, RD had stepped in and along with Kishore Kumar had completed the recordings.

Much of this is obviously hearsay. There is no written evidence of SD having chosen Rafi as the voice of Rajesh Khanna. The first and only choice was always Kishore Kumar. The recording dates which were shown to the authors by Rakesh, son of Anand Bakshi, clearly indicate that the Kishore songs were recorded earlier. They were[9]:

Roop tera mastana – 17 June 1968
Mere sapno ki rani – 28 August 1968
Kora kagaz tha yeh mann mera – 30 July 1968

While the Rafi songs were recorded on:

Gun guna rahe hain bhanware – 11 October 1968
Baagon mein bahaar hai – 5 February 1969

However, the reason why SD shifted to Rafi for *Gun guna rahe hain bhanware* and *Baagon mein bahaar hai* is not known. In all probability, he may have composed these songs for a different actor. Rajesh Khanna was initially chosen to play only one of the lead roles as hero; the son's character was slated to be played by another actor. The double role angle was introduced much later into the script by Shakti Samanta. By end-1968 -early 1969, Kishore Kumar was also extremely preoccupied with Madhubala's deteriorating health.

Therefore, all the conjuncture involving the music of *Aradhana* is probably unfounded. As was the norm, it was SD who decided on the singer. In his group, nobody interjected, unless it was a suggestion which made sense to the patriarch.

Like it had happened during the sitting of *Roop tera mastana*. Bhanu Gupta said it in as many words, 'SD had composed a folksy tune to which RD added frills, making it trendy.'[10] Pancham's friend, Badal Bhattacharya further added: 'RD had the suggestion conveyed to his father through Kishore Kumar.'[11]

During the making of *Mere sapno ki rani*, the guitarist was unable to reproduce the rhythm pattern set by Bhanu Gupta, because of which SD had to cancel the recording. There was pressure from the director, Shakti Samanta whose cast and crew, including Rajesh Khanna and Sujit Kumar were waiting in Darjeeling. At this juncture, RD had stepped in and added a mouth organ motif to the prelude, while Bhupinder Singh played the electric guitar.[12]

Rajesh Khanna[13], who had become a national rage, riding on his mannerisms inspired by Rock Hudson (his crinkling of eyes, shaking of head and dancing style), was astute enough to understand that Kishore Kumar and the Burmans, especially RD, were critical for his success. In the following years, there were instances when he would refuse anyone except Kishore as his playback. RD and Khanna had worked before in *Baharon Ke Sapne* (1967), but became better acquainted during *Aradhana*. Soon, the two began to meet frequently and spent many evenings together, which would begin with Solan Number One, and ended with Johnny Walker Blue Label!

SD kept a safe distance from his son's parties, but he did throw one after the success of *Aradhana* and also invited the press. The adulation kept pouring in, even as he was faced with a controversy from singer Subir Sen, who said that *Mere sapno ki rani* was copied from the international hit, *Tequila*.[14] SD refuted Subir's claims and defended himself by accepting that he had indeed been inspired, but from a *baich* (a long boat rowed by a group of boatmen) song of Bengal, and saw no reason to fall back on foreign tunes.[15]

The Filmfare Award eluded SD yet again. However, when Kishore Kumar won the Filmfare Best Singer award for *Roop tera mastana*, and SD himself won the prestigious National award, everything was forgotten. Today, forty-nine years later, when most of the songs from *Jeene Ki Raah*, which received the Filmfare award for best music in 1969, are forgotten, *Aradhana* remains an eternal classic.

There are a few riveting nuggets about *Aradhana*'s music which added to its uniqueness in more ways than one. For instance, SD had this strange habit of calling up playback singers weeks before the recording schedule, and putting down the phone immediately after hearing their voice. This helped him to judge their vocal condition. One day, he called up Kishore Kumar quite late at night and started teaching him *Kora kagaz tha yeh mann mera*. Both SD and Kishore were in the habit of retiring early at night, and waking up at the crack of dawn. Kishore was startled by this phone call, which surprisingly did not end with hanging up, and he was actually called upon to sing along! But Kishore was sleepy and kept yawning even as he sang his lines till SD let him go back to sleep.[16]

For the recording of *Kahe ko roye*, RD had gathered twelve musicians, while SD had eleven in mind. The father refused to budge and the extra musician was eventually paid off and released. SD's penchant for minimalism was non-negotiable, particularly when he was singing. In the same year, *Talash* also had a cracker of a solo by him.[17]

Bhanu Gupta recalled a discussion with SD in the mid-1960s. He went to meet the composer, and found him sketching boxes. 'You see,' explained SD, 'the various boxes represent the listening habits of your audience. One section listens only to classical compositions. Another might listen to rock-and-roll. A third set could be keen about devotional songs. Someone might listen to nursery rhymes, say for example *Twinkle twinkle little star*. Yet another group might love geets, or only ghazals. There are people who only listen to qawwalis. The list goes on. As you would appreciate, Hindi film music has to cater to all categories, as it has a pan-Indian presence. The work of a composer becomes that much difficult.'[18]

Talash was that kind of a film, for which SD composed multiple genre-based songs. It was the most expensive film of the time—'One crore-color colossus, Bigger than the biggest, Larger than life,' read its blurb. The American spelling of 'color' was deliberate to synchronise with brand names such as, Technicolor/Eastmancolor/Gevacolor, etc.

The hype generated around the film was so high that it became one of the first attempted victims of piracy in the history of Hindi cinema! Apparently, it was the handiwork of a gang which in cahoots with unscrupulous lab owners, had smuggled master prints out of the country and made multiple copies of the film, to be sold elsewhere.

After a few weeks, O.P. Ralhan organised a grand premiere for the film at the Apsara theatre on Grant Road in Bombay. An unfounded rumour did the rounds that the organisers planned to shower the venue with flowers thrown from helicopters! The guests included the well-heeled gentry of Bombay, including the Maharaja of Bhavnagar who was accompanied by his wife, his sister, Neila Devi and her husband Shammi Kapoor, the actor.

Despite all the hype surrounding the film, SD was missing from the premiere. 'Ralhan had a wild temperament. SD was uncompromising when it came to his work. They had major differences leading to an acrimonious situation, and SD said he was ready to walk out of the film,'[19] said Pandit Hariprasad Chaurasia to the authors.

The bone of contention was about the choice of a singer for the classical-based number, *Tere naina talash kare hai jisse.* Ralhan had rooted for Mukesh, while SD only wanted Manna Dey. The arguments between the two soon reached an impasse and the recording came to a grinding halt. Although Ralhan later conceded that he was in the wrong, the damage was done. SD was resolute in his decision to not work with Ralhan ever again. For Ralhan's subsequent films, *Hulchul* (1971) and *Bandhe Haath* (1972), he went to RD, who had arranged the songs for *Talash.*[20]

The film was a musical feast. *Palkon ke peeche se* (Rafi–Lata) was a romantic ballad with cyclic notes; *Mera kya sanam* (Asha–Mahendra Kapoor) and *Karle pyaar karle* (Asha) were Western, the former using the bossa nova rhythm, and the latter antaras and interludes where the tonic kept changing. In the traditional folk dance duet sung by Lata and Rafi, *Aaj ko juneli raat ma* (the Nepali words, *juneli raat ma* were actually the brainchild of Manohari Singh), while RD's interjection in Bengali, *Ke jaash re bhati gaan baiya,* was SD's idea. Lata had two solos, *Kitni akeli,* and *Khai hai re humne kasam,* which became one of the biggest hits during the time. SD's solo, *Meri duniya hai, Ma,* the most poignant song in the film, was lost among the more ornately arranged songs, but became a sleeper hit nevertheless.

There is a structural similarity between *Kahe ko roye* (*Aradhana*) and *Khayi hai re.* The antaras of both can be routed to the mukhda of either. That is perhaps the universality of folk. The mukhda of *Khayi hai re* is pentatonic, symptomatic of folk, while the notes, combining both the mukhda and the antara, correspond to raga Barawa—however, the progression of the song does not fit into the progression of the raga. One wonders if this was a deliberate attempt on the part of SD, to fit folk into the framework of a raga.

Despite the excellent music, *Talash* didn't do as well as was expected of it. Amongst other things, an ageing Rajendra Kumar was not the best box office draw, and looked unconvincing as Sharmila Tagore's lover.

As mentioned earlier, RD was also working on *Anokha Pyar* which had striking similarities with *Talash*. Somehow both movies were destined to get embroiled in some controversy or the other, as also delays. After numerous name changes, *Anokha Pyar* was finally released seven years later as *Phir Kab Milogee* (1974). Starring Mala Sinha, who had replaced Rajshree Shantaram (who'd migrated to the US after marrying Greg Chapman) and Biswajeet, it was one of Hrishikesh Mukherjee's weakest films and despite its music and the song, *Kahin karti hogi woh mera intezar*, it failed miserably. But by this time, RD was rocking, and this setback had little or no impact on his career.

Talking of long delays, there was yet another film that SD began working on in 1969. The blueprint of which was readied almost a decade and a half earlier in the late Fifties.

❦

Ramesh Saigal was born in Multan (now in Pakistan) and wanted to be an actor. He joined the reputed Pancholi Pictures in Lahore, but didn't rise up the ladder, ending up only as a continuity assistant. He later shifted to Bombay, and began assisting Shaukat Hussain in films like *Naukar* (1943), *Zeenat* (1945), and *Jugnu* (1947). He also assisted Prithviraj Kapoor at Prithvi Theatres and as director, his first shot featured Bijoya Das, who later married Satyajit Ray.

In mid-1951, Saigal launched a film around the theme of war and peace. Its publicity read, 'The story of a man who challenged God.' Saigal signed up Dilip Kumar and Nutan for the film which he decided to call *Shikwa* (meaning, complaint), and it pretty much turned out to be one! But somehow, Ramesh Saigal was unable to get over his pet project and on 2 March 1959, which was his birthday, he relaunched the film with a new story around childhood love, friendship, and betrayal, and chose the coalfields of Bihar as the setting. Soon thereafter, the film was renamed as *Shola Aur Shabnam*, and the setting shifted from east to the south to Titimati forest in Mysore (Karnataka). The title card read—'And introducing a new romantic team, Tarla and Dharminder (that is how Dharmendra's name was spelt).'

Shola Aur Shabnam was a sensitive story and the filmmaker made no attempts to force-fit it into the usual framework of Hindi commercial cinema. Most importantly, the film had some delightful music by Khayyam—the best being, *Jaaney kya dhoondti rehti hain yeh ankhen mujh mein* by Rafi. But alas, the film failed.

Even the failure of such a beautiful film didn't deter Ramesh Saigal, for he was convinced that he needed to make a few more films. Three years later, he launched yet another film called *Dil Daulat aur Duniya*, with SD as music director. Work began on the film and SD even recorded a duet with Kishore Kumar and Manna Dey, but the jinx was back to haunt Ramesh yet again and the film was soon shelved and the song languished in the cans.

But relentless as he was known to be, Ramesh Saigal refused to give up and in 1969 he began re-working on *Shola Aur Shabnam*— the childhood romance was edited out; the location was shifted to the iron ore mines in south Goa; Abhi Bhattacharya, who had played the sensitive elder brother in the original was given a negative role as a vicious mine-owner. His son, played by Biswajeet, was cast as the kind-hearted friend of the hero, who falls for the leading lady, Sadhana, who in turn, loses her heart to Dharmendra.

Shola Aur Shabnam now renamed as *Ishq Par Zor Nahin*, was released in early 1970. SD was given special coverage as the film's music director, the opening titles had his portrait accompanying his name and rightfully so. The film had outstanding music, especially two superlative solos by

Lata Mangeshkar. *Main toh tere rang rati* was an example of how she had actually bettered SD's original in Bengali, *Koi koi re ghunghur*. *Tum mujhse door chale jana na* had a pentatonic mukhda loosely set to the pattern of raga Todi, while a mix of minor and major progressions in the antara succeeded in creating a fabulous mood of the mysterious and elusive.

However back then, one song which was admired more than the rest was, *Yeh dil diwana hai*. Set on an off-beat rhythm, it heralded the entry of Uttam Singh, who played the fiddle in SD's music group. Recollecting those times, Uttam Singh mentioned during a concert in Calcutta[21] that SD had composed the song using only four notes. He had sung it to him with dummy words, *Dara ra dada ri*, which Singh had initially found very amusing, before it turned into a full-fledged song. The other Lata solo in the film, *O mere bairagi bhanwara* was also unique for its impish tenor and 'catch-me-if-you-can' imagery.

Meanwhile, Ramesh Saigal's luck continued playing havoc, because even *Ishq Par Zor Nahin* came a cropper. Although he had taken enough care by way of pushing the film—advertisements, photo sessions of stars, etc., he still failed to save the film.

Somehow, SD was unaffected by it all. By now he had seen this happening way too often and had learnt to alienate himself from things which were beyond his control. Perhaps destiny was steeling him to face a colossal failure in 1970…

Neeraj

Khemkaran

No one we spoke to could explain what Dev Anand was thinking when he conceived *Prem Pujari* (1970), his first directorial venture. While the Indian Army at Khemkaran (Punjab) was engaged in a strategic war with West Pakistan[1], the absurdity of Dev's version— one-man effort to decimate not only the entire Pakistani force but also an international spy ring—was puzzling to say the least! Much like Khemkaran proved for Pakistan, *Prem Pujari* could well have been Dev Anand's Waterloo, had it not been for his keen sense of music.

It was SD who single-handedly rescued the film, which was anyway jinxed, as it took more than two years to complete. According to well known writer and long time member of Navketan[2], Amit Khanna, a lot of time was wasted in seeking government approvals, considering the film was centered around war.

Dev Anand pulled all stops to promote his directorial debut and brought in HMV to pitch in marketing. A one-page ad was released which showed Dev Anand dressed as a soldier, which was henceforth to be his *Prem Pujari* get-up. Finally, after battling several hiccups, the film was released in Bombay in early 1970.

However in Calcutta, on 27 February 1970, a few Naxalites attacked cinema theatres showing *Prem Pujari*. This led to the film being summarily withdrawn a few days later, starting 3 March 1970, with the then dispensation buckling under pressure. Therefore, not only did *Prem Pujari* have a 'no-show' in the East, it sank without a trace in other parts of India as well.

It is not as if the film had no redeeming features. If the debut of Zaheeda, despite her oomph, came a cropper, Shatrughan Sinha, who also made his debut as a Pakistani Army officer, certainly made an impact. The legendary Amrish Puri also appeared in a cameo, as did the Lebanese actress Nadia Gamal, who performed the most spectacular belly dance ever seen in Hindi cinema. And there was yet another first to the film—*Prem Pujari* welcomed a budding lyricist into the Navketan camp, Gopaldas Saxena aka Neeraj. In a series of interviews to Anuj Kumar[3] of *The Hindu* newspaper, Neeraj spoke about his association with Dev Anand and SD in detail. Certain portions of the interview are reproduced as follows:

Dev and Neeraj had met at a *mushaira* in 1955–56. The actor liked Neeraj's poetry and left with the promise that if Neeraj ever wanted to write for films, he should contact him. "Ten years later, when I saw an advertisement for *Prem Pujari* in a film magazine, I wrote a letter to him mentioning my inclination to write songs for the film. Within ten days, I got a message from him inviting me to Mumbai." Neeraj was then teaching at Dharam Samaj College, Aligarh and took a leave of absence for six days to travel to Bombay. Dev Anand was looking for a poet to fill the vacuum created by the demise of Shailendra. But writing to a situation and a tune is a different ball game altogether, and Neeraj discovered that when Dev Anand introduced him to S.D. Burman. "He (Dev) put me up in a luxurious hotel in Santa Cruz and paid me Rs.1000 even before signing me. The next day, he took me to S.D. Burman, who was apprehensive about a poet's ability to write to tunes and a given situation. Dev Anand said he shouldn't worry. He should give the tune, and if I failed, I would remain his guest for six days and enjoy Bombay. Burmanda gave me a tune and said the song should start with 'Rangeela re'; it (the situation) was about a girl who sees her beloved coming to a party with another girl. It should have the elements of jealousy, satire and frustration in love. I worked the whole night and came up with *Rangeela re tere rang mein, yun ranga hai mera mann, chhaliya re….*" The next day, Neeraj went to Dev Anand's office and showed him what he had written. After reading it, Dev embraced Neeraj; he was astonished at how Neeraj could write the lyrics in one night. "He immediately took me to Burmanda's home and presented me proudly to him and said: 'See, I told you. Neeraj has done it.' When Burmanda listened to the lyrics, he said, 'Dev, you go, now we will sit together.' After he left, Burmanda admitted that he had given me this complex situation to make me give up. After that, we three began to bond."

Shokhiyon mein ghola jaye was taken from his poem, '*Chandni mein ghola jaye*'. It was his take on life, but Dev Anand wanted it to be changed according to the requirement of the film. "I changed the antara completely. *Phoolon ke rang se* was written to tune."

The above-mentioned three songs had the right mix of lyrical elements—love, compassion, eroticism, hurt, hope, and dreams. SD set the tune for one, re-used a traditional tune for another, and had a tune for the third in his kitty.

Rangeela re, in which Neeraj's lyrics complemented the tune, was fast, taut, and rhythmic. The build-up to the mukhda, just after the introductory line, '*Rangeela re, O rangeela*', was with percussion instruments like the triangle, the acoustic guitar played without a plectrum, and with the thumb hitting the area near the sound hole[4], and double bass. The main instruments converged later. The interludes had a distinct mid-Eastern feel. SD's inflections, reproduced perfectly by Lata, had enigmatic elements to it.

The song became a mammoth hit during its time and was played out several times on Binaca Geetmala. Incidentally, it also happened to be Dev Anand's favourite song from the Navketan stable.

Whether the lyrics of *Shokhiyon mein ghola jaye* was a take on life or not is debatable, but it was a melody of a lifetime. Based on Rajasthani folk music (one does feel the strains of the iconic, *Pallo latke* in it), the notes and rhythm exuded romantic love between a man and woman. The poetry had such an amazing metre that it succeeded in creating an imagery whereby one could touch the delicate, albeit surprising elements like the high-pitched humming by Kishore; the solo violin in the second interlude; or the multi-instrument build up to the third antara.

By his own admission, Neeraj's fattest royalty cheques came from the songs he wrote for Dev Anand, one of which was certainly *Phoolon ke rang se*. The magic generated by the collective brilliance of Neeraj, SD and Kishore Kumar was so stunning that it became an anthem for every man who wanted to sing to his new-found love. Apart from the lyrics, the tune was so simple that anyone could sing along, as one can even today, particularly because there is no bifurcation between the mukhda and antara, which makes it easier to recall.

In so far as which was an original version, the Hindi *Phoolon ke rang se* or the Bengali version, *Borne gondhe chhonde geetitey*, here is our explanation and only because this may perhaps put to rest a controversy which has been raging for years now. It is most likely that the SD version was recorded in the second quarter of 1969 to coincide with Durga Puja, three months before the formal release as was the normal practice. Kishore's version may have been recorded simultaneously in mid-1969, or a few months earlier, as he was preoccupied during the last quarter of 1968 and the first two months of the next due to his wife's illness. In April 1969, Kishore went abroad for a series of concerts, and only returned in mid-1969. If one were to go by this sequence of events, it seems quite plausible that SD had completed giving the finishing touches to the Hindi version which finds Dev Anand skittering around Europe, before recording the Bengali song. While the Bengali version has serenity,

Kishore makes the Hindi version sound very youthful, even while adding an additional inflection in the line, *Kayi, kayi baar.* There are the standard SD–Kishore tell-tale signs which is so typical of any romantic number, but *Phoolon ke rang se* is so removed from the commercial fare that it literally lives up to its name, *Prem Pujari*—a worshipper of love.

However, it is widely believed that SD wasn't happy with the lacklustre and uninspiring manner in which Dev had shot the song, and had complained to his team, '*Dekho, Dev ne mere gaane ka kya haal kar diya,*' (Look, what Dev did to my song), recalled Manohari Singh in an interview with the authors in 2009[5]. He also said something which was seconded by Probir Mukherjea[6]—'One is tempted to believe that Burman Dada was inspired by the structure of D.L. Roy's *Dhano dhanye pushpe bhora* for this song. Just a thought, but the merger of the mukhda and the antara, the repetition of catch words, "*pyaar*" and "*kayi baar*" do point to a similarity, both in structure and the thought process.'

The other songs of the film, including the Punjabi folk-dance-based (giddha)—*Dungi tainnu reshmi roomal*; the patriotic, *Taakat watan ki humse hai*; or the Bhupinder–Kishore duet, *Yaaron nilaam karo susti,* neither added musical nor commercial value to the album. Although the last number, featured on Anoop Kumar and Dev Anand did have a novelty element, as it was an interesting pot-pourri of multiple song genres, like geet, ghazal, and the qawwali. Also the song was structured as a mukhda-antara combination, much like *Phoolon ke rang se.*

Oddly, the title song sung by SD, which played out at the start of the film, was quite a departure from his other classics, and is least recollected. But if one wants to revisit it, then one should also appreciate Fali Mistry's cinematographic brilliance which made it such a treat to watch.

Neeraj, who had earlier worked with Roshan, Iqbal Qureshi and Shankar–Jaikishan, had the highest regard for SD and rated him as the best in the industry. Their partnership for the next film was seamless, a carry-over from *Prem Pujari.*

The Lost Gamble

Gambler (1971), produced and directed by Amarjeet under his banner, Nalanda, was Dev Anand's return to the world of noir. It had shades of Raj Kapoor's *Awara* (1951), a story of a young boy who is mercilessly abandoned by his own family. The film's leading lady was Zaheeda, who had played the gangster's moll in *Prem Pujari*. Zaheera, who had made her debut in the Bond film, *On Her Majesty's Secret Service* (1969), made her Bollywood debut with *Gambler*. Film critic Mira Hashmi defined the two ladies, Zaheera and Zaheeda as 'Best stone-faced performances by androids.'[1] Notwithstanding the fabulous production values, *Gambler* was a tepid fare.

But it did little to deter SD and Neeraj, who collaborated once again to deliver a winning score for the film. If the melody of Rafi's last song for Dev under SD's direction, *Mera mann tera pyaasa* was top-notch, Neeraj boldly broke away from the predictable gentleness reserved for love songs and took to introspecting in the last stanza, *Pata nahin kaun hoon mein, kya hoon, aur kahan mujhe jaana....* The nazm-based *Dil aaj shayar* was a poet's soliloquy for the woman of his dreams—SD was obviously in the mood for wizardry, because while he did not once stray beyond the structure, he circumvented the grammar of raga Bhairavi and played with tonics and scales relieving the listener from the monotony which comes with nazms.

As a result, both these songs are still remembered as much for their tunes as they are for the lyrics. However, Dev Anand evoked much mirth in the song for sporting the most ridiculous moustache in the history of Hindi cinema; it was as if a caterpillar had decided to walk across his face and then lost its way half way through!

Two duets, both by Kishore Kumar and Lata Mangeshkar, *Apni hothon ki bansi* and *Chudi nahin yeh mera*, were different in styles. The former was folkish, while the latter had the velocity of a speeding car with a brief detour into bossa nova just ahead of the last antara, with dominating conga beats, and lots of brass, almost reminiscent of *Roop tera mastana*. This lively and buoyant melody introduced the audiences to a new Kishore Kumar post his success in *Aradhana*.

Kaisa hai mere dil tu khiladi, the lesser-known song from the film, was a mix of SD's Bengali song, *Soite paari na bola*, with Kishore doing a rap-like freewheeling.

The film also stood out for its instrumental themes—*Gambler's Dilemma* which became the title score, as well as the leitmotif of the film. The others—*Gambler as Trumpeter*, *Gambler's New Year Party*, *Gambler Faces Another Problem*, and *Gambler in Danger*—were scattered throughout the film. All these pieces were arranged in jazz with RD adding occasional scats. Interestingly, the film had a wedding scene in which Dev leads the band with a trumpet, while the musicians in the background belt out *Mere sapno ki rani*. This song was so popular those days that no wedding in North India was ever complete without people dancing to it!

There were unconfirmed reports that initially the film had run into some trouble with the censors, because Zaheera who played the role of a dancer in it was called Indira (which happened to the first name of the then Indian Prime Minister). Somewhere along the line, her name was conveniently changed to Julie. In what is beyond offensive, in the world of Hindi cinema which has always stereotyped communities and created false, albeit cinematically convincing characters, women of questionable repute were always given fancy names such as, Julie, Nancy, or Peggy!

Of Lyrical Partnerships

In his twenty-five-year-long career, SD had three solid partnerships. The first and the most precious was undoubtedly with Sahir Ludhianvi. In a period spanning six years, their contribution to the world of Hindi film music was deeply valued for its sheer profundity, if not for volume. Next came Majrooh Sultanpuri, whose lyrics helped SD specialise in light-romantic melodies. Finally, Shailendra whose writing lent SD's music considerable heft.

Meanwhile, SD's association with a lyricist like Neeraj added yet another layer to his music—it was fast, rhythmic, easy to remember, had the masses drooling for more, but nowhere was it easy to execute even by those who boasted of professional training.

After *Gambler*, SD and Neeraj had a chance to work with each other yet again. For SD, it was like homecoming—the famous Mukerjis of Filmalaya beckoned after a gap of nearly fourteen years. While the patriarch, Sasadhar Mukerji and his other lesser-known relatives in showbiz had shifted to O.P. Nayyar, Subodh Mukerji was working with the composer duo, Laxmikant–Pyarelal for one of his forthcoming productions. Therefore, the rationale behind signing SD for *Sharmeelee* (1971) was rather puzzling…

Subodh Mukerji's son, Subhash in an interview with the authors in May 2017, spoke about his father shifting from Laxmikant–Pyarelal to SD: 'After the fiasco which happened during *Love Marriage* (1959), my

255

father lost touch with SD. Then it was in 1965 when Pancham came to our house to invite us for his marriage reception. My father honoured his request. On seeing my father at the reception, SD came up to him and after hugging him, apologised. In a matter of a few minutes, the ice melted. *Sharmeelee* went to SD as a result of that reunion. LP had actually done a very good job in both the films they did for us, *Shagird* (1967) and *Abhinetri* (1970). My father was an emotional man, and his friendship with SD did play a role in getting him back for *Sharmeelee*.'[3]

SD recommended Neeraj to the Mukerjis and as was expected, the poet-lyricist delivered on the commitment. The lead actor of the film, Shashi Kapoor, who had had a bleak run in the previous two years, was back in the reckoning with *Sharmeelee*.

The film had four popular tracks. This is not to downplay the other two in the film, as both have a terrific recall till date. Let us begin with *Aaj madhosh hua jaye re*, the raucous duet between a couple who are in the throes of passionate love. One wonders if SD was uncomfortable using the loud, jarring, multiple-echo-laden notes of dholaks in it? The reason: he detested high decibels in any form, and this dislike reflected repeatedly in his reluctance to embrace instrumentation as an alternative to simple melodic expression. As it was in the case of *Reshmi ujala hai*. Yet another seduction gem from Asha Bhosle, which was picturised in a club on Jayshree T., it had the flavour of *Raat akeli hai*—in the cadence, the gradual speeding up, and in the explosive movement from the lower to upper *sa* at the end of the mukhda—and was as delicate as the flat notes of the mukhda.

In the title song, *O meri Sharmeelee*, it appeared as if the flat notes were playing a game of hide-and-seek. Often ignored as just another rhythmic number, the song was the result of some bizarre phrasing. One does find the liberal use of both normal and flat notes in the mukhda, while the antara is purely on major scale, transitioning to the mukhda with a flat note (komal *ga*). In what was characteristically SD, one finds both the *nis* and komal *re* creeping in gently.

The song moves fast, almost as if it's a continuation from *Gambler's*

Chudi nahi yeh mera. A breezing melody, made special by Kishore's singing, and three different interludes composed in sparkling hues, it wouldn't be wrong to conclude that SD was enjoying himself thoroughly—his creativity in the prelude and interludes manifesting his enthusiasm. Initially, SD was more inclined to use long notes in antaras, but post-1960s, they began sounding more crisp, colourful and urbane. In this particular song, all the antaras ended with the question, which sounded more like a plea from the lover—*Jaaneman tu hai kahan?* (Where are you, my love?) with the last note stopping abruptly, as if to get a fresh lease of life with the first line of the mukhda.

While *Kaise kahen hum* was more like classical poetry in its long-drawn intonation of driving home the pain of the hero, the iconic song from *Sharmeelee* was however, *Khilte hain gul yahan* (the song was lifted lock, stock and barrel in the Tamil film, *Kanimuthu Paappa* (1972) as *Raadaye Nenjame*). The Kishore version was a marvellous amalgamation of youthful spirit and the beauty of Indian classical music. The same song had a sentimental version, sung by Lata, but with a very contrasting mood and entirely different sets of interludes and prelude. If one hears both versions, they actually sound very different.

The two-paced—differentiated by tempos within the same interlude—*Megha chhaye aadhi raat bairan ban gayi nindiya* was SD's special offering for Lata. It is quite likely that SD had deliberately mixed a slow mukhda with a fast interlude. Much like *Kaisa hai mere dil* (*Gambler*), he used it in *Megha chhaye aadhi raat* to show the woman's lover cavorting with another woman. The renowned filmmaker, Tapan Sinha, who was a party to the genesis of the song, recounts it in his memoirs as follows:

I wonder if any Bengali in Bombay got the kind of respect that was given to Sachinda. During my stay in Bombay, I would visit his place with my wife, Arundhati. One day I went alone and found him composing a tune. He said, "Please listen to the composition. How do you find it? Lata will sing this one...", and went on to sing the now famous *Megha chhaye aadhi raat*. His heartfelt rendition of the tune which sounded like Malhar, brought tears to my eyes and I said—"Beautiful."

Sachinda retorted, "You think it's mine? All courtesy Rabindranath!"[2]

SD's admission was clearly out of humility; the mukhda of *Megha chhaye* had little to do with Tagore. It was more reminiscent of the Chinmoy Lahiri–Pratima Bandyopadhyay duet, *Tribeni teetha pathe ke gahilo gaan* from the Bengali film *Shapmochon* (1955). Hemanta Kumar was the composer of the song, but considering this was a standard progression in raga Patdeep, it could well have been dovetailed by SD in the same fashion. However, the antara of the song did have snatches of Tagore's *Lauho tule lauho*, but wasn't by any stretch a straight lift. SD had of course referenced it but for a different song, *Leke jiya piya kahan jaaoge* in *Madh Bhare Nain* (1955).

Incidentally, the mukhda of *Megha chhaye* had been composed for another film. One day, Subodh Mukerji during a sitting session at the Jet found SD in a pensive mood, playing a composition. 'What is the matter, Sachinda?' he asked.

'You know, Subodh, a big producer had once rejected this tune,' said SD.

Mukerji loved the tune and booked it immediately. In *Sharmeelee*, he wanted the contrasting characters of the twin sisters to stand out sharply, and SD used the dawdling antaras and the power-driven interludes to establish it brilliantly.

Incidentally, the 'big producer' who'd rejected the tune was none other than Dev Anand, who had chosen *Rangeela re* over *Megha chhaye*, which was SD's original bet for the sequence.[3]

Transition—The Seventies

SD made a smooth transition into the Seventies. He had tasted success even earlier, but the quantum leap post *Aradhana* was incomparable. This pleasant change in his career however had come at the cost of certain extremely unfortunate circumstances—Jaikishan's death at the young age of forty-one in September 1971, and his partner, Shankar's struggle thereafter. Here was a man who had witnessed great successes during his career, but after Jaikishan's death, he somehow failed to hold onto his producers, including Raj Kapoor, Bhappie Sonie and Shakti Samanta. Moreover, the dipping fortunes of megastars such as, Raj and Shammi Kapoor added to Shankar's woes. Rajendra Kumar, who was once called Jubilee Kumar for his Midas touch, could do nothing right in the Seventies. Established directors like Sridhar who had previously made super hit films with him (*Saathi*, 1968; *Dil Ek Mandir*, 1963), came up with an eminently forgettable *Dharti* (1970). In spite of the sweet-sounding tracks by Shankar–Jaikishan, the romantic image of the Jubilee star faded away.

Naushad, who had shifted focus while composing for *Saathi* by opting for a symphonic and an extremely Western-sounding style, in contrast to his established 'Hindustani classical-based sound', was roped in by Rajendra Kumar and his brother, Naresh Kumar for a couple of films. Their productions, *Ganwaar* (1970), *Tangewala* (1972), or *Gaon Hamara Shehar Tumhara* (1972) were tedious and unwatchable.

259

By early- and mid-1960s, the king of melody O.P. Nayyar had also lost his sheen. His problem was his temperament—vowing never to work with Lata; calling Kishore names after *Ek Baar Muskura Do* (1972); refusing to compose for Rafi for a trivial reason; deliberately neglecting Geeta Dutt and Shamshad; and lastly, the severing of professional and personal relationship with Asha in 1972—all of which impacted his career.

The other talented composer of the time, C. Ramchandra practically gave up composing after *Rootha Na Karo* (1970), while Ravi had a rather curious graph. He remained in circulation, churning out hits like the Kishore–Asha duet, *Ek cheez mangte hain* from *Babul ki Galiyaan* (1972), *Sansar ki har sheh ka* for the thriller, *Dhund* (1973), *Mein toh chala* in the reincarnation story, *Dhadkan* (1972), the tandem, *Dil mein kisi ke pyaar ka* and the Kishore solo, *Dekha hai zindagi ko* from *Ek Mahal Ho Sapno Ka* (1975). His songs were picturised on stars like Sanjay Khan, Mumtaz, Hema Malini, Zeenat Aman and Dharmendra in the 1970s, but for some reason, he could never make it to the same league as his predecessors, or the troika of Kalyanji–Anandji, Laxmikant–Pyarelal, and R.D. Burman, who ruled the decade.

Amongst the old stalwarts, it was only SD (perhaps partially applicable to Madan Mohan and Salil Chowdhury as well, although their commercial clout had dwindled by then), who managed to keep a fine balance between quality and popularity.

The star singer of undivided Bengal was now the star composer of film songs in India. Interestingly, SD always projected himself as someone who was apologetic about succumbing to the needs of Bombay masala films. He had even gone to the extent of wanting to shift back to Calcutta, if assured of a monthly salary of five hundred rupees! Amongst other things, it was the thought of living close to his beloved Ganga which perhaps rekindled his desire to return to Calcutta. That he was deeply rooted in the music of Bengal—of Tagore, of the boatmen, of itinerant bards, of bostoms and bostomis—was something he didn't want to let go. Although he wasn't dismissive of Western influences in music, he was, by nature, conservative.

With the gradual urbanisation of India starting the late 1960s, Hindi cinema began shifting focus from the rural hinterland. This change was manifest in the way cover versions of Western theme scores were sold in small towns—notable among them were Henri Mancini's *Baby Elephant Walk* (*Hatari*, 1962), and Maurice Jarre's *Lara's Theme* from *Doctor Zhivago* (1965). The Ventures also played a significant role in propagating this kind of sound amongst people. Their versions of songs like *Tequila, Walk Don't Run, Diamond Head, Apache, Lonely Bull, Telstar, Pipeline*, etc., were legendary for their recall value. Topping the charts was the 1961 standard play album, *Theme from Come September* and *Berlin Melody*, cover versions by Billy Vaughn and his orchestra, which was not only played at paan shops across India, but also resulted in Hindi versions (*Rim Jhim* and *Dhak Dhak*), sung by Suman Kalyanpur in 1964, set to lyrics by Shailendra. This genre of music mesmerised an entire generation and succeeded in bridging the gap between the local-yokels and the city-slickers.

Given these conditions, SD had to fall in line with the demand for Western music and as was evinced, he handled the transition rather well.

It was around the same time when the Burmans decided to work separately, as did the Anands. Vijay Anand had split from Dev to start his own production company under the umbrella of Navketan, with a similar sounding name, Navketan Enterprises. (Dev's production company was Navketan International Films (P) Ltd.) *Tere Mere Sapne* was his first film as a producer-director, which was based on *Akela*, a script he had written in the early 1950s about a doctor in a mining town. After the film's release, Golide found himself mired in a controversy, for he hadn't acknowledged A.J. Cronin's *The Citadel*. However, Goldie came out unscathed, saying that the second half of the film was original and had no resemblance to Cronin's story. But it was clear for everyone to see that owing to market pressures, even Goldie had succumbed to clichés—melodrama, bad set design, unrealistic costumes, etc.—elements that were anathema to him all his life. For instance, the sight of well-dressed dapper medicos in a rural setting was an eyesore in the film. The consummate artist of *Guide, Johnny Mera Naam, Teesri Manzil* and *Jewel Thief* was missing in action, except for some brilliant, albeit grossly unreal, song picturisations. One wonders if Goldie's metier was more suited for thrillers and he had perforce ventured into untested waters.

Tere Mere Sapne (1971) was SD's third film with Neeraj. In the album, he continued with rhythmic and nimble tunes, but the Kishore–Lata duet, *Jeevan ki bagiya mehkegi* and the Lata solo, *Jaise Radha ne mala japi Shyam ki*, retained an intrinsic feel of Bengal. Both the songs were used multiple times in the film, but *Jaise Radha ne mala japi Shyam ki* needs special mention for its overt modernity, while securing the latent feel of a kirtan.

There is no doubt that composers like Anil Biswas, C. Ramchandra, Naushad, Shankar–Jaikishan, Roshan, and Madan Mohan not only brought out the various aspects of Lata Mangeshkar's singing deftly, but also her unparalleled genius which is unquestionable. So did SD, but the only difference being that he transformed her songs into visual treats, which ideally speaking, is the director's role. Sample this: while singing *Jaise Radha ne mala japi*, the passionate love of a woman for her man she considers god, sprakles through and even if one were to close one's eyes and listen, that is exactly what one sees in the mind's eye.

But in a song like this, the khol, a regular in SD's orchestration was sorely missed. Even *Jeevan ki bagiya mehkegi* used more flute, santoor, and less of rhythm. The late Manohari Singh explained the reason for this so-called deviation to the authors, 'We—Basu, Maruti and I—were with RD in Madras in mid-1970s working at Vasan Studios. It was for a film called *Laakhon Mein Ek* (1971). Studios in Chennai are usually very organised, but that particular day, there was some delay in recording, and we had to get back to Bombay because we had a back-to-back recording at the Film Centre with Burman Dada. When we reached Bombay, we were shocked to receive a message from him saying that we weren't required.

'However, Dada had a child-like temperament and after everything was sorted out, he allowed us to be acknowledged in the credits. RD who had been assisting his father in the film was already famous, and I think Dada asked boudi's (Meera Dev Burman) name to be included as assistant director. In all likelihood, she must have helped him with those Vaishnav-sounding songs. Music arrangers, Anil Mohile and Arun Paudwal, also began working for Dada around that time. We continued to play for him, in fact most of us continued with Dada's team as well.'[1]

Pandit Shiv Kumar Sharma, in an interview with an SD fan called, Moti Lalwani[2] said that in the absence of his arrangers, SD had asked him and Pandit Hariprasad Chaurasia to play the fillers in the Kishore–Lata duet, *Jeevan ki bagia mehkegi*. One would notice how the santoor plays the role of a percussion instrument in the song, in addition to the tabla and the dhol.

It now becomes clear why SD had moved away from his usual sound for this film, considering his team was away in Chennai, as was his son. As explained earlier, this particularly shows up in *Jaise Radha ne mala japi*, where one misses his hallmark layered sound. However, this song became immensely popular, as did *Jeevan ki bagiya*, notwithstanding the fact that the film wasn't a hit at the box office. Unfortunately, Lata's moving solo, *Mera antar ek mandir* which was inspired from SD's *Jodi daki okarone*, evokes little or no nostalgia amongst fans.

But for the most popular song of the film, *Hey, maine kasam li*, SD played with the tempo, and used the off-beat rhythm to his advantage, especially during the antara with Dev and Mumtaz riding doubles on a bicycle.

Talking of Mumtaz, it was her debut opposite the legendary Dev Anand, and she looked like a million bucks in the film! But what is a film without a controversy and it happened when Mumtaz had an argument with her director about roping in Hema Malini for a cameo. Goldie reasoned with her that Hema's inclusion was to boost the commercial value of the film—he needed a star to play a star. Goldie and Hema were friends from *Johnny Mera Naam* (1970) days (reportedly

263

the first Hindi film which had earned five million rupees as revenue), which he had directed for producer Gulshan Rai, and as a result of which, Hema had instantly said yes to Goldie when he approached her for a guest appearance in *Tere Mere Sapne*.

However apart from having done her friend a favour, *Tere Mere Sapne* did little for Hema Malini. But Pramod Chakraborty's *Naya Zamana* which released in 1971, compensated her adequately. With Dharmendra in the lead role which was reminiscent of his earlier films, *Anupama* (1966) and *Phool Aur Patthar* (1966), and a script which strongly evoked *Pyaasa*, *Naya Zamana* was the first Dharam–Hema film to celebrate a golden jubilee. Chakida would thereafter use the pair in all his films during the 1970s, except *Warrant* (1975).

Naya Zamana made SD return to his folk roots; it is just that he packaged it differently. It was also SD's umpteenth reinforcement of faith in Lata Mangeshkar's calibre as a singer—*Choron ko saare nazar aatein hain chor* and *Rama Rama gajab hui gaware* had the free-flowing magic of folk, sans the mushiness which comes with the genre at times. One wonders if *Rama Rama* was the song with the elusive note that SD claimed to have found in Rajasthan? Manna Dey once recounted in an interview how SD had gone missing from a film shoot in Rajasthan. He returned after a few days and disclosed that he was with a group of folk singers and amongst other things, had discovered an interesting variation of the komal *dha* note. He was so taken with it that he told the crew how it would soon find a place in some of his tunes. Well, even before *Naya Zamaana*, he did use it in a sporadic fashion in *Kaanton se kheench ke yeh aanchal* (*Guide*, 1965).

For the title song, *Kitne din aankhen tarsengi*, SD experimented with a traditional Bengali song—until then, the trend in Bengali music was to start on low notes and then graduate to higher ones. But SD went against the very grain of an age-old tradition, something he had done with utmost ease at different stages of his career. On careful hearing of the song, it becomes evident that the entire raison d'être of Bengali folk is found in the first two lines of the antara. It is safe to presume that this may have probably come as news to many of his peers, but in an act of incredible ingenuity, all SD did was retrofit the tune of *Hori din toh gelo shondhya holo* (featured on Chunibala Devi in Satyajit Ray's *Pather Panchali*, 1955). The highest note in the song followed as the punch-line in the antara, *Naya zamana aayega*, which was also used during the title run.

Duniya o duniya, the only song Dharamendra lip-syncs in the film was tailor-made for Kishore Kumar, which he delivered with characteristic confidence. The short music portions in the song were examples of what a traditionalist SD was as a composer. (In 1973, RD used a similar outline for *Mein shayar badnaam* in *Namak Haram* in one of the interludes.)

It is common knowledge that SD did not take to the avant-garde theme of *Hare Rama Hare Krishna* (1971) and let his son deal with it. In *Naya Zamana*, one gets a glimpse of how he may have sounded, had he not passed the baton to RD for the iconic Seventies' film. While, SD's understanding of the concept of flower power, with the Blues and rock-and-roll in the Kishore solo, *Wah re naujawan aaj kal ke* didn't sound laboured, his tryst with comedy in the same film, the Manna–Mahmood's *Aya mein laya, chalta phirta hotel*, failed to impress. The only novelty associated with the song was the first interlude, which was inspired from *Yeh dil na hota bechara* (*Jewel Thief*). Both songs in *Naya Zamana* were featured on the star of comedy, Mahmood, but were eclipsed by other songs in the film. Unfortunately, even *Das gayi sui*—the Bengali version of which was used in *Chaitali*—faced the same predicament. It was meant for greater glory, with its catchy tune, a multi-layered rhythm, and elegant dancing by Hema Malini, but unfortunately faded away into oblivion.

While on *Chaitali* (1975), a slight digression is mandated here. This was the film which had brought SD back to Bengali cinema after a gap of almost twenty-five years. It was a prestigious project, starring Uttam Kumar in the lead, while its producer, R.D. Bansal had the distintcion of working on four Satyajit Ray films—*Mahanagar*, *Charulata*, *Kapurush O Mahapurush* and *Nayak*. Maybe it was this which had lured SD in the first place to agree to the project.

However, fate had other plans. Bansal, who had invested heavily in *Jhuk Gaya Aasmaan* (1968), faced a terrible financial backlash after the film failed at the box office. The legendary producer of Ray's films was under such intense pressure that he was forced to abandon financing *Goopy Gayen Bagha Bayen* (1968) and *Aranyer Din Ratri* (1969). Therefore, as a safety measure, he'd roped in Rajshri Productions for *Chaitali,* as co-producers. In a few day's time, Uttam Kumar abandoned the project for some strange reasons and was replaced by Biswajit, who neither had the charisma, nor the acting skills, and most importantly, the box-office prowess of Uttam.

Alas, the opportunity to work with Bengal's superstar, who was also known for his fine musical sense and singing talent eluded SD. Around the mid-1960s, when Uttam Kumar had temporarily shifted to Bombay, Asit Chowdhury, the producer of Bengal's first Hindi colour film, *Mamta* (1966), had announced a remake of Ajoy Kar's monumental hit *Saptapadi* (1961), starring the iconic actor and Suchitra Sen in lead roles. SD was roped in to compose the music. But yet again, Uttam dissociated from the film which was given the working title of *Saat Kadam.* In the interim, there was a buzz about Rajendra Kumar replacing Uttam Kumar but finally, the film was relegated to the backburner.

Then there was more apropos Uttam Kumar. The Sinha brothers, Prasad and Girindra, who ran a production company called Sree Arup Productions in Calcutta, were the producers of *Monihar* (1966), starring Soumitra Chatterjee and Biswajeet, who played siblings in the film. After the sudden passing away of Prasad Sinha, Girindra decided to make its Hindi version and firmed up on Uttam Kumar to play the elder brother of actor, Deb Mukerji. Salil Sen, who had directed the Bengali film, was signed on to direct the Hindi version, titled *Mera Bhai.* SD was signed on as the film's music director, but alas, even this one never saw the light of day. It seemed as if SD and Uttam Kumar were not destined to work together.

Bangladesh

The year 1971 turned out to be uncharacteristically busy for SD. He was handling multiple projects, including a few which were shelved later (like *Aparna*) or were delayed releases like, *Tyaag* (1976). However, as a person, compared to what he was in the initial years, he had become socially amenable and was frequently sighted at various film parties holding a glass and making conversation.

The end of 1971 also saw him breaking the single peg rule. The Jet suddenly tranformed into an open house and there were a host of parties over wine and delectable food. The resident cook, Manu Pal, whom R.D. Burman had virtually hijacked from Sachin Bhowmick's house in 1966 following his father's illness, would lay out a fabulous feast during such soirees. There was yet another reason to celebrate that year—India had sent its forces to liberate East Bengal from the clutches of a diabolical dispensation.

The Burmans' home that evening saw many people from the world of cinema—Majrooh and Anand Bakshi, Pramod Chakraborty, Vijay Anand, Shakti Samanta, and Rajesh Khanna. The guests found an ecstatic SD greeting his guests with *Joy Bangla*.[1] SD was the man of that glorious evening, because the newly-formed Bangladesh was where he had spent his wondrous childhood—he took a nostalgic trip down memory lane and spoke about his beloved Comilla. The guests raised many toasts to him, and in what was extremely rare, he did them the honour by singing songs which evoked the beauty of his soil, including *Ami takdum takdum bajai Bangladesher dhol*, which was written by his wife, and dedicated to Bangladesh. The song was released during Durga Puja in 1971 and went on to become a monumental hit subsequently.

Alas, family politics played a spoiler and ruined an otherwise lovely evening at the Burmans' home. Meera Burman's contribution to SD's success was being openly acknowledged by guests at the party, which seemed to have incensed Rita, who anyway shared a strained relationship with her mother-in-law. After some time, Rita drove off in a huff to her house without informing her husband. Once RD realised what had happened, he followed his wife to their home. As it turned out later, the episode was more than the usual domestic spat between spouses. The next day, RD left Lino Minar and for all practical purposes, his wife as well. He checked into Caesar Palace Hotel in Khar. He would live there for the next two years.[2]

SD and Meera hoped for things to settle between their son and his wife. After all, they had been witness to such acrimonious scenes even in the past including once during a party thrown for *Aradhana's* success in late 1969. But this time around, things turned for the worse and an extremely distressed SD sought the advice of Sachin Ganguly and said that he now wished to consult an astrologer regarding his son's future, and caught an early morning flight to Calcutta sometime in 1972.[3]

Sachin Ganguly took him to an astrologer called Benimadhab Saha in Haji Zakaria Lane in Maniktala, north Calcutta. Saha was a short man and at a first glance, looked unimpressive. He was known to live a frugal life and would dress simply in a dhoti and shirt, but was legendary for his incredible gift of prophesising. His clientele included the rich and the famous of Calcutta and Bombay—Suchitra Sen, Bikash Roy, Dilip Kumar, and K.N. Singh.

As Saha was also from East Bengal and spoke the same dialect as SD, they clicked instantly. After hearing SD's version of the story, Saha said, 'Rita is blackmailing your son and there could be attempts on his life too. She is aiming for the property. But do not worry. Your son and his wife will split amicably and everything will be sorted.'

RD's divorce came a year later with little or no animosity between the involved parties. There was no scandal, no write-ups in newspapers, and no scurrilous gossip. RD disposed off Lino Minar as a distress sale, and Asha Bhosle helped him with the additional money to close the deal with Rita. According to Sachin Bhowmick, the house was sold at one hundred thousand rupees, while Asha doled out an additional two hundred thousand rupees for the settlement.[4]

Zindagi Zindagi

As is well known, during the late 1950s and Sixties, Bengali cinema was compartmentalised into two distinct genres—art house and commercial. Satyajit Ray, Ritwik Ghatak, and Mrinal Sen were acknowledged as the artistic lot, while the others who were obviously in large numbers, fell into the slot of those who hawked their wares for the sole purpose of making money. This categorisation was faulty, because Ray's films, while remaining true to the moniker of 'art', made more money than most Bengali films. This may be construed as contentious, but for many cinema lovers it was difficult to comprehend the 'art' quotient in Mrinal Sen's films, while somebody like Tapan Sinha made enjoyable, no-nonsense entertainers that were commercially successful too.

SD was friends with Tapan and the two would often spend several evenings in each other's company. It must be mentioned here that SD had eclectic taste and was friends with film directors from across the spectrum—Bimal Roy, Pramod Chakraborty, Shakti Samanta, and so on. Tarun Majumdar[1], another middle-of-the-road filmmaker from Bengal told the authors how one fine morning, he was literally hijacked by SD to his house and contrary to the tight-fistedness that was often attributed to him, he was fed to his heart's content. Majumdar would never work with SD, although he would have liked to in *Balika Badhu* (1976).[2]

Tapan Sinha's tryst with Bombay was at the insistence of Hemen Ganguly, who was an academician, film distributor, and an influential member of the industry. In 1970, Tapan Sinha decided to remake *Sagina Mahato* starring Dilip Kumar and Saira Banu, and roped in SD to score the music.

However, the film ran into several delays, as a result of which Tapan Sinha decided to start work on yet another film titled, *Zindagi Zindagi* starring Sunil Dutt, Waheeda Rehman, Ashok Kumar and Shyama. This 1972 film was based on Sinha's own Bengali film, *Khoniker Athithi*, which he had made almost a decade ago in 1959. Nariman A. Irani, the ace photographer, who had worked with SD in *Talash* (1969) volunteered to produce *Zindagi Zindagi*. Tapan Sinha, who was extremely driven by the idea of getting a toehold in the Hindi film industry, and had even bought a flat in the Pali Hill area, started meeting SD frequently over discussions on music.

There is a golden rule in Indian cinema—never remake your own film. Even someone as illustrious as Satyajit Ray had apparently warned Tapan Sinha not to risk it, but the latter was so firm in his decision that he refused to pay heed, and ended up paying a hefty price. As it finally turned out, the film flopped miserably. Even SD's music evoked no magic as was being touted earlier and alas, it also happened to be the last film in which he sang his own compositions. He sang two songs— just like he had in *Eight Days* (1946) and *Guide* (1965)—but there was something missing—his voice had lost its original suppleness and the obvious culprit was his advancing age. Even *Piya tuney kya kiya*, a song which had shades of *Sunn mere bandhu re* (*Sujata*, 1959), failed to create any impact. SD was supposed to have expressed his inability to Tapan Sinha, 'I can sing the old songs much better, but my voice does not do justice to my thoughts.' Nevertheless, *Zindagi Zindagi* won SD the National Award for Best Music Director and put him in a rare slot of being the only Indian composer to have received the award for both singing and composing.

However, in so far as Nariman A. Irani was concerned,

Zindagi Zindagi left him neck-deep in debts—he owed 1,20,000 rupees (a large sum of money those days) to sundry creditors in the market. While working as DoP for Manoj Kumar's *Roti Kapda Aur Makaan* in 1974, it was rumoured that he had borrowed heavily from his co-workers. Meanwhile, many advised him that the best way out of a debt trap was to make a successful film, and Irani decided to try his luck yet again.

He immediately started working on a concept and signed up Amitabh Bachchan to play the lead role, while Kalyanji–Anandji, who were close to the star, were brought in to score the music. When SD heard that Irani had started another film, he expressed his desire to score its music, which put Irani in a conundrum—how was anyone to tell the doyen the truth? But finally it took little effort, as SD was told that the movie was an action-based thriller and the grand old man even suggested to Irani that his son could perhaps handle its music better. The said movie was none other than *Don* (1978). While Irani and the director, Chandra Barot, didn't approach RD, Amitabh Bachchan wanted to work with SD for a film that he had partly financed, and the working title for which was, *Raag Ragini*.

Egos, Sentiments & Music

If it wasn't for a man called Bimal Roy, the world of Indian cinema would have been poorer, for we wouldn't have known about a gent called Hrishikesh Mukherjee. It was Roy who'd brought a young Hrishikesh (or Hrishida as he was called popularly) from Calcutta to Bombay during the making of *Do Bigha Zamin* (1953). Arguably one of the best editors in the annals of Hindi cinema, Hrishida later rose to become one of the best directors in Bombay. When he began his directorial journey with *Musafir* (1957), he chose Salil Chowdhury as his music composer. Gradually, when sundry producers, directors and leading stars began making suggestions about other music directors, Hrishida began to think of options.

According to Hrishikesh Mukherjee's daughter, Jayasree Mukherjee, as told to author Jai Arjun Singh, her father would select the composer based on the mood of the film.[1] This point however begs a debate. His choice of composers, ranging from Shankar–Jaikishan (*Anari*, 1959), (*Aashiq*, 1962), (*Asli Naqli*, 1962), (*Sanjh Aur Savera*, 1964), (*Gaban*, 1966); Hemanta Mukherjee (*Do Dil*, 1965), (*Biwi Aur Makaan*, 1966), (*Anupama*, 1966), (*Manjhli Didi*, 1967); Vasant Desai (*Ashirwaad*, 1968), (*Guddi*, 1971); even Chitragupta and Laxmikant–Pyarelal for *Pyar ka Sapna* (1969) and *Satyakaam* (1969) respectively; as also Madan Mohan for *Bawarchi* (1972), do not exactly vindicate her statement. Most of the composers mentioned in the list, could have well done justice to most of his films.

In early 1970, Hrishikesh Mukherjee made a shift to the Burmans, and this was purely out of deference for his producers. After *Anand* (1970), Salil Chowdhury was in demand yet again, but according to Ranabir Neogi[2], a Salil aficionado from Calcutta, there were instances when Salil would come to Mukherjee asking for work, only to be told that the producers were unwilling to punt on him. RD had already started his journey with Hrishida in *Phir Kab Milogee* (1974), after which followed, *Buddha Mil Gaya* (1971). In the interim, Hrishikesh Mukherjee did *Bawarchi* (1972) with Madan Mohan, which was a sleeper hit. *Sabse Bada Sukh* (1972), which was advertised as India's first sex-comedy, had Salil as composer, and as was expected, turned out to be a disaster. Salil's market price plummeted and Hrishikesh Mukherjee did not work with him again, except for the background score of *Naukri* (1978), which, despite being based on a story by Salil, had RD as the composer.

However, it was most intriguing that a competent director like Hrishikesh Mukherjee hadn't yet thought of working with Sachin Dev Burman! One of the reasons could be that Hemanta, Salil and Hrishida shared a camaraderie; SD was much older and hence not part of the group. But if one goes by what Tapan Sinha and Tarun Majumdar had said, then this seems far-fetched because according to them, Burman neither pulled rank nor authority when it came to forging friendships with his peers.

Yet another curious point in Hrishikesh Mukherjee's work was that seldom did he make films around the theme of music and while this was also true of many directors, it stands out in his case because he happened to be a trained sitar payer and had even perfomed in AIR, Calcutta. In fact he had once gone as far as to say that if he had his way, he would have done away with song sequences in his films! This was strange, coming from a man who had music in his family— his father, Shital Chandra Mukherjee was a dhrupad artiste and his brother, Kashinath Mukherjee (popularly known as Chotuda) played the sitar.

One wonders if his near indifference towards music was in the latter phase of his career, because he did direct a musically wondrous film called *Anuradha* (1960) which fetched him the President's award and an entry into the Berlin Film Festival in 1961. During the making of the film, Hrishikesh Mukherjee, much like the neo-realist that he was, wanted Ustad Bade Ghulam Ali Khan to score the music. But Khan saab quoted a fee which was double of the most expensive composer of the time and that had led Mukherjee to Pandit Ravi Shankar, who stepped in to do a competent job.

It was almost after a decade of *Anuradha* that Hrishikesh Mukherjee once again agreed to make a film around the theme of music and announced *Raag Ragini* in 1972 with Amitabh Bachchan and Jaya Bhaduri in the lead. Pawan Kumar, who was then secretary to Amitabh Bachchan (also to Shatrughan Sinha) was made one of the producers and Amiya (purportedly a combination of Amitabh and Jaya's names) Productions was formed. There is no evidence if Mukherjee was inspired by *A Star is Born* (made thrice, first in 1932 as *What Price Hollywood*; and later in in 1937 and 1954), but the storyline of *Raag Ragini* was similar. We would stick our neck out to say that he may have been inspired by Hollywood, than what was later said in some quarters that it was allegedly based on the tumultuous relationship between an artist-couple—Pandit Ravi Shankar and Annapurna Devi, or maybe even Kishore Kumar and Ruma Guha Thakurta.

When it came to the film's music, Sachin Bhowmick recalled Mukherjee's thoughts, as follows: 'It is a musical subject. Let's go to Sachinda, for he is the best person for it.'

SD may not have responded with words but his music was enough acknowledgement of how much he appreciated the faith placed on him by his colleagues. *Abhimaan* (1973), as the film was later renamed, became a benchmark in the 1970s for the no-frills-attached-light-music genre. If Ravi Shankar used Maajh Khamaj, Jansamohini, Bhairavi and his own creation, Tilak Shyam in *Anuradha*, SD embellished *Abhimaan* with nuances he had mastered—instruments like the tabla, guitar, the occasional touch of an accordion and the sitar, the gentle interjections of ragas Khamaj and Piloo, Rabindra Sangeet, short notes, smart phrases, the use of *Sunn mere bandhu re* in the background, and so on.

If there was one common feature in the album and something the maestro had come to be synonymous with, it was the use of bamboo flute in *Piya bina*; *Loote koi mann ka nagar*; *Teri bindiya re*; *Ab toh hai tumse*; and *Tere mere milan ki ye raina*. Especially in *Piya bina*, sung by Lata Mangeshkar, if one notices the bridge from the last line of the mukhda to the first line, it is nigh impossible to distinguish between Lata's voice and Pandit Hari Prasad Chaurasia's bamboo flute. However, the overtly classical number in the film, *Nadiya kinare*, was an exception, as its arrangement was string-based, with only a fast treble flute piece joining the second interlude to the antara. Even in *Meet na mila re mann ka*, which introduces the star-singer Subir (played by Amitabh Bachchan) to the audience, a flute-bridge was used in the antara.

Although it's nearly impossible to get two people to agree on that one song which stands out in this fabulous album, *Ab toh hai tumse* does qualify, for it has an inherent fresh and breezy feel to it. Considering it was set to tune by S.D. Burman and sung by Lata Mangeshkar, it was by no means innately Indian, as its major scale structure with a flurry of violins made it sound very Western. The song sequence defines a cinematic moment—the ascent of Uma (played by Jaya Bhaduri) as a singer, with her star-singer husband, Subir getting progressively eclipsed. Therefore, the movement of the orchestra was openly symphonic than any other song composed by SD during that period. It was a story told in three-and-a-half minutes, with a captivating guitar riff—*ga ga pa pa dha ga ga ga*—holding the tune. No other song before *Ab toh hai tumse* evoked the ambience of an auditorium, with a near-perfect symmetry between the audio and visuals.

One also notices a symmetry between two out of three duets in the film. *Teri bindiya re*, the Lata–Rafi duet, is on 7/4; the Lata–Kishore song, *Tere mere milan ki ye raina*, the climactic song in the film whose mukhda SD borrowed lock, stock, and barrel from Tagore's *Jodi tare nai chini go sheki*, is again on 7/4. Another rhythmic beauty is *Meet na mila re mann ka*, which shall forever be remembered for its coolness, for its off-beat surprises which were deliberately introduced by SD. Brojen Biswas, a close associate of Sachin Deb ratified that SD had first composed this in Bengali as, *Preme e mojechi*[3], which wasn't recorded. It probably needed the buoyancy of Kishore Kumar and the charisma of Amitabh Bachchan to make it a trend-setting song of the decade.

In a film which had top-ranking singers like Lata, Kishore and Rafi, one wonders how a little-known Manhar was given the opportunity to sing in *Loote koi mann ka nagar*. The story goes that the song was originally composed for Mukesh, but the version recorded by Manhar sounded just right for SD to retain it in the film. Much like the shloka sung by the debutant Alka Nadakarni, better known to the world as Anuradha Paudwal, which was used in a strategic scene in which the boy hears the girl's voice for the first time. Anuradha happened to be SD's assistant, Arun Paudwal's wife, but that wasn't the reason why her voice was used in the song; Dada Burman recognised a gem when he saw one!

Abhimaan gave SD his second and last Filmfare Award. Given that Madan Mohan or Jaidev never got one; Salil, O.P. Nayyar or Naushad did but just once, Lady Luck favoured him more than his peers. With *Abhimaan*, Hrishikesh Mukherjee finally found a composer for all his films starring Amitabh Bachchan, until SD decided to up and leave the world.

However, luck didn't favour one of his closest friends, undoubtedly one of the greatest Urdu writers of his time, Rajindar Singh Bedi. His 1973 film, *Phagun* (1973) starring Dharmendra, Waheeda Rehman, Jaya Bhaduri and Vijay Arora, was a great disappointment. It was worse than his first film, *Dastak* (1970) which won him awards, but failed to register with the audience. The one common thing between both his films was

277

its outstanding music—while Madan Mohan dazzled in *Dastak*, SD's music in *Phagun* was equally pleasing. It is however another matter that it went unnoticed due to the film's terrible failure. For instance, the underrated Kishore–Asha duet, *Kab maney o dil ke mastane*. Until a few decades back, many Bengalis were familiar with *Ek baar bidaye de, Ma, ghure aashi*, by folk artiste Pitambar Das of Bankura, which was routinely sung as a tribute to Khudiram Bose's sacrifice in August 1908. The tune came back into circulation in the mid-1960s when it was sung by Lata Mangehskar in Piyush Bose's Bengali film, *Subhashchandra* (1966) composed by Aparesh Lahiri, better known to the world as Bappi Lahiri's father. It needed a sheer genius to convert the first line of a heart-wrenching ballad written for an eighteen-year martyr into a playful love song, which SD did with such aplomb. Not that this was the first time, for he had done it previously too, in a slightly different manner in *Tumi je giyecho bokul bichano pothe*. What is more, he would later use the antara of *Kab maney* for the antara of *Bye bye Miss Good Night* in *Prem Nagar* (1974).

The Story of a Gypsy Girl

During 1971–1972, SD was working on multiple projects. The two main reasons for this were: production delays, and the temptation of working with good filmmakers. As a consequence, his work often intermingled, like dishes on an Indian plate, with diverse tastes, and thus creating a near explosion in the mouth.

As mentioned in the previous chapter, the ethereal backup music in *Ab toh hai tumse* from *Abhimaan* was a perfect example of such intermixing and the result was for everyone to see and hear! SD used a similar arrangement in the exceptional *Piya maine kya kiya*, which was sung by Manna Dey in Basu Chatterji's *Us-Paar* (1974).

Basu Chatterji began his career by assisting Bimal Roy's son-in-law, Basu Bhattacharya in *Teesri Kasam* (1966), and later worked with Govind Saraiya in *Saraswatichandra* (1968). It was during this period that he had written a script called *Us-Paar*, which was based on a Czech film called *Romance for Bugle* (1967), that he had watched at an international film festival. When Basu Chatterji approached the Film Federation Corporation (FFC) of India to finance his film, it was turned down for the reason that it wasn't an original idea. He then made *Sara Akash* (1969), based on a seminal novel by Rajendra Yadav, and was hailed as a promising talent in the genre of new wave cinema in India.

In an interview with the authors, Basu Chatterji recalled, 'Suresh Jindal, a businessman from Delhi, had seen *Sara Akash* in Los Angeles and wanted to make another film. I had the script of *Us-Paar.* Jindal selected SD as the composer for the film that he agreed to produce. In the interim, Jindal had also agreed to produce one more film, *Rajanigandha* (1974), and walked out of *Us-Paar.* Who knows, maybe he was hard-pressed for money. But then, he was an astute businessman. Anyway, I decided to produce *Us-Paar* myself.'[1]

The 1974 film chronicled the poignant love story of a gypsy girl called Kamli, played by Moushumi Chatterjee. Although tragic love stories and music is a potent concoction, SD was in no mood to write sentimental music, and chose flamboyance for his score.

Us-Paar also happened to be his first collaboration with lyricist Yogesh, who spoke about SD as follows: 'After working in some non-descript films, producer L.B. Lachman helped me get work in Hrishida's *Anand* (1970) and Asit Sen's *Annadata* (1972). Salil Chowdhury who was the composer for both films, was an inspiration for my writing. He told me that a new director called Basu Chatterji was looking for me. Salilda had worked with him in a beautiful film called, *Sara Akash.* I was a big fan of Basu Chatterji. I'd seen *Sara Akash* thrice. Basuda approached Salilda and asked about the lyricist of *Anand.* I had no work those days, and went to Basuda who offered me to pick between two music directors—S.D. Burman or Laxmikant–Pyarelal. I had stuck a friendship with Manna Dey after my first film, *Sakhi Robin* (1962), in which the duet *Tum jo aao toh pyaar aa jaye* (Manna–Suman Kalyanpur) was a huge hit. I was also working on a film by Prabhat Mukherjee called *Sonal* (1973) for which Mannada was the music director. When I solicited his advice, he bluntly told me to go for S.D. Burman.

'I had seen Burman Dada before, but never had the courage to talk to him. Anyway, I took a risk and went to meet him at the Jet on Linking Road, where he used to stay on the first floor. I introduced myself after giving Salilda and Hrishida's references. Burman Dada wasted little time. He had heard about Basuda, and played a tune on his harmonium and asked me to write lyrics for the same. He wanted me to write lyrics like Gulzar, for a folk-based tune. He gave me the example of *Mora gora ang lai le*. Prabhat Mukherjee had gifted me a small dictaphone (voice recorder), in which I recorded the tune. I went back a few days later with a set of lyrics, and Burman Dada said okay to the first one. The song was *Tumne piya diya sab kuch mujhko*. That's how I began my journey with Dada.'[2]

Us-Paar resurrected SD's *Bandini* avatar—the music was soft but energetic, delicate but resolute, playful but no-nonsense. And the bard in him strode and took centre stage with *Piya maine kya kiya*. Even as the first line of the song was a take-off from the bridge line, '*Yug se woh hai mera*' from *Khai hai re humne kasam* (*Talash*, 1969), the tune scripts its own path thereafter. With *mitwa*, the master of classicality, Manna Dey does an incredibly tough taan both in the opening as well as the coda, even as one sees the gypsies' caravan leaving the village, signifying the end of a tragic love story. It is safe to presume that SD had perhaps composed the tune keeping himself in mind, only to hand it over to Manna on a platter. Interestingly, Yogesh had also written the song with SD in mind. 'I would have been thankful if he had sung it himself, but that did not happen,' he said to the authors.

The only weak link in the film was a solo by Rafi, *Ai mere mann, mai hoon magan*, which added little to the album. Basu Chatterji recalled why it was included in the first place, 'You see, we have to make films to cater to a standard length or else producers have issues in selling it to distributors, who in turn have the same complaint against hall owners. After *Us-Paar* was complete, it was felt that the film was 4–5 minutes shorter in length. As I didn't have any edited script material, we decided on including a song. We went to Sachinda and told him that an additional song was needed for a sequence where the boy is waiting to meet the girl. That is how *Ai mere mann* was born.'[3]

While speaking, Chatterjee's affection and respect for the composer sparkled through. 'Sachinda was a pain in the neck, but in a lovely way! Every other day he would say, "*Basu, ekta notun sur eshche. Shune jao*" (Basu, I have just thought of a new tune. Come, listen to it), while I would be running around for money.

'He was one music director who worked harder than the producers. He would be in a state of frenzy while working, obsessed and extremely passionate. Every situation posed a challenge for him, and he worked on it until he was satisfied, only to come up with more alternatives the next day. The man was immensely talented, as talented as Salil Chowdhury, who was my favourite composer. He scored brilliant music for *Us Paar*. I would have loved to do more work with him, but unfortunately the opportunity never arose.

'During the making of *Us-Paar*, he was very upset when I'd included some pre-recorded music as background score for the climax of the film. He heard it, but didn't object. I had bought the canned music from a small-time composer at a paltry sum of Rs.15,000. If I had recorded the background score with him, it would have cost me 40,000 rupees. He probably understood the pain of a first-time producer who was working on a shoestring budget.'[4]

The last comment is particularly significant, given that SD was well into his twenty-ninth year as a composer and was still considerate towards youngsters in the profession.

However, Yogesh had a slightly different take on this. He said that SD and he had gone to see the rushes of the film and the death sequence of Raja Paranjpe (who played Mohan's {Vinod Mehra's} grandfather in the film) had disturbed SD no end. Yogesh added that he didn't like the way it was shot and decided there and then to not compose the background music.[5]

Love Triumphs Over Sickness

The gypsy girl of *Us-Paar*, Moushumi Chatterjee who had started her career with the Bengali super hit, *Balika Badhu* (1967), decided to migrate to Hindi cinema after she was offered a role by United Producers. Shakti Samanta had announced *Anuraag* (1972) with Rekha in the lead opposite Rajesh Khanna. The film however got delayed, and Samanta had to look for fresh faces. Coincidentally, singer-composer, Hemanta Mukherjee also happened to be a member of the United Producers team, and when Shaktida asked him if he was fine with his daughter-in-law acting in Hindi cinema, he gave his consent.

Anuraag was a stereotypical family drama, with large doses of sentimentality and other routine staples associated with such films. So far as its music was concerned, SD was *Anuraag*'s lead 'playback singer'. *Sun ri pavan* and *Neend churaye chain churaye* were the Hindi versions of two of his most popular Bengali solos, *Ke jaash re* and *Baanshi shune aar kaaj nai*. Lata was once again entrusted with the task of creating classics from the original Bengali.

There was a third, although not a very popular Lata song—*Mera raja beta bole*, the last lullaby composed by SD. Like *Nanhi kali sone chali* (*Sujata*), the lines had a drawn-out effect.

Anuraag also happened to be Shakti Samanta's last film with SD, as

RD had stepped in to take over the mantle. One can only speculate whether Samanta would have considered SD for films like *Mehbooba* (1976) or *Anurodh* (1977), had the maestro been alive and willing to work.

In Continuum

The Action-packed 1970s

The Seventies belonged to action drama, a genre which flourished like no other in the history of Hindi cinema. According to some accounts, the sudden spurt was in protest to Nehruvian socialism—India had been ravaged by three wars (one with China, and two with Pakistan); the poor were burdened by escalating prices; but the politicians, as always, cocked a snook at the masses and added to their coffers by indulging in unprecedented corruption. The poor-rich divide had widened to such an extent that mini revolutions were witnessed in different parts of the country. It was this churn brought about by hunger, anger and despondency which created space for the rise of the 'Angry young man' and he arrived, much like the messiah of the poor. His name was Amitabh Bachchan.

Considering there was a paradigm shift in Indian society, the film industry was naturally impacted by it. While several artists struggled to keep up with the times, many found ways to align themselves with the imminent change. The change percolated to the music industry as well. Ironically, while music was never the focal point in action-packed films, music directors had to work doubly hard to keep themselves afloat.

In September 1966, in an article in *Cine Advance*, SD argued that a song was important to a film only if it was cinematically well presented.

This one statement proved how well he understood the medium and even as action films were slowly taking over the industry, SD was singularly focussed on bettering his compositions. There is no gainsaying the fact that his music for every action-based film during the period was not only unforgettable, but also a perfect fit for the times. Despite his advancing age, the man was most willing to experiment, like using voices from outside the music fraternity. The well known actor and an alumni of the FTII, Danny Denzongpa in a chat with the authors, said,[1] 'I was the original choice for the role of a tribal (Dev Anand's sidekick) in *Yeh Gulistan Hamara*, which was released in 1972. S.D. Burman had heard me singing a tune that he liked, and composed *Mera naam aao* based on that. He wanted me to sing the song too. In effect, I was to do my own playback.

'Johnny Walker, who was a constant fixture in every Guru Dutt production, came and asked the director of the film, Atma Ram (who was Guru Dutt's younger brother), "No role for Johnny Walker in a Guru Dutt film?" Atma Ram convinced me to give up the role, which I did.

'But S.D. Burman wanted me to sing *Mera Naam Aao*.[2] Now, Atma Ram wanted some other singer, since I was neither part of the cast, nor a professional singer. Burman Dada was furious and said that he would not compose the music, as Atma Ram had no business taking decisions about the music. Atma Ram apologised profusely to Burman Dada and he finally relented.

'On the first day of the music sitting, I landed up at Burman Dada's place wading through knee-deep rain water. Dada chided me never to do that as it could adversely affect my voice. He told me to dry my legs, and have a cup of tea first.

'During the rehearsal, I wanted multiple mics around me, as my body would sway with the rhythm while singing. So, Burman Dada kept six mics and I kept swinging and singing.'

Although *Yeh Gulistan Hamara*, starring Dev Anand and Sharmila Tagore (the only time they worked together), failed to do good business,

Gori gori gaon ki gori re (Kishore–Lata), *Suno meri baat* (Kishore and chorus), and *Mera naam aao* (Danny–Lata) were chartbusters.

Alas, the film's failure proved to be the end of SD's twenty-year-old relationship with Guru Dutt Productions that had started with *Baazi*. Atma Ram offered him *Aarop* (1974), but SD passed it to his admirer-turned-friend, the late Dr Bhupen Hazarika.[3]

The song *Raina soyi soyi*, sung by Lata and chorus in *Yeh Gulistan Hamara* was the only instance when both father and son—SD and RD—sang together.

Shedding his soft, poetic, self-effacing avatar in several films like *Anupama* (1966), *Ishq Par Zor Nahin* (1970), *Naya Zamana* (1971), and *Satyakam* (1969) etc., macho-man Dharmendra decided to go for a conscious image makeover in *Jugnu* (1973). In the film, Ashok Kumar played the typical 'Dr. Jekyll and Mr. Hyde' kind of a role—he was a benevolent philanthropist during the day, and would transform into 'Robin Hood' at night, who would leave his mascot, 'Jugnu' at the scene of crime, and thus came to be called so.

In an interview with the authors, Sachin Bhowmick explained *Jugnu's* song sequences, as follows. 'Normally, Chakida (Pramod Chakraborty) and I never worked with a final script. *Jugnu* had a story outline which was fleshed out in detail by Gulshan Nanda, the well known writer. However, during the scripting, he faced a road block because he didn't know where to insert the songs. We kept breaking our heads—what could the hero do? Sing a duet perhaps? Would he sing wearing a Jugnu mask? Maybe he could, while chasing after the heroine in a car? What could the heroine do—a few dances maybe, and so on and so forth.

'This is how the song slots for *Jugnu* were created. It was decided that Dharam and Hema would be given a duet, which happened to be *Gir gaya jhumka* (Lata–Kishore). The masked avatar song didn't come to fruition, and was shifted to *Azaad* (1978), which was anyway delayed and the music was then taken over by RD. Meanwhile, the chase we had discussed was taken to the skies with Dharam wooing Hema in *Pyaar ke iss khel mein* (Kishore). Hema Malini performed two dances in the film—the classical-based, *Meri payaliya geet tere* (Lata) and the drunken rain dance, *Janey kya pilaya tuney bada maza aaya* (Lata, yet again).'[4]

SD's unshakeable trust in Lata showed up yet again in the film, especially in *Janey kya pilaya tuney*. As an accomplished singer, although she laced the number with obvious signs of drunkenness like hiccups at regular intervals, it could easily have been an Asha Bhosle number composed by RD like, *Hai bichua das gayo re* (*Jheel Ke Us Paar*, 1973) or *Sharma na yoon* (*Joshila*, 1973). But while RD preferred a layered rhythm in these similar-sounding songs, the rhythm instruments in *Janey kya* pick up right at the beginning with Kersi Lord's piano accordion creating an ambience like *Roop tera mastana* (*Aradhana*), and Bhupinder's guitar riffs setting up the mood of a romantic night. The second interlude of the song was focussed on beats, while the third interlude was created in a jazz-like fashion.

Meri payaliya, based on Marathi folk, was representative of SD's multi-layered treatment of sound. On close inspection, one would notice how the use of *Hai* to end the first line of the mukhda, lent a surfeit of rhythmic energy to the number. It was well known about SD that he desisted from overdoing what was his USP, and made the listener hanker for more!

Jugnu also happened to be one of the earliest films of Dharamendra and Hema Malini, and apart from the fact that the lead pair were seeing each other, the film was acknowledged as a benchmark for romantic love in the Seventies. *Pyaar ke iss khel mein* and *Gir gaya jhumka* were both contemporary and set to a pulsating beat. The latter, which was picturised in a park, had obvious overtones of intimacy, right down to the point where Lata imitates Kishore's disappointment of 'having lost something'. The song finally tapers off with a refusal, '*na, na, na…*', leaving the rest to viewers' imagination.

One of the prime examples of SD's comfort with change, or modernity was the title song of *Chhupa Rustam* (1973). It was his last film with Navketan, more specifically Vijay Anand's production house, Navketan Enterprises. Although the film was based on Alistair Maclean's bestselling novel, *Fear is the Key* and also borrowed liberally from *McKenna's Gold* (1969), it came a cropper.

What is most remembered about the music of the film is that it parodied one of S.D. Burman's iconic songs, *Dheere se jaana bagiyan mein, re bhanwara* as *Dheere se jaana khatiyan* (a cot) *mein, re khatmal* (bed bug). This must have not only taken a lot of courage, but also compromise, given that he was known to be impatient with superficiality. But then, he was also a man who aligned himself with changing times, and was willing to look at music from the prism of the audiences. The rest was achieved by Kishore, who not sang it with élan, but in many ways even bettered the original.

In yet another song of the film, the Lata–Kishore duet, *Bolo kya humko dogey*, SD transformed his *Ami takdum takdum bajai* tune into a trendy question-and-answer love song.

Chhupa Rustam was Neeraj's last film with SD, as he went back to teaching. His loss willy-nilly became Goldie's gain as he turned lyricist with this film for a song which was also picturised on him—*Jo mein hota* was a duet between Kishore and Asha, and probably the most Western-sounding song from SD's stable during the period.

We have said this before and would like to reiterate yet again, particularly for those who have raised questions about SD's understanding and resultant preference for Indian sounds. Although in the 1970s, he still preferred using predominantly Indian instrumentation, he was far more open to using both brass and multiple rhythms and this despite the fact that his arrangers, Anil Mohile and Arun Paudwal were no experts in the genre. But this is where Manohari Singh and Basu Chakravarty filled the gap, by assisting him from time to time, as also Maruti Rao who added magic to songs composed by both the Burmans.

Having mastered multiple styles, SD could easily fit into the role of the traditionalist as well as a renegade. His last work for a South Indian production found him doing just that.

Prem Nagar (1974) was originally made in Telugu by K.S. Prakash Rao in 1971, starring Akkineni Nageswara Rao. The film was later remade in Tamil as *Vasantha Maligai* (1972) starring one of the most prolific actors of Tamil cinema, Sivaji Ganesan.

It was the well-known Telugu producer, D. Ramanaidu who decided to make it in Hindi and insisted on top actors, much like its counterparts in Telugu and Tamil. In so far as the male lead was concerned, there was no doubt in anyone's mind—Rajesh Khanna, who by now had ceased to be just an actor and was acknowledged as a national phenomenon. While Hema Malini was signed on to play the female lead, S.D. Burman was roped in as the music director.

Generally speaking, Tamil film music was usually at par with Hindi, just that it tended to be a shade heavier and overly melodramatic. After nearly thirty years in the film industry, one would have forgiven SD if he had taken it easy, but then who was anyone to guess what the Tripura scion was planning in his head. As was expected of the man, he decided to spring a surprise and did what he was famed to do—adapt! As a result,

Prem Nagar (1974) was more about violins and sitar jhalas than the flute and santoor. He also used the electric bass guitar in a prolonged phase for the first time in his career, as if to steer *Pyaase do badan*, which remains one of Asha Bhosle's most popular songs during the early Seventies. Amongst others, the accusatory, *Ja mujhe na ab yaad aa*, the mukhda of which was the Hindi version of SD's Bengali original, *Na amare soshi cheyo na* (1971), was probably the most contextual song in the film.

But a particular song from the album however stood out for its sheer musical brilliance and popularity—even Rajesh Khanna who was known to be musically inclined, endorsed *Yeh lal rang* as his favourite song. By the time *Prem Nagar* was released, the sheen had somewhat worn off his star status, and the song almost helped him in resurrecting his career.

With *Prem Nagar* and *Jugnu* in his bag, SD was yet again acknowledged as one of the most successful music directors in the industry. Several from his peer group had either taken a back seat, or were struggling to be heard. The only competition he had was from composers who were almost two-and-half to three decades junior to him, including his son, R.D. Burman, who had truly moved with the times—his layered rhythms, peppy brass and guiding bass guitar defined the new sound of Hindi cinema. Meanwhile, Laxmikant–Pyarelal with the heavy, popular dholak-based melodies were almost like a counterpoint to him, while Kalyanji–Anandji with their soft tonality and minimalistic compositions, almost echoed the essence of SD's music.

Not only did SD measure up to the taste of the new generation, he took to shattering established norms routinely. Like he did in *Sagina* (1974) by using Kishore Kumar's voice for Dilip Kumar, who played the role of a flamboyant union leader. While it would be unfair to compare the music of the Hindi remake to the original version composed by Tapan Sinha which was definitely more inspirational—especially with *Chhoti si panchi* (sung by Anup Ghoshal and Arati Mukherjee) becoming a lyrical ballad in Bengali film music—it was high on the popularity charts during the time.

SD sang his only song, rather an antara, for another music director in Hindi cinema after 1941, if we consider *Doli mein bithai ke kahar* (Amar Prem, 1971) as his own composition. The stanza *Chhote chhote sapne hamaar, Chhoti aasha chhota pyaar* written and composed by Tapan Sinha—was used in the opening scene as well as in last shot of the film. SD's voice was fragile; a poor shadow of what it was in the 1940s.

Meanwhile, Hrishikesh Mukherjee was back and asked SD to weave in his magic yet again. This time there would be a lot of laughter as well....

The Farewell Songs

Released in mid-1975, *Chupke Chupke* was the Hindi remake of a famous Bengali film which was made twice—for the first, SD composed the music, while the second which was ready in 1971, had exceptional music by Sudhin Dasgupta.

Incidentally, SD is probably the only composer to have scored the music for a Bengali film and its Hindi version, which was released three decades after the original. While Ajoy Bhattacharya's *Chhadmabeshi* was seventy-two pages long, and stuck to the original story, except for the addition of a Socialist angle with Chhabi Biswas playing Mr. Bose, Hrishikesh Mukherjee made a couple of changes to suit the taste of North Indian audiences. Truth be told, his interpretation was rather loud, almost like slapstick comedy.

However, a few changes were rightfully introduced to suit the times and the setting. For instance, Calcutta in the Bengali version became Allahabad in Hindi; Allahabad in the Bengali version became Bombay in Hindi; and the professor of Physics became a professor of English literature in the Hindi version.

One thing was however strikingly similar; both films began with a song with opening credit rolls running simultaneously. In the Hindi version, it was *Chupke chupke chal ri purvaiyaa*, which was also picturised on Jaya Bhaduri later in the film. The impish, *Ab ke sajan saawan mein* featured on Sharmila Tagore, had the perfect lilt for it to qualify as a song for a party-like ambience in someone's living room. Lata's playful intonation, the sharp *hai* (by now, this word had become SD's trademark), the onomatopoeic *ish* (Bengali for shock or surprise), and the 'tsk-tsk' added brilliantly to highlight the frustration of a young, newly-wed couple who are barred from consummating their marriage. Somewhere amidst peals of laughter in *Chupke Chupke*, the two Lata gems were unforgettable.

The original *Chhadmabeshi* was scripted in a fashion so as to provide SD enough space to manoeuvre for music; in Hindi, there was very little scope to do that. It was probably the shortage of song situations which manifested itself in a couple of non-descript songs in the film. The Kishore–Rafi duet, *Sa re ga ma*, and the Lata–Mukesh duet, *Baagon me kaise yeh phool khilte hain* were nice songs, but not befitting a man who was at his creative best in the last quadrant of his career. Moreover, they paled in comparison to the near ethereal score by Sudhin Dasgupta in the Bengali version.

Meanwhile, SD's personal life was also in turmoil. His wife, Meera was mentally ill and it was said that her illness was the result of a deep-seated feeling that her husband had deprived her of a career that she'd so well deserved. The poor woman would be restless all day and with advancing age, she was diagnosed with dementia. It wasn't as if SD was getting any younger and in order to avoid any unpleasantness, he would stay with his son at Odena Apartments and play Patience in his free time. His other and most favourite pastime was of course, football. Jyotish Bhattacharya, who was the manager of the East Bengal team in Bombay, would often invite SD when the team came visiting and the crazy football fan would adjust his music sittings and recording dates accordingly, especially during the Rovers Cup. According to the legendary East Bengal player, Parimal Dey, whom SD addressed as Jongla babu[1], the man took care to enquire after the well being of each player. Yet another football legend, Surajit Sengupta recalled meeting SD in 1974 at Shelleys Hotel near the Radio Club in Colaba. It was said that SD would reach the hotel by 10 a.m. on match days, take his seat in the coach's room, and talk to players individually for he knew all of them by first names. He would then proceed to perform a quirky ritual—when the players would be on their way out for a match, he would stand at the hotel's exit door and touch their shoulders. This was his way of wishing the team good luck. What was most peculiar was if he failed to touch any player, he would return and complete the good luck ritual all over again. There were times when the team coach, Pradeep Banerjee (the Indian football legend, popularly known as 'PK') would actually ask SD, 'Dada, should we move?', and wait for the final nod from him. As a football fan watching an East Bengal match, he ceased to be either the scion of Tripura or the legendary music composer. S.D. Burman was like any other ordinary fan—passionate, devoted and obsessed with his team's victory.

There were times when Pancham would also accompany his father to meet with the players. It was said that SD would keep a sharp eye on his son, fearing that the players may accept his son's offer for a ride; RD was a rough driver and hence unsafe, felt his father! Surajit Sengupta recounted an incident when Sudhir Karmakar, Gautam Sarkar et al., were riding with RD on their way to Cooperage stadium, when he negotiated a sharp turn within seconds of starting his car. Suddenly, SD screamed at the team coach, 'Pradeep, who all are there in that idiot's car? Make sure nobody gets into his car tomorrow.'

Alas, that was Surajit Sengupta's last meeting with SD.[2]

SD was perhaps the only man, and most likely the only film personality in Bombay, who had two seats allotted in his name at the VIP box at Cooperage. He would sit in one, and use the other as a footrest. It was a funny sight—here was a tall, paan-chewing man, sitting in a VIP seat which had his name embossed on the back, with his legs perched firmly on the second seat which was turned 180-degrees to face him.

And then....

In 1974, S.D. Burman was engrossed in multiple assignments with several directors and producers. Pramod Chakraborty was working on a Hindi adaptation of the Spanish-English film, *Summertime Killer* (1972); Subodh Mukerji had already launched a film with Shashi Kapoor, even after the disastrous, *Mr. Romeo* (1974); and *Tyaag*, which was partially financed by Sharmila Tagore, was in the making. In continuation of his alliance with Hrishikesh Mukherjee, SD was working on two of his films at the same time. It wasn't as if he was unused to hectic schedules, but it was the illness which came as a shock.

Epilogue

Farewell

It was a red letter day for one team, and a day of deep mourning for the other. On another day, the man would have perhaps sung loudly, '*Ami takdum takdum bajai Bangladesher dhol re...*' But on 29 September 1975, he was in Bombay Hospital and unable to even comprehend the good news—Surajit Sengupta, Shyam Thapa, Ranjit Mukherjee and Subhankar Sanyal had brought East Bengal its greatest glory by beating Mohun Bagan. In what could perhaps be an apocryphal story, SD is supposed to have momentarily opened his eyes on hearing the good news, which was whispered to him by R.D. Burman.

For the fans of East Bengal Football Club, Durga Puja had arrived early that year. But for the Burman family, a tragedy was looming ominously just a month away.

The Bombay traffic police had to step up its security arrangements to help Sachin Dev Burman manoeuvre his way through the streets of Bombay for the last time. A city that he had reluctantly embraced, but once he submitted to its charm, there was no looking back, except this last time when he would not return. It was during a rehearsal session in November 1974 when SD had fallen seriously ill and was rushed to Bombay Hospital. The end came less than a year later at home, on the afternoon of 31 October 1975.

That success came to S.D. Burman is well known, but what was unique was that he was fortunate to have witnessed his son rise to unprecedented heights, even as he himself was at the top of his career. Unlike several others who recede during their twilight years, the decade preceeding SD's death was most fulfilling in terms of his career, although he had one major personal upheaval that devastated his otherwise calm mind. Shakti Samanta once mentioned during an interview that SD died a 'very sad man'.[1] Although he didn't elaborate on the reason, it is quite likely that his wife Meera's vulnerable mental state had broken his heart. Later, RD is also said to have acknowledged that his father might have lived for a few more years, had his mother been in a state to take care of him. However in the final analysis, the sixty-nine-year-old SD left this world as a contented man, and apart from his musical legacy, he left his wife and son enough money to tide over any eventuality.

That S.D. Burman lived on even after his death and not in the trite manner of remembering a legend on certain dates after his passing, became evident when the radio crackled and played his songs from Hrishikesh Mukherjee's *Mili* (1975), featuring Kishore's sonorous solos. Additionally, Pramod Chakraborty's revenge saga, *Barood* (1976) was up for release; *Arjun Pandit* (1976) was nearing completion; Samir Ganguly's *Deewangee* (1976), for which the maestro could only manage to complete a song, was waiting to be showcased in theatres. That left *Tyaag* (1976), which was delayed due to SD's death, as its background score was pending, while the title score was adapted from SD's *Ishq Par Zor Nahin*.

But SD did not live to hear these albums. From a living legend, he had transformed into a living memory. Life went on, and much like the ending of *Mili*, in where the lead pair fly off to an unknown destination...

Amongst other things, the one thing that *Mili* did was put an end to a misunderstanding between SD and Yogesh—a story that dated back to *Chupke Chupke*.

In 1973–74, SD had asked Yogesh to write the lyrics for *Chupke Chupke*. In deference to the old man, Yogesh went and met SD quite a few times, but then stopped, as SD would not follow up on the meetings. One day, director Basu Chatterji ran into Yogesh and asked him if he was writing for *Chupke Chupke*. Yogesh repeated what he had been through with SD. Basu heard him out and later said that he had spotted lyricist Anand Bakshi, Hrishikesh Mukherjee and S.D. Burman together a couple of times. The penny dropped, Yogesh knew that he had been replaced.

A year later, Yogesh received a message from his neighbourhood store (he didn't have a telephone those days and would get his calls there) that S.D. Burman wanted to meet him. When the two met, SD asked him if he was still upset about *Chupke Chupke*. Yogesh made a joke about of it and laughed it off. SD then explained to him that considering his writing was more attuned to folksy numbers, he had not encouraged him for *Chupke Chupke* which required a modern outlook. Yogesh politely reminded SD that he had written for Salil Chowdhury, which was nothing if not modern. It suddenly dawned upon SD that he had been unfair to the young writer and asked Yogesh to write the lyrics for *Mili*. His rapprochement with a colleague was almost like penance, because shortly thereafter, during the rehearsal of *Badi sooni sooni hai*, SD collapsed and was rushed to hospital where it was confirmed that he had suffered a paralytic stroke. It was later discovered that it ran in his family; his grandfather too had succumbed in the same fashion. Along with other doctors who attended on him, his personal physician from Calcutta, Dr. Himanshu Sen, was also flown in at the insistence of RD.

After three months in hospital, mostly in Intensive Care, SD was brought back to the Jet. But RD realised that his father now required constant monitoring, considering he was partially paralysed, strapped to a wheel chair, and decided to move him to his penthouse at Odena Apartments. Around the third quarter of 1975, SD had to be moved to Bombay Hospital yet again and stayed for more than a month. This time around there was no great improvement in his condition and he gradually slipped into a coma. The doctors suggested that he spends his remaining days at home, and hoped that the sound of his own music may help him come out of the crisis.

The monsoons came and went, and it was now autumn in Bombay. The audio tape with *Aaye tum yaad mujhe*, *Maine kaha phoolon se* and *Badi sooni sooni hai*, sung by SD was in Yogesh's possession. 'I handed them to Panchamda,' said Yogesh[2], a man who is known for his unshakeable integrity. There was work to be done, and RD stepped in to dutifully complete the album, and stuck to minimalistic instrumentation just the way his father would have liked to do. Yet another song had been written for *Mili*, titled *Dusht Raakshas*, a term Hrishikesh had liberally borrowed from Oscar Wilde's *Selfish Giant*. However, owing to SD's health, the song had to be shelved.

Once during a sitting session of *Aaye tum yaad mujhe*, one of SD's assistants, Bablu Chakravarty, kept insisting on a rhythm accompaniment, till Kishore Kumar snubbed him, 'Keep it simple, just the way Yogesh had hummed it just now.' It was clear that Kishore Kumar did not wish to tamper with SD's final offering. The two shared a special relationship and Kishore Kumar had unflinching loyalty and respect for his mentor. Had it not been for SD's keen ear, Kishore Kumar may not have ended up a serious singer, but only fabulous at mirthful songs. It was SD who sifted through layers of Kishore's eccentricities to discover the molten, glowing talent at the core. What was most touching was that SD would nurture and care for Kishore's voice, cautioning him against performing in too many stage shows or asking the manager of a theatre to, 'Switch off the air conditioner at once!' on hearing Kishore cough during the premiere of *Prem Pujari*.

At one level, their relationship was more like a friendship between equals! There were occasions when SD would suddenly stop his car in the middle of a road on sighting Kishore Kumar and start singing a tune, oblivious of the cacophony created by the honking of cars.

Kishore Kumar also recounted an instance how once while he was on his way to another recording, SD had virtually hijacked him! Kishore was driven all the way to an open field miles away from the city, and made to run on grass by Sachinda. Finally, when Kishore was out of breath, SD began coaching him to sing 'oyi lala ding lala' from the song, *Paanch rupaiya barah aana* (*Chalti Ka Naam Gaadi*). There were very few people in the world Kishore Kumar would listen to and SD was perhaps the last.

During his superstardom days, it was widely known that Amitabh Bachchan neither needed crackling music nor beauteous heroines to carry a film forward. But even he, whose name had become synonymous with success, felt the void post *Mili*. The astute actor knew that after SD's passing, his films would rarely have the kind of music that had genuine connoisseurs as its fans.

Unlike *Mili*, somehow Hrishikesh Mukherjee's *Arjun Pandit* has little recall. The film was based on one of Banaphool's story, which had been made into a Bengali film called *Arohee* (1964) by Tapan Sinha. It is rather unfortunate that the film has very few digital prints in circulation, considering that not only was it amongst the director's best works, but it also won Sanjeev Kumar the Filmfare Award for Best Actor. So far as its music was concerned, while *Dil mera uda jaye* (Kishore) was routine, the Lata solo, *Bolo pritam kya boli thi* featured on the late Srividya (daughter of the legendary Carnatic singer, the late M.L. Vasanthakumari), was a composition to die for. As SD did not live to complete the background score, Hrishikesh Mukherjee liberally borrowed from Salil Chowdhury's title score for *Anokha Daan* (1972) for *Arjun Pandit*.

As mentioned earlier, for Pramod Chakraborty aka Chakida, SD was like family. His *Barood* with a vengeful Rishi Kapoor in the lead also released post S.D. Burman's demise. It was also interesting to note that never before did any of Rishi's films have someone as senior as Sachinda composing the music—keeping with his trendy, youthful image, it was either Laxmikant–Pyarelal or RD. It was rather endearing to note that here was a man who'd started his career almost at the same time as Rishi Kapoor's grandfather Prithviraj and was also someone who had made his father and uncle, both known for their acting and not singing prowess, croon! A little nugget which may have made *Barood* the second Rishi Kapoor film to have music by Dada Burman—the actor was almost signed up for *Us-Paar*, until he was replaced by Vinod Mehra. Enough evidence of how well Sachin Dev Burman had settled into Gen Next!

The Legacy

So, like many may ask today: what was S.D. Burman's legacy? For one and which is a no-brainer, R.D. Burman, who drew inspiration from his father's uncompromising commitment to music. SD had also left behind a wealth of tunes, a few of which RD borrowed and used in films like *Kinara* (1977), *Shaukeen* (1982), *Anusandhan* (1980), *Kudrat* (1981), *Chor Ho Toh Aisa* (1984), *1942: A Love Story* (1994), etc. RD openly acknowledged the source of these tunes, to the extent that he used the original mukhda of *Din dhal jaye* (*Guide*, 1965) in the antara of *Ab ke na saawan barse* (*Kinara*), jocularly terming it as '*baap ka maal*' (father's property), albeit complimenting the original composer's genius in a backhanded way. Therefore, in a way, and as a natural corollary, SD's legacy was reflected in his son's tunes—from the generous sprinkling of rural folk to modern orchestration.

It would however be unfair to not establish a fact regarding R.D. Burman's own musical journey. Beginning the late 1960s, RD had already set out on his own, ironically at his father's insistence. He was advised to come out of the shadow of sundry musicians like, Madan Mohan, Roshan and even his own father, and work on a new identity for himself, which he did rather successfully. Not only did he create the 'RD brand', but post 1971, S.D. Burman came to be known as 'R.D. Burman's father'. In more ways than one, Rahul Dev carried forward

Sachin Dev Burman's legacy, because he was part of his father's team and had imbibed several nuances closely.

Apart from R.D. Burman, there were other contemporaries who could have carried forward SD's torch—for instance, Jaidev and Hemanta Kumar Mukherjee. As is well known, Jaidev was SD's assistant for several years, and Hemanta, due to his decades-long association with him, understood the kernel of his music. But unfortunately, Hemanta had receded into near oblivion after his spectacular music for *Khamoshi* (1970), both as a singer and composer. On the other hand, Jaidev, for all his acclaim and the respect he commanded, was not perceived to be in the big league, not even by Navketan, for whom he had composed the immortal, *Hum Dono* (1961).

If there was one duo who showed their reverence for S.D. Burman in the best possible way, then it was the late Kalyanji, and his brother, Anandji. They emulated SD's style of composing, including his minimalistic arrangement, in Shankar Mukherjee's *Mahal* (1969); Goldie Anand's *Johnny Mera Naam* (1970); *Blackmail* (1973); or Anil Ganguly's *Kora Kagaz* (1974), amongst others.

But then no two composers are alike. At best, Kalyanji–Anandji were good at emulating a style, not creating one which would stand the test of time. Ravindra Jain was one composer who, by his own admission, had modelled himself on SD. Much like Sachinda, he also began his career in Bengal as a music director for a theatre group in Calcutta. Two of his compositions in Sudhendu Roy's *Saudagar* (1973), *Tera mera saath rahe* (Lata) and *Door hai kinara* (Manna Dey) had SD's notations etched all over—for instance, in the former, the kirtan-like patterns between the antara and mukhda, and the way the khol was used was evidence that SD's influence had crept into it in more ways than one. The song clearly has similarities with *Yeh kisne geet cheda* (*Meri Surat Teri Ankhen*) and *Main toh tere rang rati* (*Ishq Par Zor Nahin*), although, by no stretch of imagination, was it a blatant copy.

In time, Ravindra Jain became the preferred music composer for the makers of the great Indian-family social dramas—Rajshri Productions. His compositions for films like *Chitchor* (1976), *Geet Gata Chal* (1976), *Dulhan Wahi Jo Piya Mann Bhaye* (1977), etc., were simple and soft musical compositions based on folk or a raga with very few accompaniments.

It was a pleasant coincidence when Ravindra Jain had stepped in to complete a project called *Deewangee*, post SD's death. He went on record to say that he wrote its music the way, 'Burman Dada would have himself composed.' But as mentioned earlier, in the early 1970s when 'action-packed films' took precedence over sweet family sagas, Jain had no big-budget tailwind to give him the critical momentum. Even in the genre of 'family socials', he remained confined to the Barjatyas of Rajshri and other small houses. For those who grew up in the Eighties, Ravindra Jain's music was very much part of their collective memory, as he was a competent composer, albeit a niche one.

While many may lament the complete absence of SD's brand of sound in current times, it needs to be categorically mentioned here that it would have been nearly impossible to follow his oeuvre. Lest one forgets, his music was a product of his childhood, and most importantly, Bengal. If one were to make a comparison, then it would be safe to say that it was much like what Calypso was to Harry Belafonte. For both these musicians, their art form wasn't just typical of them, but almost 'proprietary'. It may be recalled that SD's early tutorials in music were from wandering minstrels, nomadic bards, unlettered boatmen, and house helps who also sang while going through their routine chores. Unless one understood the grammar of the terrain, with music being one of its main aspects, it was willy-nilly impossible to create that kind of a sound. It was not a straitjacketed secret sauce that could be transferred from one to another. It should also be remembered that despite embracing modern forms of music with great aplomb, every film of his dragged the listener back to the backwaters of Bengal. It was perhaps his way of reiterating his roots and paying homage to a tradition. Therefore, any attempt to emulate SD's music in bits or pieces may evoke nostalgia, or perhaps work as a tribute to the master, but an effort to sound like him may only result in derision.

What would be more appropriate is to treat his legacy like heritage, a treasure trove which allows everybody to rummage, but seldom steal. Moreover, his legacy was more 'static' than dynamic; it existed; it exists even today, but is more like the breeze that his beloved bauls from Bengal sing about—omnipresent, yet intangible. The same holds true for many others—Madan Mohan and his ghazals, or Roshan and his qawwalis. Eternally incomparable. And inimitable.

S.D. Burman made a successful career in Bombay, but nowhere was he what we understand today as a 'Mumbaikar'. He was the last of the Bengali bhadraloks, the genteel Bengali who not only wore his roots on his sleeve, but stuck to every marker of a bygone era—his sojourns to Kolkata during Durga Puja; his obsession with football, or the East Bengal team; his quirks of going on fishing expeditions; his box of paan, out of which he would only part with one for that someone special; his starched dhuti-panjabi; his skin-coloured pump shoes or Kolhapuri chappals; and most importantly, his refusal to correct his heavily accented Hindi, even while working in an industry which not only revolved around the language, but also produced stalwarts like Shailendra, Sahir and Majrooh. Along with the likes of Bimal Roy, Anil Biswas, Salil Chowdhury, Hemanta Mukherjee, and Hrishikesh Mukherjee, he was a perfect example of securing Bengali hegemony in post-Independent Bombay film industry. Even his wife, Meera Dev Burman, despite her astounding talent as a writer-musician, was a typical Bengali woman who followed the strictures laid down in her community. For instance, she would always refer to Sachin Ganguly and Sachin Bhowmick as Ganguly and Bhowmick respectively, never to utter her husband's first name even once, by mistake.

Except for a few occasions, like the liberation of Bangladesh in 1971, which he celebrated with much pomp and show, or his son's wedding reception, S.D. Burman was known to keep to himself, despite the flamboyance which was mandatory in his profession. Even the monthly subscription of ten rupees to the Musicians' Association would be dropped from his balcony into the hands of composer Suresh Kumar, who would be standing below to catch! Seldom did he smile; there are very few photographs of him which show him guffawing or enjoying the company of friends, unlike his son, whose lifeline was his large circle of friends. His uprightness won him respect, and even during his low phases, he neither displayed desperation, nor courted controversies for the simple reason that nobody could pierce the impenetrable aura and his exceptional talents which were incomparable.

S.D. Burman's musical career was neither a stroke of luck nor a miracle; there were no patrons nor godfathers to guide him through his career. One wonders how many people in showbiz would have his kind of perseverance because the first time he tasted success was when he was nearing forty. He was known to be content in that old-fashioned way, taking one step at a time, composing one classic and then moving to the next. All through his life, he made it clear that music was less of a career and more about devotion—he owed it to the rivers, birds, soil and the breeze of his childhood home, where music was free to be had, provided you knew how to nurture it.

Is is interesting to know how the world at large, not necessarily music lovers or his fans, remember the great Sachin Dev Burman. He was awarded the Padmashri in 1969, and in 2007 a stamp was issued by the Department of Post and Telegraphs in his honour. His love for the paan was immortalised by his close associate, Shailendra in the song, *Paan khaye saiyaan hamaro* (*Teesri Kasam*, 1966). But what is most unfortunate is till date, not even a road has been named after him, either in Kolkata or Mumbai. In what can only be termed as shameful, the Comilla palace in Bangladesh (where he was born), was converted into a poultry farm in the late 1950s by the Pakistan government. Even today, despite several pleas by music lovers in India and Bangladesh, the palace remains in a state of utter neglect. During a visit to the palace while writing this book, the caretaker of Chartha estate, who was kind enough to show the authors around, drew a blank about the Burmans!

Back home in Kolkata, his house may have been razed to the ground, had it not been for Abhijit Dasgupta (a television journalist) who raised a protest to the then Mayor of Kolkata Municipal Corporation, Subrata Mukherjee in 2003. The Mayor understood the significance of such a disastrous move and swiftly declared the house a Heritage Asset, Grade IIB, in 2003–04[1]. However, while the government order barred the demolition or even remodelling of the building, no steps were taken to preserve the house. It stands there like a forgotten relic, with its gates locked forever, and the plaster peeling off its walls. Amongst other things which are in a complete state of dereliction, the broken letter box in the house is a sad reminder that there shall be no more messages to and from the great Sachin Dev Burman.

In a world which forgets the dead within hours of their passing, there were thankfully a handful of S.D. Burman's admirers who genuinely lamented his passing, for he left their dreams unfulfilled. For example, the renowned director Tapan Sinha regretted how he had ignored a suggestion from friends, including the author, Santosh Kumar Ghosh, to get SD to sing Tarashankar Bandyopadhyay's poetry, one of the most talented writers in the post-Tagore era. Alas, SD passed away before that could happen. Similarly, lyricist Pulak Bandyopadhyay could never get SD to sing his, *O dayal, bichar koro* (which was later sung by Akhil Bandhu Ghosh). SD always insisted on singing his own Bengali compositions, despite many brilliant singers around him. For instance, and rather strangely, once singer-composer Dipankar Chattopadhyay was so desperate to sing SD's compositions that he had threatened to consume poison, if denied the opportunity![2] Such juvenile behaviour however did little to shake SD's resolve. One wonders what if SD had relented and used Manabendra Mukherjee[3] and Nirmalendu Chowdhury[4] to sing his compositions. There is no doubt that both were masters of the semi-classical and folk genres respectively, and who knows, maybe Hindi cinema would have been musically richer. In the 1990s, RD had once said how his father never had the opportunity to work with Pandit Ajoy Chakrabarty, a classical maestro who may have done justice to his father's *raagpradhan* songs[5].

There were times when SD's reluctance to adapt to situations worked in his son's favour. Apart from several accounts recounted in this book, there is an interesting anecdote which may sound rather convoluted, but did result in adding heft to Pancham's discography. This happened around 1967–68 when Nachiketa Ghosh had composed two Bengali basic songs for SD, which as a rule, he refused to sing. The songs were later bought over by Arabinda Mukherjee who created special situations to fit them in his film *Nishipadma* (1970). *Ja khushi ora bole boluk* and *Na na na aaj rate aar jatra shunte jabona* became landmarks, winning Manna Dey his second National award. The unprecedented success of the film and its music prompted Shakti Samanta to buy out Mukherjee's script. Subsequently, Pancham composed *Kuch toh log kahenge* and *Yeh kya hua* for identical situations in the Hindi version of the film. Suffice it to say, had SD not turned down the offer, there might have been no *Amar Prem* (1971).

As a householder, SD left this world with a few unfulfilled desires, but two continued to plague him for years during his lifetime. First, he wanted to see his son settle down with a nice Bengali girl; second was the passing away of his father, Nabadwip Chandra without having heard a single recorded song of his. SD had dedicated his first book *Surer Likhan*—a compendium of twenty-five notations of his songs to his departed father.

Maybe, in some faraway world, Boro Karta waited patiently to hear his son sing—*Chhote chhote sapne hamaar, chhoti aasha chhota pyaar....*

Endnotes

Prologue

1. Tower Hotel still stands at 27 B C D, A P C Road, Kolkata, opposite Sealdah main station.
2. Brigadier Bhattacharjya passed away on 15 October 2015.
3. Brick walls made on one side of the streets in Kolkata.
4. *Amrita Bazar Patrika*, 17 January 1944.
5. *Amrita Bazar Patrika*, 22 January 1944.
6. Sushil Majumdar was freelancing, having left Bombay Talkies at that time, and was not on the payroll of Filmistan.

Karta

Historical Musings

1. The *Imperial Gazetteer of India*, Journals of Asiatic Society, Rajmalas, etc.
2. Stories about Comilla were collected from various sources including Nabadwip Chandra's book, *Abarjhanar jhuli*; also, members of the Tripura royal family who wished anonymity; also, authors' visit to Comilla, and subsequent meetings with Golam Faruk.

Comilla Days

1. Comilla stories are from multiple sources, including publications by Tripura Government (contributors—Rajeshwar Mitra, Robi Nag, Girindra Majumdar,

310

Rabin Sengupta, Ramaprasad Dutta, Mahadev Chakrabarty, S. Suresh Kumar Sinha, et. al.); also, authors' visits to Comilla.
2. Interview of S.D. Burman.

Calcutta—1925–1931

1. Hindustani classical music finds roots in North India. What came to Bengal was a mix of several genres—the first known existence of music in Bengal could be attributed to Buddhist devotional songs—*Chorjapodo*, said to have emerged between seventh-fourteenth century AD. In the twelfth century came Jayadev's *Geet Govind;* from Punjab came the tappa through Ramnidhi Gupta (popularly known as Nidhubabu) in the late eighteenth century. Itinerant performers popularised kirtans, kabi gaan, etc., while Dasu Roy's *Panchali* made its way into the homes in various forms, the most popular of which was *Lakshmi's Panchali*. Dhrupad, which flourished in several places during Akbar's rule in Delhi, and Man Singh Tomar in Gwalior, came to Bengal via the religious route. Thumri was imported to Bengal from Lucknow by Wajid Ali Shah. Later, Badal Khan, a septuagenarian sarangi player who used to accompany khayal singers, came to Calcutta from North India in the early twentieth century. Archisman Mozumder, a Mumbai-based classical music aficionado, attributes the spread of khayal in Bengal to Badal Khan. The blind singer, Krishna Chandra Dey, was a disciple of Badal Khan. In 1925, SD started learning Hindustani classical music under Krishna Chandra Dey.
2. *Incomparable S.D. Burman,* H. Q. Chowdhury, Toitomboor Publications, Dhaka, 2011.
3. *Shono go dakhin hawa,* Jayati Gangopadhyay, 2006.

Calcutta—1932–1944
Renaissance & Basic Songs

1. While Rabindranath Tagore is well known, the other three were lesser known outside of Bengal. D.L. Ray's poetry had satire, and his music was influenced by the West. Atul Prosad Sen, having settled in Lucknow, added aspects of the thumri and ghazal. Rajanikanta Sen's songs were mostly around patriotic sentiments. The poetic quartet led to the genesis of the modern Bengali song.
2. Interviews with Amal Banerjee of SaReGaMa India, September 2013.

Hindusthan

1. Interviews with Amal Banerjee of SaReGaMa India, September 2013.
2. Interview with Sovon Lal Saha, Kolkata, December 2012.
3. For the songs in question, Karta might have been influenced by Nazrul Islam. He had composed similar-sounding songs, like *Kon kule aaj bhirlo tori* in Manj Khamaj, or the folk-based *E kul bhange o kul gore*. The second number was popularised in the 1940s by Dhiren Das (father of comedian, Anup Kumar Das). An interesting aspect in *Daaklo kokil* was the use of the word 'Taal pukur', which was a pond in Comilla, and is also part of Nazrul's poem, *Babuder Taal pukure*.
4. Today, Taal pukur has disappeared owing to urbanisation.
5. Interview with Sachin Ganguly, Kolkata, December 2012.
6. Interview with Goutam Ghosh, Kolkata, February 2015.
7. Interview with Indrajit Banerjee, November 2011.
8. Article by musicologist Suresh Chakrabarti in the book, *Bhati Gang Baiya*, edited by Shymal Chakrabarty, Akshar Publications, Tripura, 2001.
9. Interview with Debasish Roy, Kolkata, November 2015.

The Wedding

1. Interview with Anuradha Gupta, Kolkata, June 2014; she passed away in December 2014.
2. Interview with Dipankar Dasgupta, June 2012 & June 2014.
3. *R.D. Burman: The Man, The Music*, Anirudha Bhattacharjee & Balaji Vittal, Harpercollins India, 2011.
4. ibid.
5. Interview with Debasish Roy, Kolkata, November 2015.

Varman—Bombay 1944–1949

Filmistan

1. *Jeevan Naiya*, Aajkaal publishing.
2. ibid.
3. Interview with Probir Mukherjea, December 2012.
4. Interview with Kalyani Kazi, December 2013.

5. Interview with Abhijit Dasgupta, January 2016.
6. The journalist, Salil Ghosh, who was very close to Varman and had interviewed him extensively, wrote a letter to the *Desh* magazine in 1970 mentioning that Sushil Majumdar's *Begum* (1945) was Varman's debut for a Bombay production. However, the credit was given to Hariprasanna Das. Sachin Ganguly, in an interview with the authors also mentioned that there were instances of his guru writing music for films where his name did not appear as the music director.
7. *Filmfare*, June 16–30 1985.
8. Advertisement in a few dailies of Kolkata, August 1946.
9. ibid.
10. A report in a few dailies of Kolkata, late 1946–early 1947.
11. A report in a few dailies of Kolkata, late 1946.
12. Advertisement in a few dailies of Kolkata, June 1947.
13. Mohini Chowdhury, like Ajoy Bhattacharya, was also a rank holder in Senior Cambridge. However, he could not pursue higher studies due to financial constraints and took up a job with the postal department. He later became the secretary of the renowned scientist, Dr Meghnad Saha.
14. A report in *Filmindia*.

The Would-be Stars

1. A report in *Filmindia*, February 1949.
2. A blurb in newspapers, late 1949.

HMV, Bombay & Bengali Songs

1. Interview with Sachin Ganguly, December 2012. The recordist was a Chinese gent called Mr Leo, who was one of the few Chinese working in the music industry.
2. A blurb in newspapers, early 1949.
3. Interview with Sachin Ganguly, December 2012.
4. A report in *Filmindia*.
5. Interview with Abhijit Dasgupta, January 2016.
6. Interview with Sachin Ganguly, December 2012.
7. ibid.
8. Interview with Abhijit Dasgupta, January 2016.

Sachin Dev Burman

Romancing Bombay Talkies

1. *Jeeboner Jalsaghare*, Ananda Publishers, 2004.
2. *Bollywood Melodies: A History of Hindi Film Songs*, Ganesh Anantharaman, Penguin Books India, 2008.
3. Interview with Sachin Ganguly, December 2012.

41, Pali Hill: The Anands

1. In his autobiography, S.D. Burman mentions how Dev Anand was very fond of his music. Although this was true of the Hindi music that the maestro made and after he met with Dev Anand, it seems rather implausible in so far as Burman's Bengali music was concerned, simply because, much of it preceded even before the two came to know each other. However, one branch of the Anand family—Uma Anand, the wife of Chetan Anand was a Bengali, and it is quite possible that Dev Anand was introduced to some of Sachin Dev's music through her and her illustrious father, Gyanesh Chandra Chatterji, Professor of Philosophy at Government College, Lahore.

The Gamble

1. *Sahir Ludhianvi, The People's Poet*, Akshay Manwani, Harpercollins India, 2013.
2. A poster of *Afsar* is available in *Cinema Modern: The Navketan Story*, Sidharth Bhatia, Harpercollins India, 2011.
3. An email exchange with Sadanand Warrier, 24 September 2014.

Sabbatical, Insignificance & More...

1. Publicity material of *Saz* in newspapers, early 1951.
2. Publicity material of *Baba* in newspapers, 1951.
3. *Ogo Mor Geetimoy*, Sahityam, 2001.

The Noir Turnstile—One

1. Interview with Shiv Shankar Bhattacharya, Kolkata, December 2015.
2. Interview with Ketan Anand.
3. *Cinema Modern: The Navketan Story*, Sidharth Bhatia, Harpercollins India, 2011.
4. Interview with Ketan Anand.
5. Excerpts from *Filmindia*, 1951–1954.

Devdas

1. Interview with Rinki Roy Bhattacharya.
2. ibid.
3. A blurb in newspapers, such as, *The Times of India* and magazines, such as, *Filmfare*, etc.
4. Email exchange with K.L. Pandey, 21 September 2013.
5. Interview with Sachin Ganguly, December 2012.
6. Interview with Kalyani Mitra Pillai (daughter of Kamal Mitra).

The Noir Turnstile—Two
House Number 44

1. Interview with Biman Mukhopadhyay, September–October 2009.

Funtoosh

1. *Cinema Modern: The Navketan Story*, Sidharth Bhatia, Harpercollins India, 2011.
2. *Chetan Anand: The Poetics of Film*, Uma Anand, Himalaya Films, 2007.
3. *R.D. Burman: The Man, The Music*, Anirudha Bhattacharjee & Balaji Vittal, Harpercollins India, 2011.

Pyaasa—The Haves & Have-nots

1. The crushing of the insect may have been inspired by the first scene of *Les Diaboliques* (1955) by Henri-Georges Clouzot, where the vehicle throws the paper boat out of the puddle of water.

2. *Kothaye Kothaye Raat Hoye Jaye*, Pulak Bandyopadhyay, Ananda Publishers.
3. Interview with Mubasher Bukhari, Lahore, November 2015.
4. Interview with Kersi Lord, August 2008.
5. Figures, courtesy: Biswanath Chatterjee.
6. *Guru Dutt : A Life in Cinema*, Nasreen Munni Kabir, Oxford University Press, 1996.
7. Interview with Dipankar Chattopadhyay, Kolkata, April 2010.
8. Interview with Sachin Ganguly, December 2012.

Dev & Filmistan

1. Interview with Subhash Mukherjee, March and May, 2017.
2. ibid.
3. Interview with Anuradha Gupta, Kolkata, June 2014.
4. Information provided by Chandra Sanyal, daughter of Anoop Kumar.
5. Interview with Subhash Mukherjee, March and May, 2017.
6. Tripura Government's brochure celebrating 100 years of S.D. Burman.

Navketan, Asha & Kishore

1. *Romancing with Life*, Dev Anand, Penguin India, 2007.
2. Bengali composers often referenced each other's compositions. At the time, Sudhin Dasgupta was on a two-year contract with Guru Dutt. Salil Chowdhury had also referenced Dasgupta's, *Ei chaya ghera kalo rate* for the first line of *Suhana safar aur yeh mausam haseen* (*Madhumati*, 1958).
3. Multiple interviews of Kishore Kumar.

Sujata

1. Interview with Tulika Ghosh, October 2013.
2. Interview with Debu Sen, Mumbai, 2012.
3. Interview with Sumit Mitra, Kolkata, May 2013.
4. According to writer and filmmaker, Arabinda Mukherjee—interview published in *Mukhopatro*, by Eastern India Film Director's Association in December 2002—he had written the original scenic treatment of Subodh Ghosh's *Atmaja* which was later renamed *Sujata*. Bimal Roy did not acknowledge the same. Suffice it to say that Arabinda Mukherjee was quoted in it as saying: 'Sujata

was made by Bimal Roy. When I saw the film, I found that my scenic treatment had been used in a major way. I felt honoured, despite the fact that my name was not even mentioned in the credits.'
5. Interview with Debu Sen, Mumbai, 2012.
6. Interview with Probir Mukherjea, December 2012.
7. Interview with Debu Sen, Mumbai, 2012.
8. Interview with Sachin Ganguly, Kolkata, 2012.

The Sixties

1. Interview with Subir Sen, November 2011.
2. Interview with Gautam Chowdhury.

Flashback—Kaagaz Ke Phool

1. *Guru Dutt: A Life in Cinema*, Nasreen Munni Kabir, Oxford University Press, 1996.
2. Interview with Chandrasekhar Rao, September 2011.

Musicals, Noir & Family Planning

1. *Manzil* has a spectacular scene depicting the arrival of sound in India through the re-creation of a publicity campaign for India's first talkie, *Alam Ara* (1931).
2. *Aapki Parchaiyan*, Rajnikumar Pandya, R. R. Sheth, 1995.
3. Interview with Bhanu Gupta, Kolkata, June 2007.
4. Interview with Sanjay Sengupta, December 2011. As told to him by Utpal Chakrabarti of Melody, Kolkata.
5. Interview with Ashim Samanta, Mumbai, 2012.
6. An interview of S.D. Burman.

Bandini

1. *Mera Kuch Samaan* (Hindi), Gulzar, 1994. Translation in English, Aritra Bhattacharyya.
2. *Hindi Film Geet Kosh*, Volume III, Harmandir Singh 'Hamraaz'.
3. *In the Company of a Poet: Gulzar in Conversation with Nasreen Munni Kabir*, Rupa, 2012.

4. *In Search of Lata Mangeshkar*, Harish Bhimani, Indus, 1995.
5. S.D. Burman had moved into the Jet in the mid-1950s; his letter pad, printed in 1956, had the name of his house embossed on the top right-hand corner.
6. Lata Mangeshkar recorded *Mora gora ang* for S.D. Burman in *Bandini* in December 1960; *Filmfare*, January 1961.
7. *Bimal Roy: The Man Who Spoke in Pictures*, Rinki Roy Bhattacharya, Viking, Penguin India, 2009.
8. Nutan's son, Mohnish Bahl was born in August 1961, at Dr Ajinkya's Maternity Home—the same where Nutan was born.
9. Interview with Bela Sengupta, September 2015.
10. Bird identified by wildlife enthusiast and entrepreneur, Bhaskar Dutta.
11. Interview with Ratna Mukherjee, Bhagalpur, December 2013.
12. As told to the authors by Tulika Ghosh, November 2012.
13. Interview with Sumit Mitra, Kolkata, May 2013.

The Unsure Years
A Village Tale

1. Interview with Kersi Lord, 2008.
2. As told to the authors by Debasis Mukhopadhyay, February 2012.
3. Interview with Sachin Ganguly, December 2012.

It Happened One Night

1. Interview with Sachin Ganguly, December 2012.

The Endless Night

1. *Swarasha*, Vishwas Nerurkar.

Hasrat

1. *Filmfare*, 1984, a quiz on S.D. Burman by Raju Bharatan.
2. Interview with Sachin Bhowmick, 2010.
3. ibid.
4. Tripura Government's brochure celebrating 100 years of S.D. Burman.
5. This was the Eighth World Youth Festival, organised by the World Federation of Democratic Youth (WFDY) and the International Union of Students (IUS).

Shakeel

1. An email from Rinki Roy Bhattacharya, 25 May 2014.
2. The road in front of Tata Memorial Hospital in Mumbai is named after Dr E. Borges.

Dev Anand—Phase II
Guide—The Uncut Version

1. *Romancing with Life*, Dev Anand, Penguin India, 2007.
2. *Filmfare*, August 1962.
3. *Ek Hota Goldie*, Anita Padhye, Anubandha Prakashan, 2017 edition.
4. Reviews published in *The New York Times,* and *Time* magazine.
5. Confirmation by the marketing coordinator, Chicago Film Festival, via email on 11 April 2013.
6. Indira Gandhi, who cleared the film, apparently told Dev Anand—'You talk very fast.'
7. Interview with Sachin Ganguly, December 2012.
8. *Rasrang,* Diwali issue, 1966, translated from the Marathi by Kaustabh C. Pingle.
9. *Incomparable Sachin Dev Burman,* H. Q. Chowdhury, Toitomboor publications, Dhaka, 2011.
10. Interview with Dinesh Shailendra, Mumbai, 2011.
11. Interview with Kishwar Jaipuri.
12. Interview with Manohari Singh, March 2009.
13. *The Desai Trio*, Nilu N. Gavankar, AuthorHouse, 2011.
14. *Filmfare*, February 1966.
15. *Filmfare*, 1986.

Filmfare Awards: Myth & Reality

1. In all probability, readers until then were unaware of the changes made to the nomination system, and letters followed. One such letter by a reader called Seshkar from Vizag, published in the 22 February 1963 issue, had this to say: I am keen that the FF awards should reflect reader views faithfully. The awards are supposed to be given only on the basis of votes polled. The principle, democratic in nature, is welcome. But I doubt whether the public verdict

is the sole factor behind the awards. The doubt gained ground with the 9th Annual Awards. Some of last year's awards smack of 'behind the scenes' forces. Such forces, if they do exist, should be kept to a minimum, so that the readers' verdict may be respected. Otherwise, the purpose of furnishing entries becomes meaningless.

This was followed by a remark by the Editor – 'The system has been changed.'

Teen Deviyan

1. Rasikeshu, a radio show featuring Anil Biswas.
2. Interview with Simi Grewal, 2011.
3. Interview with Badal Bhattacharya, June 2006.

Jewel Thief

1. *R.D. Burman: The Man, The Music*, Anirudha Bhattacharjee & Balaji Vittal, Harpercollins India, 2011.
2. Interview with Amrut Rao, Mumbai, September 2008.
3. *Enchantment of the mind: Manmohan Desai's films*, Connie Haham, Roli Books, 2006.
4. Several interviews of Dev Anand.
5. Interview with Manohari Singh, August 2008.

SD

The Watershed Years
1969

1. Interview with Sachin Ganguly, December 2012.
2. *Kothaye Kothaye Raat Hoye Jaye*, Pulak Bandyopadhyay, Ananda Publishers.
3. Interview with Sanjay Sengupta, January 2015.
4. Letter from S.D. Burman to Sachin Ganguly, 3 February 1969.
5. An email from Rupali Guha, 18 June 2014.
6. Interview with Rakesh Bakshi, who confirmed that the two songs, *Dhan waalon ka yeh zamana* and *Anjaane mein inn hoton pe* were recorded on 6 March 1964 and 12 December 1964 respectively by Lata Mangeshkar.
7. Interview with Sachin Ganguly, December 2012.

8. *Hindustan Standard*, January 24–29 1970.
9. Interview with Rakesh Bakshi.
10. Interview with Bhanu Gupta, January 2007.
11. Interview with Badal Bhattacharya, June 2006.
12. An email from Bhupinder, 1 July 2011.
13. *Akhri Khat* (1966), which is cited as Rajesh Khanna's first signed and released film on most websites and in books, was actually his fourth signed and second released. It commenced months after *Raaz*, *Aurat* and *Baharaon ke Sapne*. The actual release dates of the films were: *Raaz*, 26 January 1967; Mumbai, 3 February 1967; *Akhri Khat*, 9 June 1967; *Aurat*, 7 July 1967; and *Baharon ke Sapne*, 17 July 1967.
14. Interview with Subir Sen, Kolkata, November 2011.
15. Quoted several times on different platforms.
16. Kishore Kumar's interview after the passing of S.D. Burman.
17. Shakti Samanta's interview on the recording of the song.
18. Interview with Bhanu Gupta, January 2007.
19. Interview with Pandit Hariprasad Chaurasia at his ashram in Bhubaneshwar, September 2012.
20. Interview with Manna Dey, Bankura, 1983.
21. Uttam Singh, Kolkata, January 2013.

Neeraj
Khemkaran

1. Brigadier S. P. Bhattacharjya was in Khemkaran working as an engineer in the army in September 1965. According to his son, Joy Bhattacharjya: 'Khemkaran could have been the biggest disaster in the history of Indian warfare. India actually had a situation where Pakistan launched a lightning attack using tanks of which we were not even aware. When the war started in 1965, India thought that Pakistan had one armoured division that was fighting our armoured division in Kashmir. Pakistan actually took their second armoured division, of which we were unaware, to the Khemkaran sector and made the thrust. Had Pakistan got through Khemkaran, it could have been Ajmer next, and Delhi could be reached straight through the Ajmer–Delhi highway. This was a huge Intelligence failure. I remember how they would brag, "Delhi in 30 days. We'll be eating breakfast in Jaipur and lunch in Delhi."'
2. Interview with Amit Khanna, 2013.

3. Interviews from *The Hindu* reproduced with Kumar's permission.
4. Demonstrated by Bhanu Gupta to the authors, Kolkata, June 2007.
5. Interview with Manohari Singh, 2009.
6. Interviews with Probir Mukherjea.

The Lost Gamble

1. Interview with Mira Hashmi.

Of Lyrical Partneships

1. Interview with Subhash Mukherji, May 2017.
2. *Chalacchitro Ajiban*, Tapan Sinha, Deys Publishers, 2009.
3. Interview with Subhash Mukherji, May 2017.

Transition—The Seventies

1. Interviews with Manohari Singh, 2007–2009.
2. Facebook messenger discussion with Moti Lalwani.

Bangladesh

1. The People's Republic of Bangladesh was founded in March 1971. The phrase, 'Joy Bangla' was coined during the war.
2. Interview with Sachin Bhowmick, 2010; with Mili Bhattacharya, August 2008.
3. Interview with Sachin Ganguly, December 2012.
4. Interviews with Sachin Bhowmick.

Zindagi Zindagi

1. Interview with Tarun Majumdar, August 2009.
2. ibid. The music of Balika Badhu was composed by R.D. Burman as SD had passed away.

Egos, Sentiments & Music

1. *The World of Hrishikesh Mukherjee: The Filmmaker Everyone Loves*, Jai Arjun Singh, Penguin India, 2015.
2. Interviews with Ranabir Neogi, 2001–2015.
3. A well-recorded statement by Brajen Biswas.

The Story of a Gypsy Girl

1. Interview with Basu Chatterji, April 2015.
2. Interview with Yogesh, Mumbai, 2009 & 2011.
3. Interview with Basu Chatterji, April 2015.
4. Interview with Yogesh, Mumbai, 2009 & 2011.
5. Interview with Basu Chatterji, April 2015.

In Continuum
The Action-packed 1970s

1. Interview with Danny Denzongpa, Mumbai.
2. Unconfirmed sources say that the Aao Naga tribe of Nagaland found the line, *Mera naam aao* offensive. Hence, in video (especially YouTube) versions of the song, all lines with the word '*aao*' have been completely edited out. Even IMDB mentions Johnny Walker's screen name as 'Tuna's boyfriend' and not 'Aao'.
3. Interview with Bhupen Hazarika, Jadavpur University, March 1988.
4. Interview with Sachin Bhowmick, 2010.

The Farewell Songs

1. Interview with Pratik Dey, son of Parimal Dey.
2. Interview with Surajit Sengupta, Kolkata, 30 November 2012.

Epilogue

Farewell

1. *Star & Style*, 11–24 October 1985.
2. Interviews with Yogesh, Mumbai, 2009–2012.

The Legacy

1. The court order came via Assesse number 110902500510, 2003-04. Clause: Building cannot be broken down. External changes limited to horizontal and vertical addition and alteration of the building in compatibility with the heritage building may be granted.
2. Interview with Dipankar Chattopadhyay, 2010, corroborated by Sachin Ganguly to the authors, 2012.
3. To appreciate how Manabendra Mukherjee might have sounded under SD, one could listen to an alaap in Ahir Bhairav sung by him in the seminal film, *Sare Chuttar* (1953). The composer of the film was Kalipada Sen.
4. Nirmalendu Chowdhury's folk songs, especially bhatiyali, were extraordinary. SD being a pioneer in the field, may have utilised his services in the industry. Those interested in listening to him may refer to ECLP 2336 (ID:14968)
5. Interview with Ajoy Chakrabarty, August 2009.

Index

Biswas, Anil, 49, 65, 160, 262, 306
Biswas, Brajen, 130
Biswas, Chhabi, xviii, 293
Bitter Rice, 81
Biwi Aur Makaan, 273
Blackmail, 304
Bombai Ka Babu, 155–156, 158, 195
Bombay film industry, 33, 35, 173,
 177
problems faced by, 233–234
Bombay Labs, 171
Bombay Talkies, 33, 35, 59–63, 75,
 83, 134, 237
Bond, James, 70
Boot Polish, 84
Boral, Rai Chand, 15, 20, 28, 43
Bose, Bela, 176
Bose, Khudiram, 278
Bose, Nitin, xviii
Bose, Piyush, 278
Bose, Satyen, 134
Boundary Commission of Bengal, 47
Brahmo Samaj, 43
Brando, Marlon, 188
Buck, Pearl S., 194, 197
Buddha Mil Gaya, 274
Bullet, 218
Burma (now Myanmar), 3
Burman, Meera Dev, 4, 26, 49, 51,
 110, 225, 235–236, 263, 268, 298,
 306
Burman, Naren Dev, 19
Burman, Rahul Dev (R D Burman),
 6, 68, 80, 130, 153, 165, 171, 197,
 200, 225, 245, 260, 268, 284, 288,
 291, 303–304, 309
Burman, Sachin Deb (or Shachin

Karta or S.D. Burman / SD or
 Pancham), xvii, xviii, xix, 6, 63,
 66, 68, 104–110, 113–114, 117,
 135, 150, 164, 176, 192, 199–202,
 205–206, 210, 213, 219, 225, 227,
 234–235, 249, 253, 286–292,
 294–295
 absence from Bengali music, 74
 admitted to hospital due to ill
  health, 297
 appeared for senior Cambridge
  examination in 1955, 118
 article in *Filmfare* magazine,
  39–40
 awarded Padmashri in 1969, 236
 in Calcutta
 from 1925-31, 12–15
 from 1932-1944, 16–17
 recorded first song, 23
 completion and registration of
  house in 1949, 54
 composing principle, important
  aspect of, 203
 death of, 298
 earned reputation of composer,
  173
 family vacation in 1959, 146
 faults in Hindi language, 20
 first composition, 30
 gold medal from Dr Katju, 22
 house-hunting spree, 19–20
 Indian fakir tag, 94–95
 inspired by wandering minstrels
  and ustads, 94–95
 legacy of, 303–309
 lyrical partnerships, 255–258
 mantra to his son, 71